Voices of Fayette City, Pennsylvania

Voices of Fayette City, Pennsylvania

Recollections from the 1940s

by

Eric J. Moskala

Preface

A few years ago, I wrote a book about the early history of Fayette City from its founding in 1800 to its peak, at least in terms of population, in the 1920s. The 1930s were not kind to Fayette City. The demise of the local coal industry and the onset of the Great Depression took a heavy toll on the small town and left it with steep challenges as the decade of the 1940s approached. The goal of this book is to capture what it was like to live in Fayette City during this impactful decade which challenged the entire world and not just this little town in the northwest corner of Fayette County, Pennsylvania.

Fayette City was probably not much different from any of the other small towns in the mid-Monongahela River Valley. Towns like Brownsville, Newell, Belle Vernon, and Monessen on the east side of the River and Roscoe, Allenport, Stockdale, California, and Charleroi on the west side were heavily dependent on the coal and steel industries and relied on the River for transportation and recreation. In order to assist the reader who may not be familiar with Fayette City, I briefly review the early history and geography of Fayette City in Chapter 1 and the role of the town's weekly newspaper, the Fayette City Journal, in Chapter 2. Hopefully these two Chapters will provide the foundation for better understanding the events of the 1940s.

Two primary sources of information were used as the basis for this effort: interviews with people who actually lived in Fayette City during the 1940s, and four consecutive years of the weekly Fayette City Journal newspaper. I interviewed more than thirty people for this project. The interviews were conducted according to the principles and best practices developed by the Oral History Association at oralhistory.org. The names of the interviewees, or narrators as I like to call them, and their birth years are provided in Appendices I and II. Considering that the population of Fayette City was only about 1500 during the 1940s, it was truly remarkable finding so many people to interview. The narrators were almost evenly balanced between male and female which hopefully provides a balanced view in terms of this demographic. The majority of the narrators were born in the 1930s with most of them being born in the early 1930s. During the 1940s, Fayette City had six distinct neighborhoods. Each of these neighborhoods is represented by narrators with the exception of the sparsely populated Johnson Hollow. About half of the interviews were conducted in person. The remaining interviews were conducted over the telephone. Recordings of the interviews are archived at the library of the California University of Pennsylvania, Fayette City's cross-River neighbor. A list of questions for the interview was usually provided to the narrator before the interview took place to give the narrator some time to recall their precious memories. The interviews were usually conducted one-on-one although there were times when other family members joined the conversation. Excerpts from the interviews are called out in a special text box throughout the book. I have kept the editing to a minimum (see Editorial Note) to retain the integrity of the interviews.

The second source of information for the book was four consecutive years of the weekly Fayette City Journal from October 1944 to October 1948. More than 200 issues of the weekly newspaper were scoured for details of what life was like in the 1940s. Access to the newspapers was generously provided by James Enoch Eley, a lifelong Fayette City resident, business owner, and civic leader. The editor of the Journal over this four-year span was Allan Keenan. His brother James joined him as assistant editor of the Journal in 1947. Allan left the newspaper business in October of 1948 to pursue a career in the ministry. His brother collated all of the issues for which his brother was the editor and bound them in two hardbacked books. With rare exception, it is nearly impossible to find complete copies of any of the weekly papers, let alone four consecutive years, which were published by the local communities mentioned earlier. This extraordinary resource supplied unprecedented insight into the ups and downs of living in Fayette City in the 1940s.

The history of any town can be presented in layers. Government data provides important information on population, average family income, land mass, property values, number of businesses, etc. While very useful, this type of information gives no insight into the specific issues facing a town. Weekly newspapers like the Fayette City Journal provide the next layer of granularity offering details about such things as community activities, local government elections, births, deaths, and issues facing the town, to name just a few. Real life, however, is lived between the headlines. The recollections of the narrators offer the most detailed and intimate portrayal of everyday life. The numerous, original, black and white photos provided by many of the narrators add color to their voices. A combination of these three sources of information is offered here to give more than just a partial portrait of life in Fayette City during the 1940s.

Chapter 1 begins with a schematic of Fayette City drawn by my sister Vanessa Moskala Pugh. The map highlights the various neighborhoods of Fayette City, the locations of its seven churches and seven bars, and the locations of the town's key landmarks such as the schoolhouse, baseball field, jail, ferry dock, and coal mines. The remaining Chapters begin with an illustration that was inspired by a story of one of the narrators. It is up to the reader to identify which story is represented by the illustration! The illustrations for these Chapters were prepared by professional illustrator Joe Sorah at jsorahdesign.com. The Chapters are arranged mostly by topic and not chronologically, although the World War years which occurred at the beginning of the decade are mentioned early on and the Sesquicentennial which occurred at the end of the decade is mentioned last.

If you have never been to or heard of Fayette City, Pennsylvania, I hope this book will give you a glimpse of the community during this incredible decade. If you ever lived in Fayette City or visited it often during the 1940s, or if you know of people who did, or even if you live there now, I hope this book brings a smile to your face and evokes memories of an era the likes of which we may never see again.

On the cover...
Top Row: Joanne Cunningham Manetta, Larry Moskala, John Vargo, Judith Dewar Shearer, Pauline Vargo Baker
Second Row: Ella Marie Auther Davis, Leila Breckenridge Steiner, Joe Vargo, Nancy Ferree Johnson, Grace Hough Martin
Third Row: Constance Moskala Grados, Georgia Jean Arrow, Georgia Nicholson Slezak, June Cramer Yevincy, Willard Jones
Fourth Row: Kathleen Walton Stimmell, James Eley, Jack Young, Barry Hindmarsh, Raymond Moody
Bottom Row: William (Bill) Williamson, Linda Russell Nelson, George (Mike) Hancock, Audrey Tiernan Repka, Jack Gargan

Dedication

This book is dedicated to everyone who lived in Fayette City in the 1940s and made it a place that evokes such strong and wonderful memories of days gone by.

This book is also for my grandparents Minnie Natola Moskala and Frank Moskala, Mary Mullen Miller and Hugh Miller, parents Edward and Dorothy Moskala, and siblings Connie, Larry, and Vanessa Moskala who resided in Fayette City over this period of time. In some small way I am sure they contributed to and benefited from the strong sense of community that permeated the town.

Acknowledgements

First and foremost, I want to thank the thirty-two people who participated in the interviews for their kindness and generosity. My sincerest wish is that they are pleased with the final product. Without them, there would be no book. They brought to life the true spirit of the 1940s that otherwise would have been relegated to the author's interpretations of a bunch of newspaper articles. I also want to thank everyone who contributed photographs and other historical documents. A special thanks to James Enoch Eley for letting me borrow his bound copies of the Fayette City Journal. It was an incredible privilege to be able to pour over those newspapers and absorb the flow of history over that four-year period. Thanks also to Bob Decroo for sharing his artifacts and postcards from Fayette City.

Second, I want to thank my sister Vanessa Moskala Pugh for drafting the schematic found at the beginning of Chapter 1. The map is an indispensable tool for understanding the events of the 1940s in their geographical context. I want to thank Joe Sorah for patiently listening to me as I described my thoughts for the illustrations and capturing the essence of the narrators' stories. I also want to thank Kathie Owens for reviewing the text and making many valuable suggestions for improving the flow of the narrative.

I also want to thank the California University of Pennsylvania for agreeing to archive the audio files of the interviews and to make them accessible to anyone upon request.

Finally, I want to thank my family, Aaron and Maria, who let me work mostly uninterrupted for hours every day and supported me with their love and understanding.

Editorial Note

I tried to keep the excerpts from the interviews as close to the original texts as possible. When it seemed necessary to adjust for syntax and to improve clarity and flow, I made minor edits to the texts. In every case, however, I tried to maintain the "voice" of the narrator and the integrity of their story. Anyone wanting an unedited version of the interviews may find them at the library of the California University of Pennsylvania.

I should also note that the narrators often referred to friends and neighbors by surname. I tried my best to identify the proper spelling for these names. In the event that I misspelled any of them, I apologize in advance.

Finally I should mention that I knew a few of the narrators from my time as a youth in Fayette City. Further, almost all of the narrators knew at least one of my immediate family members including my grandparents, parents, and older siblings. Although these common touchpoints brought a sense of familiarity to the interview, I strived to keep the focus of the interview on the narrator and his or her family.

Table of Contents

FAYETTE CITY

CIRCA 1950

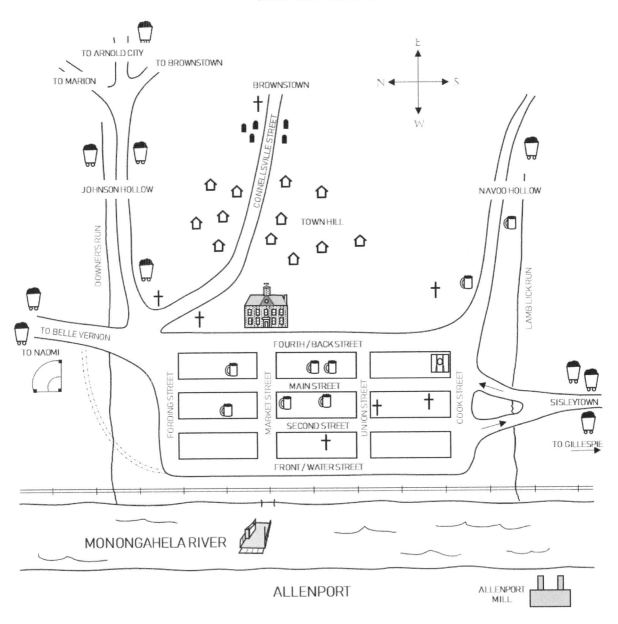

CHAPTER 1 The Early History of Fayette City

Perhaps no other region west of the Appalachian Mountains has more historical significance with respect to the formation and development of the United States than southwestern Pennsylvania. In the mid-1700s, the long-fought French and Indian War found theatres here including George Washington's defeat at Fort Necessity outside of Uniontown and General Braddock's losing fight for Fort Duquesne at the Battle of the Monongahela. After the Revolutionary War, the Whiskey Rebellion in southwestern Pennsylvania provided the first true test for the newly formed United States and resulted in President Washington sending thousands of troops to the region to squash the insurrection. The National Road, also known as the Cumberland Road, was constructed between 1811 and 1837 and brought pioneers from Maryland to Brownsville, Pennsylvania and beyond. From Brownsville, travelers could choose to continue west on the National Road or navigate the Monongahela River to Pittsburgh and then west on the Ohio River. Later in the 1800s, coal, coke and eventually steel, from southwestern Pennsylvanian enabled unbridled growth and development throughout the region and attracted millions of immigrants from central and eastern Europe searching for a better life.

In the late 1700s, Westmoreland County comprised the entire region of southwestern Pennsylvania. In 1783, Fayette County was carved out of Westmoreland and named after the Marquis de Lafayette, the French military officer who fought in the Revolutionary War and commanded American troops in several battles. The Mason-Dixon Line formed the southern border of Fayette County. The Monongahela River formed its western border. Tucked away in the northwestern corner of Fayette County is a small town originally known as Freeport. Freeport, which later became Cookstown and then Fayette City, was established by Colonel Edward Cook in or around 1800 and is the second oldest town on this stretch of the Monongahela after Brownsville (established 1785) and before Belle Vernon (established 1813).

Colonel Cook, a friend of George Washington's and a voice of reason during the Whiskey Rebellion, owned hundreds of acres of land in Fayette and Westmoreland Counties including a tract known as Whiskey Mount for the role it played in the Whiskey Rebellion. As tradition would tell it, Colonel Cook and his friend Joseph Downer laid out the streets and lots of Freeport using a clothesline. The fifty-one lots were sixty feet by one hundred and twenty feet. The layout consisted of four streets (Front, Second, Third, and Fourth) running parallel to the Monongahela River and four streets (Fording, Market, Union, and Cook) running perpendicular to the River. Front Street would come to be known as Water Street for obvious reasons. Third Street would become known as Main Street as businesses started to populate the town. Fourth Street would often be called Back Street because the steep hill to its east prevented easy development. The triangular piece of land at the head of Market Street was dedicated to public use and later became the location of the public school and Methodist Church.

Historical Population		
Year	Population	% ±
1840	411	--
1850	972	136.5
1860	820	-15.6
1870	889	8.4
1880	867	-2.5
1890	931	7.4
1900	1595	71.3
1910	2005	25.7
1920	2018	0.6
1930	1594	-21.0
1940	1598	0.3
1950	1404	-12.1
1960	1159	-17.5

Most of the early inhabitants of Freeport were of English, Irish, or Scottish descent with a smattering of Germans for good measure. Freeport officially changed its name to Cookstown in 1825 in honor of its founder to avoid any confusion with another town also named Freeport that had been established earlier on the Allegheny River north of Pittsburgh. The final name change occurred in 1854 when Cookstown was retitled Fayette City after the Marquis de Lafayette, the namesake of the County as well.

As the population of Fayette City grew, new homes and businesses expanded up the hill to the east of Fourth Street, up the hollows at the north and south ends of town, and on a narrow strip of land along the River at the south end of town. The hill was accessed by Connellsville Street which makes the steep climb up the hill behind the public school building before taking a hard left turn and continuing to climb. The public cemetery found just beyond the top of the hill became the unofficial town boundary. The cemetery actually consists of three cemeteries: the Woodvale and Fayette Public Cemeteries on the south side of Connellsville Street and the newer Mount Auburn cemetery laid out in 1874 by undertaker Samuel Mansfield on the opposite side of the street. This hilltop neighborhood would appropriately become known as "town hill" while the original part of town would often be referred to as "downtown" (or as the colloquialism "downstreet" by some residents.) Around the turn of the 20th century, Andrew Brown, the banker, land developer, and owner of the farmland beyond the cemetery, laid out the village of Brownstown, sometimes referred to as Fayette City Heights, allowing for further expansion to the east.

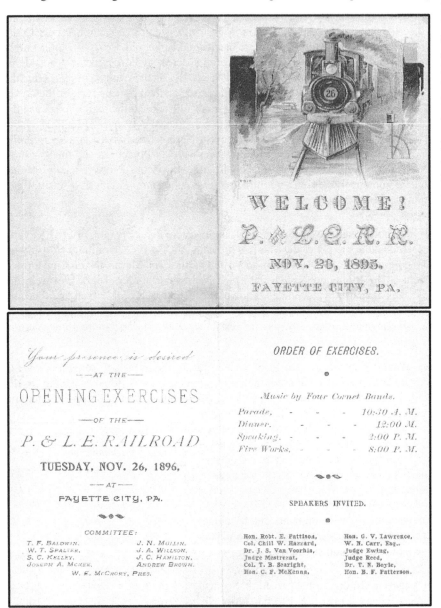

Invitation to opening exercises celebrating the arrival of the railroad in Fayette City. Top: Outside of invitation. Bottom: Inside of invitation.

The hollow at the north end of town was occupied before the founding of Freeport by Colonel Cook's friend Joseph Downer who used the creek, now known as Downer's Run, which runs through the hollow to build a grist mill and later a sawmill. In 1840 James Hamer constructed the Fayette City Woolen Factory on Downer's Run and operated the Factory until 1887 when heavy rains washed out the Factory and other mills along the creek. Because of Hamer's extended success in the hollow with the Factory, the hollow was often called Hamer Hollow. By the end of the 1890s, however, life in the Hamer Hollow was about to take a dramatic turn.

Throughout the latter half of the 1800s, Fayette City desperately sought a railroad connection to Pittsburgh. The Pennsylvania and Lake Erie (P&LE) railroad was extended from McKeesport to Belle Vernon in 1889. Completing those last couple of miles from Belle Vernon to Fayette City proved to be a nearly insurmountable task. However, six years later, on November 26, 1895, Fayette City's dream of a railroad was finally realized. In what was surely the grandest celebration Fayette City had ever seen, the first locomotive made its way into town. Flags lined the railroad tracks and more than 1000 people stood at the trestle to welcome the first train and its passengers. An elaborate ceremony was held at the Odd Fellows Hall by invitation only and included numerous distinguished speakers expounding on the significance of the event.

Just five years later, in 1900, Fayette City had another cause for celebration: its centenary. The program for the centenary consisted of parading, speechmaking, a bike race, music, and, most notably, fireworks. The fireworks provided more than the usual thrill. As the story goes, the stands for observing the pyrotechnics were built too close to the place where the fireworks were stored. At the start of the display, one of the fireworks accidentally set off the rest of them resulting in unexpected excitement and some of the spectators being burned.

The turn of the century proved to be a prosperous time for Fayette City. In 1901 the railroad was extended upriver to Brownsville and a double track system was added from Fayette City to Pittsburgh. The coal boom, which was made possible by the new railroad, attracted immigrants, primarily from Eastern Europe, causing the population of Fayette City to nearly doubled between the years 1890 and 1900. Two of the town's landmark buildings, the bank building and the Masonic Temple, both on located on Main Street, were built during this time. These three-story buildings

Postcards of Main Street before (top) and after (bottom) construction of the bank building at the turn of the 20th century.

were exceeded in height only by the Odd Fellows Hall which was constructed in 1885. The new Presbyterian Church was dedicated in 1902. The headquarters of the Fayette City Council of the Junior Order of United American Mechanics was constructed on a lot on Fourth Street in 1904. The YMCA was organized in 1904 and their own building was dedicated three years later. The 20th century was clearly off to a bang in Fayette City.

Now that the railroad had arrived in Fayette City, the massive coal deposits that filled Hamer Hollow could finally be tapped and easily transported down river to Pittsburgh. In an announcement that coincided with the opening of the railroad in 1895, the Johnson Coal Company (sometimes incorrectly spelled Johnston) declared its intent to open a new mine, the Arnold Mine, just a hundred or so yards up the Hollow from the intersection of Fording and Fourth Streets. More mines followed and the formerly quiet Hollow quickly became engorged with railroad tracks used to transport the seemingly endless natural resource. Such was the dominance of the Johnson Coal Company in the Hollow that Hamer Hollow became known as Johnson Hollow, as it is still called today.

Arnold City, about a mile from Fayette City, up the Monongahela river, is the product of the Johnston Coal Mining Company, and is one of the most flourishing hamlets along the river. The coal company has 100 houses already up or building, having let a contract for 50 some weeks ago. Figures are now being taken on 50 more dwellings, to be erected as soon as the other 50 are finished. The houses are to be built separately, each on a lot 40x120 feet, fronting on streets laid out by the company. The town has grown so fast within the last year that a large addition is to be built to the town school during the summer vacation.

Pittsburgh Daily Post
July 2, 1899

The second Arnold Mine, Arnold No.2, was opened in 1898 at the end of the Hollow, about a mile from Fayette City. A year later, Arnold No.3 was opened between the first two mines. In order to provide for the hundreds of necessary workers for the mines, the Johnson Coal Mining Company constructed a patch town known as Arnold City

Postcards of the corner of Main Street and Union Street before (top) and after (bottom) construction of the Masonic Temple. The building on the corner in the top picture was known as the Baldwin House. The office and residence of Dr. J.M.H. Gordon was located next to Baldwin House.

located on the hill directly above the Arnold No.2 mine. The company store for the patch town was located at the base of the hill leading out of the Hollow to Arnold City. The hill to Arnold City is just one of the options for exiting the Hollow. A left turn at the company store climbs to the town of Marion (or Fairhope). A right turn on to what the locals call Shaft Hill ascends to Connellsville Street returning to downtown Fayette City through Brownstown and town hill. A loop from downtown, through Johnson Hollow, up Shaft Hill, and down through Brownstown and town hill to downtown provides a nearly 3-mile scenic tour of the area.

> "Navoo Hollow was at the end of town. There were coal mines down there. On Sundays, my cousins and I would walk from Johnson Hollow around what we called the loop to Navoo Hollow. Usually the coal miners lived there, like the Slovaks. There weren't too many Italians that I remember, but a lot of Slovaks and Russians. They lived in their little houses there. They didn't associate much with the other people in town. But that was our Sunday outing. It was quite a walk."
>
> -Shirley Ferree Stilgenbauer

> "Something else we'd like to do was we enjoyed long walks with my cousin and sister. On Sunday afternoons, we would take these long walks. We had a choice of a Navoo Hollow or Johnson Hollow loop. With Navoo Hollow, you can walk to the end and turn around and come back. Johnson Hollow, you could walk through the Hollow, walk the loop through Brownstown and then down the hill to town again. That was a big, big thing for us. We used to do that quite often."
>
> -Nancy Ferree Johnson

> "One of the things we would do on Sunday afternoon we would walk the loop what we called it. You would go up Johnson Hollow, and then up through and around Brownstown and come down town hill. That was like a big Sunday."
>
> -Georgia Nicholson Slezak

At the south end of Fayette City, Navoo Hollow forms the other boundary of town hill. Lamb Lick Run creek runs down the Hollow and exits into the Monongahela River just as Downer's Run does from Johnson Hollow. The road going up the Hollow begins as an extension of Cook Street before becoming Navoo Hollow Road. Navoo Hollow was the location of one of the first glass factories in Fayette City. The glass factory was originally constructed in 1844 and saw several changes in ownership before its final demise at the turn of the 20th century. The tenement houses that were part of the glass works became inhabited with coal miners who flocked to Fayette City during the coal boom. Town hill and Brownstown are connected to Navoo Hollow by Hill Street which descends to the Hollow near the Woodvale Cemetery and offers an alternate route for a loop around town.

The origin of the name "Navoo" is somewhat of a mystery. The editor of the Fayette City Journal, Fayette City's weekly newspaper established in 1900, asked his readers in a February 1945 issue if anyone knew the origin of the name. Unfortunately, no response was ever reported in the Journal. However, circumstantial evidence points to at least one plausible hypothesis for the name's origin. In the Upper Monongahela Valley Business Directory of 1890, the glass works in the Hollow was referred to as the Nauvoo Glass Works. A 1904 map of Fayette City published by T.M Fowler also refers to the hollow as Nauvoo Hollow. The word "Nauvoo" is of Hebrew etymology and means "they are beautiful". The complete Hebrew word Nauvoo is fairly rare and appears only in the Old Testament book of Isaiah. The word Nauvoo was made famous by Joseph Smith, founder and leader of the Latter Day Saints Church. In 1840, fleeing persecution by the state of Missouri, Joseph Smith purchased the small town of Commerce, Illinois and renamed it Nauvoo. Nauvoo, IL to this day attracts visitors from far and wide because of its historical importance

> "How *beautiful* upon the mountains are the feet of him that bringeth good tidings."
> Isaiah 52:7

to the Latter Day Saints and its offshoots. So what's the connection to Fayette City? Stories of Mormons in Fayette City date back to at least 1886 when it was reported that members of the local Reorganized Church of Jesus Christ of Latter Day Saints (RLDS) refused to take medicine recommended by the town doctor, relying instead on church elders to lay hands on the sick for healing. It is entirely possible, although still speculative, that Nauvoo Hollow was named by someone from the local RLDS, particularly considering the bucolic scenery in the Hollow. The spelling of the word Nauvoo appeared to vary in period newspapers. While the earliest spelling seemed to be Nauvoo, several examples of the spelling Navoo were evident by the 1940s including references in the Fayette City Journal. At first blush, the Navoo spelling appears to be a simplified and more phonetic spelling of Nauvoo. What is clear, however, is that both spellings were used for the same location. The Navoo spelling will be used here from this point forward.

Just to the south of the entrance to Navoo Hollow and the southern entrance to Fayette City is the small neighborhood known as Sisleytown. In 1801 Lewis Sisley bought a 175-acre tract of land called "Sewardton" from John Seward. The original Sewardton tract adjoined the southern border of Colonel Cook's Whiskey Mount tract. Sisley laid out the tract in plots forming the tiny village of Sisleytown. A few years later, in 1808, Sisley purchased from Thomas Strawn an additional 77-acre plot along Lamb Lick Run where he built the first of several iterations of sawmills to inhabit the location. Sisleytown was the location of one of the first glass factories in or around Cookstown as well as the home of Justus Blaney, Cookstown's first potter. Continuing south from Sisleytown, Gillespie Hollow with its copious coal mines marks the beginning of one of the richest coal fields in all of Fayette County.

Clay pot produced by J.L. Blaney, Cookstown, PA.

Fayette City's neighbor across the Monongahela River to the west is the small, unassuming hamlet of Allenport in Washington County. Originally known as Independence, Allenport was founded in 1850 with the name change occurring in 1865. Around 1820 ferry service between Allenport and Cookstown was put into place and continued until the 1964. For decades the two towns discussed the possibility of a constructing a bridge between them. The original 1881 proposal had the bridge landing at Market Street in Fayette City. Subsequent proposals made the connection from Bridge Street in Allenport to Union Street in Fayette City. Plans to build a toll bridge were approved by President Hoover in 1931 but were never realized due to the onset of the Great Depression. Yet another proposal to connect the two towns was made in 1946, this time connecting at the north end of Fayette City. The planned route ran through Johnson Hollow, crossed the River north of the waterworks and connected with Allenport Hollow. It too failed to gain support. Allenport remained largely unaffected by industry until 1917 when the Pittsburgh Steel Company announced plans to build a plant to produce tube steel on bottom land bordering the Monongahela River. This stroke of good fortune would have a profound impact not only on Allenport, but also on Fayette City as well.

Such were the neighborhoods and neighbors of Fayette City by the 1940s. Although downtown, town hill, Johnson Hollow, Navoo Hollow and Sisleytown were really only separated by hundreds of yards, the topographical barriers between the neighborhoods significantly reduced the interactions between their inhabitants. Only a smattering of homes was located in Johnson Hollow and Sisleytown. Navoo Hollow with its connection to the mines was slightly more populated, but still not as heavily as town hill and downtown. Most of Fayette City's residents lived on town hill while businesses dominated the downtown area.

The topography of Fayette City not only made it difficult for neighborhoods to interact, but also made it particularly prone to flooding. With the River and town hill forming boundaries to the west and east, respectively, and the two Hollows and their creeks at the south and north ends of town, downtown Fayette City would effectively become cut off from the world in times of high water. The low-lying intersection at Fording, Fourth, and Connellsville Streets and the entrance to Johnson Hollow was and still is a particularly troublesome spot. The slightest flash flooding prevents traffic in all directions. This persistent problem led the Borough Council in 1945 to create an emergency road connecting Front Street and Route 711 to Belle Vernon to circumvent the intersection during flooding. The unpaved road was a welcomed escape route during high waters. Unfortunately, its infrequent use and less frequent maintenance often left it a challenge to navigate when most needed!

Coal production dominated the economy of Fayette City from the late 1800s to the early 1900s. By the mid-1920s, however, many of the large mines surrounding Fayette City including the Apollo, Fayette City, and Arnold No.1 mines were exhausted. The surge in Fayette City's population during the first two decades of the 1900s was significantly reversed by 1930. The onset of the Great Depression exacerbated the situation even further. At one point during the Depression the unemployment in Fayette City reached 40 percent. Such were the conditions at the beginning of the 1940s, a decade that would challenge Fayette City like no other and bring with it heartbreaking lows to open the decade and exhilarating highs to close the decade.

An Editorial!

WHY MUST FAYETTE CITY SUFFER?

That old old story about the high water, which has caused many inconveniences and hardships to Fayette City residents, is again a topic for discussion. Everyone seems to have a remedy or plan but few have tried to get action. While the road is closed everyone wants to get action, but just as soon as the water subsides the project is a forgotten issue.

Fayette City's plight is now news for the Pittsburgh newspapers. Just as soon a the river gets a little above normal they report route 711 thru Fayette City is closed to traffic due to high water. The radio even comes in with their share by broadcasting the news that Fayette City is plagued wih high water.

Why all the concern over high water? Here is the reason. Fayette City, which is located across the river from the Allenport Works of Pittsburgh Steel and is just five miles from the Monessen plant of the same company, has many men who are vital to the war effort in their employ. When the water is high these men lose valuable time in getting back and forth to work, in some cases are late, and this past winter were unable to get around the high water due to hazardous conditions on alternate routes.

Another way the high water hinders the war effort is that this route is used by three coal mines and truckers must stop hauling coal from these mines because alternate routes are not safe for travel.

Now is the time for action so let us all get behind Council and help them to succeed in their efforts to secure an emergency road.

Fayette City Journal
March 2, 1945

As Flood Waters Surrounded Fayette City

Flood waters once more descended upon Fayette City as pictured above. The water started to come into the borough early last Saturday morning and continued to rise until about midnight. The emergency road was used until about 5 p. m. when it too became covered with water.

Fayette City Journal
February 20, 1948

REFERENCES

Coode, Thomas H. *Bugdust and Blackdamp, Life and Work in the Old Coal Patch*. Comart Press, 1986.

DiCiccio, C. *Coal and Coke in Pennsylvania*. Commonwealth of Pennsylvania, Harrisburg, 1996.

Pittsburgh Steel Company Monessen Works, Monessen Pennsylvania (historic-structures.com) http://www.historic-structures.com/pa/monessen/monessen_steel1.php

Soroka, Mark (2016, December 12) Small Town Life: Life goes in in Allenport despite economic downturn. *The Herald Standard*.

Wikipedia contributors. "Fayette City, Pennsylvania." *Wikipedia, The Free Encyclopedia*. Wikipedia, The Free Encyclopedia, 7 Dec. 2021. Web. 8 Dec. 2021.

CHAPTER 2 The Fayette City Journal

History

Numerous small towns sprung up along the banks of the Monongahela Valley in southwestern Pennsylvania during the 1800s. As these towns grew in stature, one sure sign of success was the establishment of a local newspaper, usually of the weekly variety. The Brownsville Clipper (est. 1853), the Belle Vernon Enterprise (est. 1886), the Charleroi Mirror (est. 1891), the Roscoe Ledger (est. 1897), the Monessen News (est. 1899), and the Monongahela Daily Republican (est. 1889) are some prime examples. Fayette City joined the ranks in 1900 when the Fayette City Journal published its first issue.

Fayette City Journal
October 13, 1944

It was announced in the Monongahela Daily Republican on March 19, 1900, that a new weekly paper to be called the Fayette City Journal will soon be issued and that Carson W. Beam will be the editor and proprietor. Beam learned the newspaper trade as a typo on the Ligonier Echo in Ligonier, PA. In April of 1900 the first issue of the Journal was released as a 4-page "six column quarto". By November of the same year, the Journal became "a seven column eight-page paper with patent inside". (The term "patent inside" refers to preprinted newspaper pages sold to newspaper publishers to provide them with content at a nominal cost. One side would be preprinted usually with some form of advertisement or other syndicated material. The newspaper owner was free to print whatever they wanted on the other side.) In April of 1901, the Daily Republican congratulated Beam on the publication of Volume 2, Number 1 of the Fayette City Journal celebrating one year in print.

Mr. Beam quickly became active in the Fayette City political scene and was elected Justice of the Peace in 1905. It was not uncommon for Beam to use his editorial voice at the Journal to express his displeasure about issues ranging from public drunkenness to nude bathing in the Monongahela River. Beam's tenure at the Journal was short lived, however, when he sold his interests in the Journal to M.G. Beck in 1905, bragging that he started the newspaper on

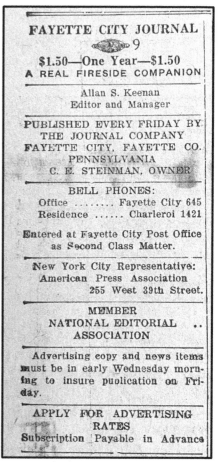

Fayette City Journal
October 20, 1944

The Fayette City Journal

PUBLISHED WEEKLY IN THE INTEREST OF FAYETTE CITY, WASHINGTON AND JEFFERSON TOWNSHIPS AND SURROUNDING COMMUNITIES

VOL. XLV. NO. 25   FAYETTE CITY, FAYETTE COUNTY, PENNSYLVANIA. FRIDAY, NOVEMBER 24, 1944   FIVE CENTS PER COPY   ESTABLISHED 1906

$12.50! Beam's departure from Fayette City was only temporary. In late 1906, Beam, then editor and proprietor of the newly established Youngwood Journal, reacquired the Fayette City Journal in a joint venture with C.L. Gilbert. Beam's second stint in Fayette City was not destined to go well either. Just a few years after reacquiring the Journal, he wrote this scathing editorial about some of the town's citizens.

> "Oh yes, you old backbiters and stick-in-the-mud individuals, Fayette City is some day going to have a factory and will forge right ahead not withstanding your "cold-water" efforts. You won't do anything yourself nor give any encouragement to others who really have the best interests of the town at heart and are trying to do something. If there is a town with more irresponsible persons who have more to say and less influence than this we would like to hear of it. There are a whole lot of people with whom patience ceases to be a virtue, but who seem to be able to get an audience with persons who should have more "gumption" about them."

In February of 1909, less than 10 years after establishing the newspaper, Beam sold the Journal to E. D. Steinman. Carson W. Beam, died in 1935 at the age of 65, spending the last 19 years of his life associated with the advertising department of Rosenbaum's store in Pittsburgh.

Edward Deletombe Steinman Sr. was born in 1861 in South Charleston, Ohio. While learning the tinning trade in his father's shop, he wrote articles for the South Charleston Sentinel newspaper. The young Steinman also took up an interest in the telegraph, a new technology at the time. His interest in telegraphy led to a job with the Pennsylvania railroads where he became the ticket agent for the Baltimore and Ohio City railroad in Pittsburgh. Looking for something to call his own, Steinman acquired the Journal from Beam and moved his family to Fayette City. Steinman and his wife Clara had four children, one daughter, Laura, and three sons, Edward D. Jr., Herbert, and Harry, all of whom would come to play a role in the newspaper business. The Steinman's learned very quickly after acquiring the Journal that printing a weekly paper left little time for anything else. Edward and Clara worked side by side to prepare the paper for publication. The children practically grew up in the Journal office and helped out in various departments as soon as they were old enough.

The Fayette City Journal printing office was located at 315 Main Street in Fayette City. The narrow building stretched from Main Street to Fourth Street and had two apartments on the second floor. The Steinmans lived in an apartment in an elegant house caddy-corner to the Journal and next to the Presbyterian manse. The apartments above the Journal office did not appear to be a significant source of income for the Steinmans generating only $180 per year in the early forties. After accruing delinquent taxes on the property from 1932 through 1940, the Steinmans, claiming little revenue from the printing office for a number of years, reached a compromise settlement of $200 to offset the $507 delinquent assessments.

Edward D. Steinman
Fayette City Journal
October 26, 1945

16

Steinman, like his predecessor Beam, eventually became involved in Fayette City's civic scene and served as Burgess for twelve years, during which time Clara served as operator of the Journal. Steinman's term as Burgess was not without controversy. In 1935, councilman William Conlon accused Steinman of violating a borough code by accepting a contact with the borough to furnish supplies and materials in excess of $10 in each instance, even though Steinman's wife had, by that time, become the official operator of the Journal. Steinman declared "I'm within the law and I'm not worrying about it." The matter was eventually dropped.

Edward Steinman remained the editor of the Journal until 1944 when, at the age of 83, illness forced him to find a replacement. On October 1, 1944 Steinman relinquished his post and leased the Journal to Allan S. Keenan of North Charleroi. Keenan learned the newspaper trade under the direction of his father James in the composing room of The Daily Republican in Monongahela,

Facade of the Fayette City Journal office looking north on Main Street.

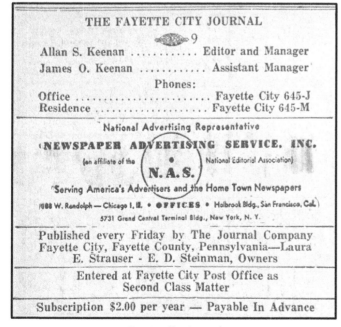

Fayette City Journal January 3, 1947

Pennsylvania. Just over a year later, in October of 1945, Edward D. Steinman passed away. Considered the dean of the Monongahela Valley newspaper publishers, his death was mourned, and his accomplishments celebrated in local newspapers. He was buried by the Bake Funeral Home in Fayette City. Ownership of the Journal was passed from Clara Steinman to her children Laura and Edward, Jr..

Allan Keenan went on to run the Journal for four years. Midway through his tenure, he hired his brother, James, as assistant manager, and increased the cost of an annual subscription from $1.50 to $2.00 per year. During Keenan's tenure, the Journal had more than eight hundred subscribers including locals and out-of-towners alike. Keenan took an active role in the community and often advocated for bettering Fayette City with such projects as building a new honor roll to honor World War II veterans, building an emergency road that could be used during high water, and fighting to keep open Fayette City's railroad station. He was staunchly conservative and in the postwar years preached against the perceived threat of nascent communism in nearly every issue of the Journal. By the summer of 1948, the quality of the Journal was clearly in decline. Local news items that traditionally dominated the front page were replaced by syndicated columns and articles borrowed from neighboring newspapers. Unsurprisingly, in October of 1948, Keenan left the Journal to pursue a higher calling. He entered the Church of God Bible School at Cleveland, Tennessee where after three terms he graduated as a licensed minister.

With the departure of Keenan, Steinman's daughter Laura (now Strauser) and son Edward, took over the newspaper temporarily while looking for a buyer. It took a couple of years, but eventually, in 1951, a buyer was found. Henry M. Badzik, a longtime owner of a printing company in Donora purchased the Journal and kept it open until March of 1957. Loss of vital help to the armed forces Selective Service System, a trend throughout the county to the reading of larger dailies, rising costs, and lack of local support were cited as causes for the paper's demise. The final edition, Volume LVI, Number 37, contained a heart-breaking guest message in the form of an obituary from Mrs. Laura Strauser that read:

> "Goodbye is such a little word
>
> To say what is in our heart.
>
> We do not like to take this road
>
> But all friends soon must part.
>
> I am but a weekly newspaper.
>
> I had tried so hard to do
>
> The many things that are required
>
> With help that is too few.
>
> Fifty-seven years I have told
>
> Of births and marriages and death.
>
> Of happy times and sad ones too
>
> And of those that have crossed our path.
>
> But now my journey is really over,
>
> For help you cannot get.
>
> So, I must follow comrades who
>
> Have long proceeded me in death.
>
> I bid adieu to all my friends
>
> And hope they will think kindly
>
> Of the past – the fun we had.
>
> Times make these changes sadly."

The Steinman family spent more than 40 years associated with the Fayette City Journal. Clara, the matriarch of the family, officially retired from the newspaper business in 1951 with the sale of the Journal, although she remained at the editorial desk until her 81st birthday. She died in 1961 at the age of 92. Edward D. Steinman, Jr. served in the

BUSINESS OPPORTUNITY

In October, 1944, the owners and publishers of this newspaper leased the plant to Mr. Keenan, who has directed the operation of the printing establishment and publication of the paper since that date.

Mr. Keenan has expressed his desire of relinquishing his position as editor and manager and retiring from the business as of October 1, 1948 with intentions of entering other fields of endeavor.

The management of the plant will therefore revert to the owners, Mrs. Laura E. Strauser, of Lock Four, and Edward D. Steinman, Jr., of Upper Darby.

Applications for position of editor and manager of the printing and publishing business will be considered and can be made in person to the owners as well as to Mr. Keenan.

An opportunity is thus afforded for someone who is desirous of entering the journalistic field to step into a position where they can get practical experience and at the same time receive remuneration commensurate with their ability to hold the business now enjoyed by the Journal and to add to the present well established patronage.

Mrs. Strauser can be reached through the Journal or at 316 Isabella Ave., Lock Four. Mr. Steinman, who is presently employed in the composing room of the Philadelphia Inquirer, one of leading daily newspapers in America, can be reached also through the Journal or by writing to 233 Kingston Road, Upper Darby, Pa.

Fayette City Journal
September 10, 1948

"At first we lived above the Journal office on Main Street......We lived on the second floor. Well, they had the office downstairs and then we lived in the apartment upstairs. I would go in there, into the office down there. There would be printing machines. You could smell the ink."

-Georgia Jean Arrow

"I remember that building. It's gone right now, but yeah, they made the Fayette City Journal. There was two apartments upstairs. We went up the steps or else you come in the back street in the back. We were in the back apartment so we could, we didn't have to go up those steps. We used the back entrance and that."

-Eleanor Welsh Owens

"It (the Journal Office) was a great big, long building on Main Street, and they had the presses. I used to go in there all the time. They had a prep room. Then the backroom where they printed, where they printed the paper. Most of the stuff that was in the paper was national and they bought it from other people, you know...And then they'd have lots of local news."

-Joanne Cunningham Manetta

"I used to go in there. I used to do posters when I was a kid. They would sell these big sheets of poster board. I would buy them in there. I read it every week, kind of because, you know, you never know in a small town like that your name might show up....My uncles, who lived in Fayette City when they were young, they moved to other places in Pennsylvania because they were coal miners and mines closed. They had to go find other mines if they wanted to stay in the mines. One was a big boss. He was a manager of the mine. You could get it sent to you every week, that weekly paper. They got it and when they stopped getting it, they were awful disappointed. They said it keeps us on track with our families and everybody."

-Bill Williamson

"Well, I just knew, I think as I recall, it came out weekly. And it had, it would have been "Mary was visiting Mr. and Mrs. Jones", they would list and "Mary visited Joe's last weekend, they went out for dinner." I mean they had little human-interest stories. It would have little write ups about some of the sports in there and advertisements for places to eat. Joe Bell's movie theater items might be in there. But it was sort of a lifeblood. Back then you didn't have television and a lot of other things. It provided a good venue for local information. If soldiers were home on furlough, it would list when they came there and when they were going back."

-Jack Young

"Well, I remember that it (The Fayette City Journal) wasn't very good. There wasn't much in it except political stuff. But here's one for you. In 1948 I fancied myself a sportswriter. And I wrote up a small summary of the World Series of that year. The World Series in 1948 was Cleveland Indians versus the Boston Braves. Yeah, I think that's who it was. The Indians won it in four straight. But anyhow, I wrote up a little summary of that and submitted it for publication in the Fayette City Journal. And they printed it!"

-Mike Hancock

military during World War I and rose rapidly through the ranks. After the War, Edward served as a national service officer of the Disabled American Veterans. He was a member of the composing room staff of the Philadelphia Inquirer newspaper when he died at the age of 66 in 1959. Edward Jr.'s son, Edward D. Steinman III, who also worked in the Journal office as a youth, was a decorated veteran of World War II flying dozens of missions over southern France, northern Italy and Yugoslavia. Herbert worked in the printing business at Masontown, PA. The youngest son, Harry, worked for the Washington Observer. The daughter Laura ran the Journal from the time of Keenan's departure until Badzik purchased the paper in 1951. The Steinmans were truly a remarkable family and served the citizens of Fayette City and the United States with distinction.

By the 1950s "The Golden Age" of the weekly local newspaper was quickly coming to an end. The Fayette City Journal was not alone in its demise. The Roscoe Ledger published its last issue in 1952. The Belle Vernon Enterprise closed shop in 1954. The Charleroi Mail, which absorbed the Charleroi Mirror in 1923, followed suit in 1960. The same reasons that caused the Fayette City Journal to close - greatly increased production costs, a trend toward the reading of larger dailies, and lack of local support - were also cited as causes for the end of these weekly publications. In reality, though, the world was changing quickly. Owning an automobile was becoming within reach of every family, as was owning a television. People were becoming more mobile and more aware of life beyond their city limits. But make no mistake, these weekly publications were the lifeblood of small towns for many decades and can be credited with creating communities with remarkable strength, compassion, and unity.

Layout and Content

The format of the Fayette City Journal remained remarkably consistent throughout the decade of the 1940s. Columns and writers would come and go. Even the comic strip section saw some minor changes when "Nancy" and "Mutt and Jeff" were introduced in 1945. At the beginning of the decade the Journal was a nickel an issue. By the end of the decade the cost for the weekly had risen by just a penny to six cents. The Journal usually consisted of eight pages. On special occasions such as Christmas and New Year's, the Journal would be extended to twelve pages to accommodate all the advertisements and well wishes from local businesses and individuals. The Journal even reached sixteen pages when delinquent property taxes for Fayette County were reported. On very rare occasions, like in December of 1944 and January of 1945, the Journal was limited to only four pages when flooding and snow prevented syndicated material from reaching the paper's office by car or rail thus limiting the issues to local news only.

The syndicated material typically consisted of four pages. During the war years, these sections often contained articles and numerous photographs of the military and European war theatre. The comics section consumed most of an entire page and contained such strips as "Sparky Watts", "Reg'lar Fellers", "Virgil", "Pop", "Raising Kane", and "Private Buck", and starting with the last issue of 1945, "Nancy" and "Mutt and Jeff". The serial story was a popular section as well. Each week a chapter of a short story would be published enticing readers to return the following week for the next installment. Titles during the mid-1940s included "Girl Overboard" by George F. Worts (19 issues), "Country Cured" by Homer Croy (25 issues) "Thunderhead" by Mary

Front entrance to the Journal office looking south on Main Street. Photo courtesy of Judith Dewar Shearer.

O'Hara (27 issues), "Last Lover" by Helen Topping Miller (21 issues), and "Valley of Revenge" by Jackson Cole (21 issues). The syndicated pages also contained advertisements for medicinal products such as Bengay, Doan's Pills, Balsam of Myrrh, Kellogg's Powder and Vicks VapoRub, no doubt reflecting the needs of the weary laborer. Other columns included "Household Memos", "Gay Gadgets", "What to Do", "Household Hints", "Woman's

World" and "Kathleen Norris Says" for the lady of the house, and "The Bible Today" and "Sunday School Lessons" for the church goer. Finally, the "Classified Department" offered a variety of help wanted, personal, real estate, and wanted ads from across the country.

Beyond the syndicated pages, the Fayette City Journal was strongly focused on local news and activities. The headlines often recounted the latest political elections, updates on meetings of the town council, local school news, new business openings, fund drives, activities of the American Legion and Lions Club, community parades, picnics and carnivals, and of course local sports news. On rare occasions, a major news story like the end of World War II, the murder of a local teenage girl, or the closing of the town's train station would capture the headlines. More on these big stories in a later Chapter.

Apart from the headline news and the occasional editorial, however, the front page often contained several reoccurring columns related to topics of community interest. During the war years, the column "Among Those In Service" provided updates on the accomplishments, promotions, injuries, and visits home of the young men and women from Fayette City and its surroundings communities. When a soldier was killed or wounded inaction, the Journal would often provide a standalone article describing the event. These unfortunate incidents occurred all too often and will be discussed in more detail in a later chapter.

Another favorite front page column was entitled "As We Look Backwards" which recounted stories that appeared in the Journal ten, twenty, thirty and sometimes even forty years earlier. Rarely containing any tidbits of hard news from decades ago, this section usually recounted marriages, birthdays, meetings, illnesses, and school activities.

Among Those In Service
★ ★ ★ ★ ★   ★ ★ ★ ★ ★

STANLEY MARCUS
Staney Marcus of the U. S. Navy stationed at Miami, Florida is home visiting with his mother, Mrs. Julia Marcus and also with friends here.

GEORGE MAST
George Mast, son of Mr. and Mrs. Alex Mast was recently promoted to the rank of Sergeant. The young Sergeant is stationed somewhere overseas.

FRED BEDNAR
Pfc. Fred Bednar, formerly of Gillespie is now stationed at Tampa, Florida. He is the son of Mr. and Mrs. George Bednar.

WILLIAM HYNES
William Hynes, son of Mr. and Mrs. Jack Hynes of Sisleytown recently arrived safely somewhere in England. He is in good health and says "hello" to all his many friends here at home.

CLAYTON PROPES
A telegram received by the parents of Cpl. Clayton Propes, informed them and his wife that he had arrived safely in the "States" after 15 months in the South Pacific. Clayton is a graduate of the local high school and is serving with the U. S. Marines.

ROBERT J. ELGIN
Cpl. Robert J. Elgin, 22 year old son of Mr. and Mrs. John Elgin, Fayette City, R. D. 1, has been promoted from private first class at the 155th Army General Hospital in England. Cpl. Elgin is an operating room technician assisting in the operations performed at this hospital which are bringing about the recovery of wounded soldiers. Cpl. Elgin received surgical technician's training at Billings General Hospital, Fort Benjamin Harrison, Indiana.

CLARENCE STARK
Lt. Clarence Stark of the U. S. Navy has been moved from Norfolk, Vrginia to Brooklyn, New York. Lt. Stark, a former local resident, prior to his entering the service was coach at Uniontown and formerly coached at Marion.

WILLIAM AND ROBERT CRAFT
William and Robert Craft, sons of Mr. and Mrs. Sherman Craft arrived home recently to enjoy the coming holiday season with family and friends. Both brothers are members of the U. S. Navy. William is a graduate of Marion High and Robert a graduate of Jefferson High School.

JOHN B. TRAVERSARI
John B. Traversari, Y 3-c returned to his duties Wednesday morning, after spending some time visiting his wife, Violet Mae Traversari, baby daughter, Donna Maria and with his parents, Mr. and Mrs. Domenick Traversari, all of Fayette City, R. D. Y 3-c Traversari is stationed at the Naval Air Station at Norfolk, Va.

PAUL COOPER
Paul Cooper arrived in Italy November 1, after leaving England in October. Enroute to Italy he stopped in Cherbourg, France for a few days, then on to Italy. There Pvt. Cooper visited the cities of Florence and Piso. While in Piso, he saw the famous leaning tower. He is now serving in the 85th Infantry Division of the 5th Army under the command of Gen. L. K. Truscott. Pvt. Cooper is the husband of the former Margaret Hamer.

WAYNE R. SMITH
Pfc. Wayne R. Smith, U. S. M. C. R., nineteen year old son of Mr. and Mrs. Charles Smith of Belle Vernon, R. D. serving in the Marianas Islands in the Central Pacific. continued on page eight

Fayette City Journal
December 22, 1944

The column in the top left-hand corner of the front page was a special location, at least judging by the content usually found there. In the early 40s, this prime real estate was occupied by the town-favorite column "'Round About Town". The column was a combination of local trivia, gossip, rumor, complaining, and idle speculation. But perhaps the most important tidbit of information in this column was the weekly update on the activities of the so-called Rose

As We Look Backwards

Through the Files of Your Community Newspaper

TWENTY YEARS AGO
FRIDAY JUNE 12, 1925

St. Edwards Church wrecked when ground settles into mine.

Miss Sara Renstrom of Fayette City, who is a student at Lasell Seminary for young women in Auburndale, Mass., has renewed her application for enrollment for the 1925-26 term.

At a meeting of the local school board held last Friday evening, a resolution was passed designating Belle Vernon High School as the school where pupils of Fayette City, of high school age, shall attend this coming year.

Mrs. Simeon Humphries, nee Allie Rutter, died in the Mercy hospital, Friday, June 5, aged 40 years.

Miss Mary Hagerty spent a few days visiting at the home of Mr. and Mrs. Heath near Rehoboth.

THIRTY YEARS AGO
FRIDAY, JUNE 11, 1915

Born to Mr. and Mrs. Daniel Tolan, a daughter, June 8.

Albert Allen Beeler and Miss Jennie Sowden, both of Fairhope and Arnold City district, were united in marriage at the home of the bride, Wednesday evening June 9.

Out of the 35 registered candidates in the pony contest conducted by ten merchants of Fayette City, which ended June 1, Dale Howes, 6 year old son of Mr. and Mrs. John Howes, came out the winner and the pony and cart were delivered to him.

Walter Vaughan, son of Mr. and Mrs. T. P. Vaughan of this place, has graduated from the Cincinnati College of Music with the highest honors.

Fayette City Journal
June 15, 1945

As We Look Backwards

Through the Files of Your Community Newspaper

TWENTY YEARS AGO
FRIDAY NOVEMBER 27, 1925

Annastacia Stublarac, daughter of Mr. and Mrs. George Stublarac and Mr. David Sudac of Swissvale, Pa., were united in marriage in Charleroi, Wednesday, November 10.

The Holly Troop of Girl Scouts held their Thanksgiving Party on Monday evening.

James P. Miller's famous Scotch Collie dogs are beginning to be widely known throughout western Pennsylvania and Ohio.

Slippery Highway still causes many accidents.

Mr. and Mrs. J. H. Wilson entertained Saturday afternoon with a birthday party in honor of their daughter, Georgetta.

THIRTY YEARS AGO
FRIDAY NOVEMBER 26, 1915

John Furlong, aged 33 years, died in the Charleroi-Monessen hospital Thursday from loss of blood following an accident on the Arnold City branch of the Lake Erie Railroad.

David Authers of Niagara Falls, former resident of Fayette City, was married to Miss Merrian Calvert Keller at the bride's home in Lewistown, New York, Wednesday November 17.

The Union High School of this place defeated the Scholastic gridiron club of Uniontown here Thanksgiving.

R. G. Knight has had placed in front of his store one of the niftiest novelties. It is a contrivance which holds roasted peanuts and keeps them hot.

Fayette City Journal
November 30, 1945

Look Who's Here!

Mr. and Mrs. George Grados, Fayette City are the proud parents of a baby daughter born on Christmas Day. The couple have three other children, two girls and a boy.

Fayette City Journal
December 9, 1944

Look Who's Here!

Born to Mr. and Mrs. John Vargo of Cook Street, Fayette City, a son, weighing seven pounds, one ounce, September 25, 1944, at 2:47 p. m. in the Charleroi-Monessen Hospital.

Born to Mr. and Mrs. Willis Chalfant of Fayette City, R. D., a son, weighing five pounds, one ounce, Monday, September 25, 1944 at 9:37 a. m. in the Charleroi-Monessen Hospital.

Fayette City Journal
October 3, 1944

Look Who's Here!

Mr. and Mrs. Raymond Barker of Connellsville St. are the proud parents of a baby daughter born on Saturday evening February 2, 1946 in the Charleroi-Monessen Hospital. Mrs. Barker will be remembered as the former Thelma Hicks.

Fayette City Journal
February 8, 1946

Look Who's Here!

Born to Mr. and Mrs. Thomas Cramer of 326 Second Street, a son, eight pounds, twelve ounces, Monday July 9, 1945 at 8:07 a. m. in the Charleroi-Monessen Hospital.

Born to Mr. and Mrs. Thomas Matalo of Fayette City, R. D. 1, a son, nine pounds, Sunday July 8, 1945 at 11:45 a. m. in the Charleroi-Monessen Hospital.

Fayette City Journal
July 13, 1945

Fayette City Journal
October 20, 1944

Room Kid. The identity of the Rose Room Kid was apparently a well-kept secret although he certainly did seem to get around. What was clear, however, was that readers returned week after week to find out what he was up to. In June of 1946, the light-hearted 'Round About Town column was replaced by the uber conservative column "Washington Flashes" by Peter Lektrich, a good friend of Allan Keenan. Lektrich, a Republican who ran for state office but was soundly defeated in the heavily Democratic district, offered insight into the machinations of Washington, DC and how Fayette City might be affected by their outcome. The column lasted about six months before being temporarily replace by "As We Look Backwards". In August 1947, a new column, "The American Way" made its appearance. The American Way emphasized, among other things, the virtues of Biblical principles, positive thinking, free enterprise, the dangers of organized labor and socialism, and the perceived threat of nascent communism. Contributors to the column included leaders of the National Small Businessmen's Association, noted national economists, and the popular motivational author Dr. Norman Vincent Peale. By 1950, the syndicated The American Way was replaced by locally written articles of general interest.

Other articles often found on the front page included "Look Who's Here" announcing recent births, and its counterpart the "Obituaries". (These two columns appeared on other pages as well.) The birth rate during the war years was exceptionally low for obvious reasons. Immediately after the war, Fayette City, like the rest of the country experienced a baby boom.

Births from "Look Who's Here"		
(*annualized for partial year data*)		
Year	*Births*	*% ±*
1944	28*	--
1945	28	0.0
1946	44	57.1
1947	91	106.8
1948	99*	8.8

Despite the sharp rise in births in the latter half of the 40s, the population of Fayette City decreased by more than 12% over the decade. Continued decline in the local coal mining industry accounted for some of the population drain. The plentiful jobs in neighboring towns like Monessen and Charleroi, no doubt, persuaded people to leave Fayette City to ease the commute to work.

Off the front page, several sections and advertisements graced the interior pages of the Journal. The numerous businesses in Fayette City advertised their goods and services weekly. These businesses and their advertisements will be explored in detail in the next Chapter. Businesses outside of Fayette City, most notably in Belle Vernon, Brownsville and Charleroi, also used the pages of the Journal to reach potential customers. Movie theatres in the area were particularly prolific advertisers. It wasn't uncommon for the Ritz and Verdi theatres in Belle Vernon, the Coyle, Menlo, and State theatres in Charleroi, and the Plaza, Strand, and Bison theatres in Brownsville to all have advertisements in the same issue. Of course, Fayette City's lone theatre, the Bell Theatre, was also a weekly advertiser.

'Round About Town

The mail bag this week brings forth another name in the contest to name the oldest resident in Fayette City. This candidate is not a resident of Fayette City proper, but since we have had so few responses from local residents we wish to enlarge the contest and include Washington and Jefferson Townships. The letter this week names John D. Perry of Fairhope as being 94 years of age. Mr. Perry has six children, twenty-two grandchildren and twenty-two great grandchildren.

Local people are wondering what is taking place along Main Street at one of the City's favorite tap rooms. The exterior and interior are being renovated with paint. Look on the back page of this week's paper and you will find the answer.

Fayette City Journal
October 13, 1944

Perhaps the most popular sections of the newspaper were the weekly "Local Topics" and "Local and Society" sections. It wasn't uncommon for the Local Topics section to take up a significant part of a page. A typical entry consisted of two or three lines of text provided by readers describing, among other things, who went shopping to far off places like Pittsburgh or Charleroi, who had callers in their home, who was on vacation, or who was suffering from illness. Having your name appear in this section connoted a certain amount of prestige and importance in the community. Some people even seemed to use the section almost like a diary of their weekly activities. For example, nearly every move of the beloved hometown hero, Major League baseball player Jimmy Russell, was documented in this section. Whether visiting home in Fayette City, attending spring training in Florida, or a vacationing in New York City, Jimmy's whereabouts were always in the news.

Entries in the Local and Society section often covered similar content compared to the Local Topics but provided much more detailed descriptions. This section routinely described announcements of engagements to be married, wedding ceremonies, family reunions, baby showers, and meetings of church groups, and various clubs like the American Legion Auxiliary, the Women's Club, sewing clubs and ladies card clubs.

Mr. and Mrs. Fred Renstrom were recent callers in Pittsburgh.

Jimmy Russell is home again after spending a week hunting in Kane.

Mrs. Minnie Brightwell of Grace Street is still confined to her home due to illness.

Mr. and Mrs. David Mathewson and Mrs. Melrose Gardner were Monday visitors in Charleroi

Mrs. Benjamin Holliday and Mrs. Gilbert Young were Pittsburgh visitors last Friday.

Mrs. Claude Davis and daughter, Nancy Ann were callers in Charleroi last Saturday afternoon.

Mrs. Ella Sneed of Monessen visited recently at the home of Mrs. Thomas Marriott on Main Street.

Rev. Sommers of Brownsville and Rev. Smith of Madison were callers in Fayette City last Friday evening.

Mrs. Alfred Makepeace, Mrs. William Hetherington and Mrs. Clarence Young were callers last Thursday in Pittsburgh.

Fayette City Journal
December 15, 1944

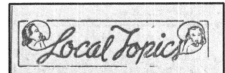

Miss Flo Gater was a business caller in Pittsburgh on Tuesday.

Mrs. Minnie Brightwell is visiting with her daughter, Mrs. Alec Abercrombie, in Verona.

Audrey Dewar and Nancy Ferree returned home Monday from a week's stay at Camp Redstone.

Jimmy Russell of the Boston Braves spent Sunday evening at his home here.

Dana Baldwin has returned from a week's vacation at Canadohta Lake.

Mr. Harry Shanks is visiting with Mr. and Mrs. R. L. Croushore in Margate, New Jersey.

Mrs. Roy Mossburg entertained the N.C.T.S. Class at the Methodist Church last Friday.

Fayette City Journal
July 23, 1948

Details of weekly worship services were provided in the "Church News" section. For a town of its size, Fayette City had a remarkable number of churches, seven to be exact, including the Presbyterian Church, the Church of Christ, the Latter Day Saints Church, the Christian and Missionary Alliance Tabernacle, the Methodist Church and two Catholic churches, St. Eusebius and St. Edwards. All but St. Edwards advertised their services in the Journal. St. Eusebius discontinued their entry in the mid-1940s. A few churches outside of Fayette City also advertised in the Journal including the Allenport Methodist Church with its female pastor, the Christian Science Church in the city of Monongahela, and Braznell's Christian and Missionary Alliance Church.

Local & Society

SHOWER HELD IN HONOR OF FORMER MARGARET COPE

Mrs. Adolph Miron, the former Miss Margaret Ann Cope was guest of honor, when her mother, Mrs. Russell Cope of Fairhope entertained at a miscellaneous shower in the social rooms of the Marion Presbyterian church.

Forty friends were in attendance and the evening was pleasantly spent playing typical shower games. During the first part of the evening a brief program consisting of readings by Mrs. Richard Hamer and Mrs. Ethel Hamer and group singing followed, with the entire program lead by Mrs. C. C. Houseman.

Later in the evening, Mrs. Cope served refreshments and Mrs. Miron was presented with many lovely and useful gifts. Her husband, Pfc. Adolph Miron is stationed in the state of California.

LEGION AUXILIARY MEETS LAST WEEK AT HAMER HOME

The regular meeting of the Ladies American Legion Auxiliary was held Friday evening September 7 at the home of Mrs. Samuel Hamer.

Durng the business meeting, the ladies agreed to give $5.00 to the local Girl Scout Troop and to donate the local school, their piano.

Guests present were Mrs. Adam Authers, Mrs. Frank Grummer, Mrs. Philip DeRienzo and Mrs. Frank McKenna, who are the local Gold Star Mothers. To each was presented a Gold Star Pin and a membership card for a year.

Later in the evening a lunch was served by the hostess.

SINGING CLASS MEETS LAST MONDAY NIGHT

The Singing Class held their meeting Monday evening at eight o'clock in the Methodist church with about forty members and guests present.

The program consisted of a saxophone solo by James Ridgway, piano solos by the Misses Agnes Wallis and Nancy Ann Davis. A quartette made up of the Rev. Mary Elizabeth Kunselman and Mr. Harper of Allenport and Mrs. Thomas Marriott and son James rendered several selections, followed by a vocal solo by Mrs. Fred Brightwell. Everyone enjoyed the program and the singing of old time hymns.

A number of guests were present from Allenport.

The next meeting of the Singing Class will be held Monday October 1 in the Latter Day Saints church. All members are urged to attend and bring a friend.

MRS. RUSSELL COPE HOST TO CARD CLUB AT HER HOME

Mrs. Russell Cope of Fairhope was hostess last Thursday evening at her home to members of her card club.

Five hundred was the main diversion of the evening and prizes were received by Mrs. John Toth, Mrs. James Davis, Mrs. Fred Leithold. Mrs. Howard Jones was a guest at the meeting.

Lunch was served later and the next meeting will be held at the home of Mrs. Leithold.

Fayette City Journal
September 14, 1945

Fayette City Journal
August 10, 1945

The back page of the Journal often contained reports on the Fayette City Borough Council Budget Resolution, the Jefferson Township Audit Report, and the Auditor's Report for the Fayette City School District. The most interesting part of the back page, however, had to be the local Classified ads. These ads were usually few in number. Categories included Wanted to Rent, Wanted to Buy, Help Wanted, Business Services, For Sale, Property for Sale, Legal Notices, In Memorial, and Card of Thanks sections. The In Memoriam and Card of Thanks entries were particularly poignant. Since Fayette City was

Fayette City Journal
July 14, 1945

such a small town, when someone died, everyone knew about it and probably knew the deceased. The bereaved family would often be flooded with copious amounts of food and offers of help from neighbors. In response, the grieving family would offer a Card of Thanks expressing their appreciation in the form of a Classified ad.

It was mentioned earlier that Allan Keenan, the editor and manager of the Journal from 1944 to 1948, was staunchly conservative and began to rail against the perceived threat of communism during the second half of his tenure. In addition to publishing the weekly column "The American Way" and an occasional editorial about communism, Keenen published an anticommunism cartoon in nearly every issue of the Journal beginning in the latter part of 1947. A couple of examples of the cartoons are included here to give a flavor for what many parts of the country, not just Fayette City, were seeing in local papers. Even though these cartoons were published more than 70 years ago, they would probably find use in some of today's publications!

Fayette City Journal
August 16, 1946

26

Fayette City Journal
August 29, 1947

Fayette City Journal
November 7, 1947

27

GEORGE STUBLARAC

Fayette City Journal
May 31, 1946

Finally, it is worth noting a significant change that occurred with the Fayette City Journal in the 1940s. Photographs that appeared in the Journal were usually either provided through syndicated sources or were professionally made headshots of politicians or other people of importance. Photographs of *current* events never appeared in a timely manner due to a lack of skilled resources for preparing the photoengraved plate required for the printing process. After the end of World War II, the G.I. Bill offered returning veterans the opportunity to launch a new career. George Stublarac, one of Fayette City's own veterans, took advantage of the opportunity. In the spring of 1946,

Next week will see the opening in Fayette City of the first photo-engraving plant ever to be attempted in the upper Monongahela Valley.

George Stublarac, a well known local young man who was discharged from the U. S. Army several months ago has been at engraving school where he was just recently graduated will be the owner of the local plant.

For the past several weeks he has been busy at his storeroom on Market Street, installing dark rooms, water and electric facilities in preparation for the opening next week.

A photo-engraving plant has long been a need in the valley and with the opening of the local plant newspapers of this vicinity will have access to a place where they may obtain news pictures for reproduction almost immediately. Schools who publish yearbooks will also find that it will be very convenient to have their plates make locally.

The local plant will be equipped for line cuts, half tones and color plate work.

Fayette City Journal
September 6, 1946

after he was discharged from the armed services, Stublarac enrolled at Tasope, better known as The Aurora School of Photo-Engraving in Aurora, Missouri with the goal of opening a photo-engraving plant in the Monongahela Valley that could provide photographic plates suitable for local newspapers, union newsletters, school yearbooks, and so on. Shortly after graduating from Tasope, Stublarac opened a small shop in Fayette City on the corner of Market on Fourth Streets across from the Bake Funeral Home. With this new capability now available in town, the Journal was able to publish photographs of local current events in a timely fashion. The first of Stublarac's photographs, a photo of the Lions Club of Fayette City, appeared in the Journal on September 20, 1946. This photograph and some other photographs of Fayette City taken by Stublarac are shown here.

LIONS CLUB OF FAYETTE CITY

photo by Johnson-plate by Stublarac

Pictured above are members of the Fayette City Lions Club who attended a recent meeting at the Central School House in Jefferson Township. Reading left to right 1st row: Glenn Mills, George Rainey, Stanley Smith, Vincent Boag, Robert Premoshis, Miller Boag, Edwin Hindmarsh, George Hancock, Andy Eberhoch, Allan Keenan; 2nd row: J. H. Renstrom, Paul P. Jesick (club president), John L. Bake, Jasper Hare, Rev. G. L. Smith, Jacob Secrist, Howard McCrory, John Nelson, Russell Newdorfer, Ernest Partington, Dr. J. R. Connelly, C. E. Davis; Back row: Walter Wozniak, Joseph Moravek, Dr. W. E. Trezise, Norman Humphries, Stephen Vesely, William Gaskill, Rev. E. J. Knepshield.

Fayette City Journal
September 20, 1946

TRUCK CRASHES DOWN TOWN HILL

Pictured above are photographs of the huge trailor that skidded on Town Hill, causing the driver to lose control. The accident which occurred last Friday at noon attracted a large crowd of people. The trailor was headed for a Monessen store and was loaded with new furniture. The driver stated that he became lost and in following the directions of a district resident was directed to his destination by the way of Town Hill. No one was **injured, however the truck could** not be removed until the next day, causing the hill to be blocked off.

Fayette City Journal
December 27, 1946

WINTER SCENES TAKEN HERE

Pictured above are scenes of the present snow and cold wave. The upper photo shows the frozen Monongahela river taken from the ferry landing looking towards Pittsburgh. The lower photo shows the snow as it appeared when looking up Navoo Hollow.

Fayette City Journal
February 28, 1947

In addition to printing the weekly newspaper, the Journal office offered printing services for a variety of items such as letterheads, envelopes, handbills, campaign cards, pamphlets, and even matchbook covers. The use of union printers was highlighted in weekly advertisements for the Journal's services. The Journal office also sold a variety of stationery including crepe paper, picnic goods, poster paper, and novelties. The Journal company announced the closing out of their entire stock of stationery in August of 1948, which proved to foreshadow the demise of the newspaper less than a decade later.

It's easy to see how the weekly content of the Journal informed, strengthened and united the small community. The "Local Topics" and "Local and Society" sections gave readers the opportunity to see what their neighbors were up to. The "'Round About Town" section offered some light-hearted local gossip. And the "Look Who's Here" and "Obituaries" sections kept people apprised of who was coming and going, so to speak. Nearly everyone in town had the opportunity for his or her name to appear in the paper at some time throughout the year. As Bill Williamson, one of the narrators in this section, said "You never know in a small town like that when your name might show up."

Matchbook cover printed by the Keenan brothers in the late 1940s.

"It (The Fayette City Journal) would come out once a week. My parents would usually buy it or have it delivered or something."

-Pauline Ann Vargo Baker

"Me and Connie used to work for the newspaper, selling the paper. The paper come out once a week. We went knocking door to door. Nobody wanted to buy a paper. I'm not sure if it was a nickel or not. I think that's what would they charge, a nickel. We got so much for selling papers."

-Larry Moskala

"I remember that (The Fayette City Journal). I think the Steinman family maybe had that. I remember there was, I don't know, the Rose Room Kid seems to come to mind. I don't know who that was or anything. But I remember people saying well, we got to find out what the Rose Room Kid was up to this week. And then the Steinmans for a time lived in that house, which would be across from the Presbyterian Church."

-Georgia Nicholson Slezak

"It (The Fayette City Journal) was over on Main Street and Jimmy Keenan ran it for a while...I used to sell papers up the Hollow. It was a nickel. Not too many people bought a paper."

-June Cramer Yevincy

REFERENCES

Baldasty. Gerald J. *The Commercialization of News in the Nineteenth Century*. University of Wisconsin Press, 1992.

Paglia, Ron (2015, March 5) Fayette City Bid a Fond Farewell to Community 'Voice'. *The Valley Independent.*

Wikipedia contributors. "Charles S. Martz." *Wikipedia, The Free Encyclopedia*. Wikipedia, The Free Encyclopedia, 15 Dec. 2020. Web. 6 Dec. 2021.

CHAPTER 3 Businesses, Bars, and Banks

Businesses

The Evening Standard (Uniontown, PA)
June 27, 1930

Beginning in the late 1800s and continuing until the early 1940s, the major newspapers of Fayette County, Connellsville's The Daily Courier and Uniontown's The Evening Standard, would publish the county's annual "Mercantile Appraiser's List". By law, licenses were required of "All dealers and vendors of whatsoever kind of goods, wares, and merchandise" and of "All proprietors of eating houses, gasoline filling stations, billiard and pool rooms, and all peddlers, beer parlors, brokers, auctioneers, theatres, moving picture or shows of whatever kind." Retail businesses were grouped by township or borough as shown here for Fayette City in 1930 and 1940. Wholesale businesses, restaurants, billiard/bowling establishments, public amusements, and brokers were reported by county-wide groups. (It should be noted that accurate spelling wasn't a hallmark of these lists. It should also be noted that the businesses in the "Retail" list sometimes overlapped with businesses in the non-retail county-wide groups. Furthermore, the classifications between retail and non-retail seemed to vary from year to year.)

Before examining Fayette City's business in the 1940s, it is helpful to review the town's business environment in 1930, the start of the Great Depression. By the beginning of the Great Depression Fayette City had already been experiencing the effects of the downturn in the local coal industry. Yet the number of retail businesses was still a healthy 39. In addition to these businesses, there were one broker (Louis Miller, owner), three restaurants (Crystal, Wiley Johnson, Kalanaras, owners), three billiard businesses (Cribbs, Kalanaras, and one other owner), and two wholesale businesses (the Atlantic and Pacific Tea and Keystone Stores). No movie theatre was listed. The list for 1940 was a bit shorter with only 33 businesses listed under retail. There were also two brokers (Miller Reality and Strawn), one billiard business (Fleming Pool), a couple of wholesale businesses (the American Store at 301 Market Street and the Great A&P at 216 Main Street) and one public amusement (Bell Theatre). Several restaurants – Riverview Grill, Union Grill, Livi's, Flemings, and Hamer Dairy Bar – were listed under the retail establishments. The Fayette City Journal was not listed. (A good example of spelling inaccuracies is the oft misspelled "Livi" name. The 1930, and 1940 lists incorrectly show "Lit" and "Levi", respectively.)

For a town of its size, only 1500 citizens during the 1940s, Fayette City had a remarkable array of businesses. In fact, Fayette City was known by its neighbors as the town which had everything a person could need including doctors and funeral homes, barber shops and beauty shops, grocery stores and hardware stores, restaurants and bars, clothing stores and feed stores, and even a bowling alley and a movie theater. Most of Fayette City's businesses advertised in the Fayette City Journal at one time or another throughout the year. A handful of businesses including

The Daily Courier (Connellsville, PA)
June 15, 1940

Fayette City Journal
October 13, 1944

Bake Funeral Home, A.E. Strawn Real Estate, George M. Ferris Plumbing and Heating, McCrory Funeral Home, Williams' Pharmacy and Bell Theatre advertised nearly every week.

The majority of the businesses were located on Main Street and Market Street with a smattering on Second Street. Town hill had Scully's confectionary, Wilbur Evan's Flower Stand, and Cussy's Barber Shop on Connellsville Street, Johnson's Photography on South High Street, and Mary Ellen's Beauty Shop. Brownstown had Chalfant's convenience store. Johnson Hollow had a bike shop while Navoo Hollow was known for its two bars, the Red Onion and Humphries. But Main and Market Streets was where the action was, so much so that on Saturdays the sidewalks were packed with shoppers, movie goers and patrons of the many bars.

Some of the many stores on Main Street included Athey & Hough, Samberg's, the Economy Store, A.E. Strawn Real Estate and Insurance (later replaced by Wm. J. Coursin Real Estate and Insurance), Fleming's Bowling Alley and Pool Hall, Williams' Pharmacy, Kuhns Confectionery, Charles Gillette's Shoe Repair and the Fayette City Journal. Joe Ciavarra's Tailor Shop moved from its original location at the corner of Main and Market Streets to the center of the 200 block of Main Street.

Fayette City Journal
June 6, 1945

Fayette City Journal
October 19, 1945

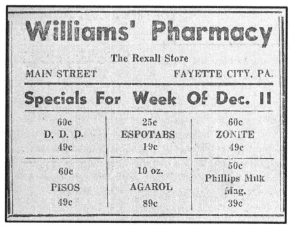
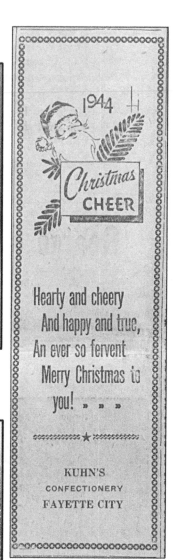

Fayette City Journal
May 7, 1948

Ciavarra's Tailor Shop on Main Street.
Photo courtesy of Vanessa Moskala Pugh.

"There was Premoshi, you know, the hardware store. That's where everyone's TV came from. And you know what? My uncle Charlie, my sister's going to say I got it wrong, but she would say it was uncle Frank, uncle Frank. My dad's uncles that came from Italy. The one uncle, I'd have to clarify that with my sister, had the shoe repair shop in Fayette City, and that was located across, let's see... Do you know where Norman Humphries used to live on in Fayette City? You know it's dilapidated now. But it was a great house that was on the right-hand side going out towards Belle Vernon. Well, his house and then there was a small store, and my uncle had the shoe repair shop there where he repaired shoes, put soles on shoes, and whatever. And this was whenever the cleats on shoes were a big thing, as girls, you know, that have the cleats on their toes of their shoes and the heels. Anyways, I remember one day I thought when I got off the school bus, I thought, oh gee, I'm going to go visit Uncle, it must have been Uncle Frank. Uncle Frank, I'm going to have him put cleats on my shoes. Here I have no money. And I go into the shop and said, "Uncle Frank can you put cleats on my shoes?" He said, "Sure". He put the cleats on and everything...I said thanks, and I went home. My mother was so mad. She says "Georgia, you take this money up and pay him. He's not going to do that for nothing". He wouldn't take the money. Yeah, he wouldn't take the money. But he was a shoe repair person. He had that business. And then there was a Jewish place across from where the hardware store eventually was. It used to be a Jewish place. Samberg's"

-Georgia Jean Arrow

"Well Sambergs had a store. Do you remember Sambergs, Jane and Lou? They lived up on the hill. They were such nice people. They had a little, I guess you would call it a department store. All kinds of little things in there. They were so nice and kind and you could go in and buy. I remember getting some blue jeans in there, socks, underwear. It was just a nice store. They were so nice. Billy Ciavarra and his dad had the tailor shop. They were very good at making things, very, very good at doing alterations. I know that Gladys Miller and her sister Flo, were on, that's Market Street. Flo had a little store there too with all kinds of little, I guess I would say for women, ribbons, scarves, hats. Of course, Gladys had the insurance and then she, I think she would collect bills for like the water company and the gas. I think she did that. I would hang out in the drugstore, penny candy, you know, that was Uncle Bob. We called him Uncle Bob. They were really really good to my sisters. They kind of adopted my sisters and I. And I'd go in there and Uncle Bob would take me down to the cellar and he'd say look at all these drugs. Oh my, I don't wanna see all those drugs. But he was so kind. Jim Davidson work there. You'd go in and get a Coca Cola, get some penny candy, and ice cream, ice cream, ice cream."

-Judith Dewar Shearer

"Let me see here. Up on this side, of course a drugstore there. A drugstore and, let me think, it seems to me Stockton's store was across on the other side of the street at that time. Then they moved to the corner. Across the corner, there was Flo Gator and her lady store there, where Mac's barbershop is. Of course, Moravek's store was on the other corner. And down further, of course, Dr. Trezise was down the street there. Across was Fred Holder's garage. It's kind of falling in now. You know where Benny Sara lived? Right next there used to be Fred Holder's garage, mechanical repair shop.. Across the way down on the other side, Freshwaters had a garage down there. And what else? Steve Figel had his garage and it's where the Pitstop is now. He had a Gulf station there. But I don't know what years I'm into now, you know. There was, let me try to think, the bowling alley, there was a bowling alley in there. There was a bowling alley. I don't know if it was a bowling alley and then the drugstore and then the bar. I think it was a bowling alley, then a bar, because it seems to me they used to sell beer or something. You could go to a window in the bowling alley and they would like hand it through the window, through the wall like, it was like an opening and that's how you'd get your beer and stuff. So it must have been right next to it, the bar and bowling alley. They were like connected. And let's see, up further the hardware store, of course it was at one time Premoshis, but it was somebody before that too."

-Jack Gargan

"The Clover Farm and Eley's used to have a little store over on Main Street at the end there going up the Hollow. The jail was behind there. Nobody ever got put in that jail. I don't think they used it. Oh there was Scully's up on the hill. Of course, there was the movie theater Joe Bell and Isabella owned. Isabella was not his wife. That was his sister. And she went out there. Stockton's, then it was, then Stockton's was the A&P. That's about all the little stores, I think. Well, of course, Kuhns and of course Canigiani's. Did they say Canigiani's was a pool hall? Oh, and then Flo Gator had a millenary shop where Mac's barber shop is up in there. Maybe she was on the corner and her sister ran the water office. Her name was Gladys, I think. Gladys Miller and Flo Gator. I think they were sisters, but I'm not sure. But they were from Allenport. They came across on the ferry every day. Flo Gator had like hats and gloves and scarves and stuff like that in there. That's what I remember. Anyway, she might have had other stuff. I don't know."

-June Cramer Yevincy

"Oh the other thing I remember, Hamers had a little, like a dairy bar on the corner. That would be the, it was the Five and Ten building. They were the first people to have soft serve ice cream. I can remember that. That would be Sam Hamer and Naomi, his wife, they opened that. That would be back probably in the 40s and that was a big thing that soft serve ice cream. Then they later opened down on Main Street because when my mother went back to work, we would eat lunch in there a lot. The other thing too was Charles Kuhns had like a newspaper stand. They sold ice cream. You could get an ice cream cone for a nickel, a double for 10 cents. That was big. And my oh we got a quart of hand pack ice cream from Kuhns. That was really good. Jean Gardner worked in there and she was, she could really pack the ice cream in there really good. That's when the Pittsburgh Press was big time. And what we would do on Saturday nights the Pittsburgh Press had a comic strip Boots. On the front page they had paper doll cutouts every Saturday night. And we would look forward to getting the Press paper. And then we would make our own clothes for those paper dolls and then color and do things. Paper dolls was the big thing. They cost 10 cents a package at the Five and Ten in Charleroi. That was a big, big form of enjoyment, things that we played with as kids, playing with paper doll girls. Some other people that lived next door to the school was the Mosko family. I don't know that Margie Mosko, was she still living? She had motorcycles and she had a taxi cab. I think she had the first taxi cab at one time. But also there was a Craft family that had a taxi company. That was on Main Street. They had a little, there had been a bakery in there at one time. And then Crafts had the taxi store. That would be almost next to Kuhns I think. And at one time there was even an A&P store in that facility there. I can remember that. And then in front of the bank building, Doodles had a barber shop. We had how many barbers? We had Fuzzy Opfar. He was up by Livi's on Main Street. Doodles was down in that, it was like the cellar part of the bank building. I think Mac McKevitt came later in time. Oh, we had hairdressers. Geraldine Jones had a shop. It was also up in that Five and Ten building at one time. And then I think she later moved down on the corner of Second and that would be Market. There was a shop in there."

-Georgia Nicholson Slezak

"Doodles had a barber shop downstairs. That's what I can recall. Then we had, let's see, we had another barber shop next to where Moravek's store was. George the barber. That was him. George Stefnik, he had a barbershop in there. And right down here on the hill as you go around the bend right going down the hill here, Cussy England he had a barber shop. It was a house. They had a barber shop right there."

-Jack Gargan

Grocery stores were also plentiful with Waugaman's, Stockton's, Moravek's, Acme, and a very small A&P all finding space on Main Street at some time during the 40s. Acme occupied the large, brick Five and Ten Building at the corner of Main and Market Streets for part of the 40s. Stockton's would eventually move into this building from their location directly across on Main Street in the 1950s. Only Stockton's and Moravek's endured well beyond the end of the decade.

"I can remember too, we did most of our grocery shopping at the Clover Farm, which was Moravek's. And again, we had a store bill. You didn't go in with a shopping cart. You went in and they waited on you, even all the canned goods and everything. The Moraveks would be the old folks. Paul was old Mr. Moravek's name and I forget Mrs. Moravek's first name. And then they had, Jo was the wife. I believe the oldest son did a lot of the meat. There was Paul. Paul served in the Navy. Mildred was the mother of my classmate, Bill Janeri. They had Bill and Mary Jo. Olga, was the youngest girl, she became a teacher. I mean, I remember all of these people in Fayette City. At that time, Fayette City had two hardware stores. There was, Weightmans had one which is where the Presbyterian Church had their social building, I guess you would call it. Across the street at one time, there was, Waugaman's had a small grocery store, which was kind of next to the post office. I remember that becoming later a liquor store, a state store. And then we had the Clover Farm. We had Stockton's and we had the Acme store, which was run by Charlie McKevitt, Charlie McKevitt's family."

-Georgia Nicholson Slezak

"There was four grocery stores. We had Moravek 's, Stockton's, the Acme Store and Waugaman's meat market. Now, it, more or less, kind of went out of business whenever I was about seven or eight years old. But the other ones were there."

-Grace Hough Martin

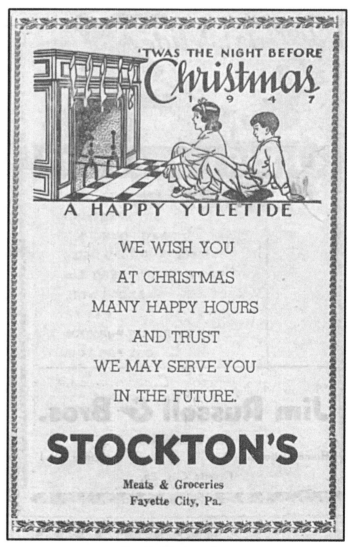

'TWAS THE NIGHT BEFORE Christmas 1947

A HAPPY YULETIDE

WE WISH YOU
AT CHRISTMAS
MANY HAPPY HOURS
AND TRUST
WE MAY SERVE YOU
IN THE FUTURE.

STOCKTON'S

Meats & Groceries
Fayette City, Pa.

Fayette City Journal
December 19, 1947

"The Clover Farm store and Stockton's. Stockton's, there was a little wee house where the bank was started. It was a little house there and then the Acme store was across the street. Well, we used to, Charlie McKevitt was the manager of the Acme store that was across the street from Riverview Grill. On Saturday, Saturday night, when they'd close, we would carry his groceries, I'd carry his groceries down, he lived by the ferry in that big house on the left. And we'd carry his groceries down and then we'd come up and he'd give us all the bread and cakes and everything that was, would be old, you know, on Monday. And we had a picnic.

There was Fuzzy's barber shop. Doodles, the barber, was down underneath the bank building. And Fuzzy's was up next to Levi's. I remember them. Fuzzy Opfar and Spike Opfar, that was the brother, he was the cop. Spike."

-Joe Vargo

"Of course you had the A&P store. McKevitt's dad ran the A&P. He had eventually that Stockton's store. The Clover Farm run by the Moravek family. That was a neat, friendly family type of arrangement. I remember my mother sent me down after the Moravek's Clover Farm store closed. I'd go around the back door and knock on the door and say my mother needs a quart of milk and she forgot to get it. They would go get it and I'd pay him. You also could call in your order at Clover Farm and they would pick it and pull it and have it for you if you went. Sometimes they would deliver your order to your location in Fayette City, whether it be downtown or uptown up on the Hill."

-Jack Young

The Fayette City Hardware and Appliance Company and William Weightman and Son Hardware competed for business on Main Street with an occasional quarrel over the price of shovels.

"Premoshis hardware store. I remember the first television I ever saw was at Premoshis. They got a totally black and white little television set. Nobody had television. They put televisions in their front window facing the sidewalk and a put a little speaker there and people would come and stand or bring a seat to watch the movies at Premoshis's store. We had, I think Samberg's department store. Weightman's hardware store. Sam Hamer had a nice ice cream sandwich shop."

-Jack Young

GREETINGS NEIGHBORS NEW YEAR 1948

• BENJAMIN FRAN
MADE THE MOST C
ERYTHING . . . MADE
GOLDEN MINUTE C
WE HOPE THAT YOU
WILL MAKE THE M
COUNT IN 1948, ANC
EVERY ONE OF THEM
ADD TO THE SUM
OF YOUR HEALTH AND
HAPPINESS.

Wm. WEIGHTMAN
& SON
HARDWARE
Fayette City, Pa.

Fayette City Journal
December 31, 1947

William Weightman and Son Hardware at the corner of Union and Main Streets. Photo courtesy of Valinda Weightman Truax.

Holiday Season
Christmas 1947

In This Joyous Season of Christmas

we want to renew all our old friendships, want each of you to feel your importance to us, and to realize that without you the story would have been quite different.

A very Merry Christmas to all of you, friendly people of this community!

Fayette City Hardware
and Appliance Co.
Robert T. Premoshis

Fayette City Journal
December 24, 1947

The Bake Funeral Home at the corner of Fourth and Market Streets and the George McCrory & Son Funeral Home on Main Street vied for the opportunity to bury the dead. John Bake learned the undertaker trade from the Mansfield family who had their own funeral parlor on Main Street and laid out Mount Auburn Cemetery many decades ago. The Methodists in town seemed to favored Bake while the Presbyterians and Catholics went to McCrory, no doubt reflecting the church memberships of the owners. Howard McCrory, the "Son" in George McCrory and Son, was a larger-than-life character, literally and figuratively, and a pillar of the community.

JOHN L.
BAKE

Funeral Director
Ambulance Service

FAYETTE CITY, PA.
Fourth and Market Streets

Phone: Fayette City 711

Fayette City Journal
October 13, 1944

ALMANAC

"Of the two evils, the least should be chosen"—Erasmus

JANUARY

29—Kansas admitted to Union as the 34th State, 1861.

30—Hitler repudiates Treaty of Versailles before German Reichstag, 1937.

31—President Roosevelt devalues the American dollar, 1934.

FEBRUARY

1—Washington Naval Treaty signed, 1922.

2—Mexico accepts peace terms demanded by U.S., 1848.

3—Income tax amendment becomes law, 1913.

4—Major Gorgas launches anti-yellow fever drive in Havana, 1901.

Geo. M.
McCrory
& Son

FUNERAL
DIRECTORS

—24 Hour—
AMBULANCE
SERVICE

Phone 768
FAYETTE CITY

Fayette City Journal
January 26, 1946

"Well, he (Howard McCrory) was so personable, you know, he, when you went to view your loved one, he would come out to the casket and he would say, if there's anything you want to change, you let me know and we'll change it. You know, if the makeup wasn't right or the hair wasn't right or the suit or whatever. He did everything he could to please you. He was one of a kind."

-Audrey Tiernan Repka

"My dad was good friends with Cocky McCrory, too. Now there's, you talk about characters. He was something. He was a work of art. He was a joker. He was, he was well known out at the restaurant out there, Sweeney's. That was one of their watering holes. They used to go out there. They put Sweeny's on the map, I think. They had good Stony's beer back in the day, that was nice and cold and fresh. That's when Stony's was good. Howard McCrory, he, my dad died in 1950, no 1965. And Howard, Cocky handled it. They said that there was always a contest on who was the biggest person, him or my dad, you know size wise. He said the question was answered. I guess my dad was bigger. My dad was. He was a big man."

-Barry Hindmarsh

"I worked at McCrory's at 13 years old. I mean in the morgue and the kitchen. I think Helen his sister, I think she, you know, was the one that, she took care of the kitchen and cooking and things and stuff, I think. But ain't nobody better than Howard McCrory, nobody better than Howard McCrory. Good guy. Yep."

-Eleanor Welsh Owens

"The funeral homes. There was a difference in the funeral homes. The McCrorys, who my dad's sister married Victor. Anyway, the McCrorys would bury Catholics where Bakes I don't think would. I know my dad and Howard, they always call him Cocky, they tried to get in the Masons and they were blackballed, because I think there was something back then. They were looked down upon. Fayette City, I guess it certainly had its amount of prejudice. But it never rubbed off."

-Georgia Nicholson Slezak

Market Street offered an assortment of smaller businesses. Hamer's Dairy Bar occupied a small shop at the corner of Market and Fourth Streets, across from Bake Funeral home. Sam Hamer, the store's owner, purchased the unoccupied bank building on Main Street and moved the Dairy Bar to this large location in 1946. Other businesses on Market included Stub's Photo-Engraving (see Chapter 2 for details), Flo Gator's Dress Shop, Glady Miller Real Estate and Insurance, Canigiani's Shoe Repair and an adjacent Pool Hall. At one time Ciavarra's Tailoring occupied the corner of Market and Main before moving to a location on Main Street.

"Hamers had an ice cream parlor there, which was kind of one of the highlights of Fayette City. There had been, eventually an Acme store came in to what was referred to as the Five and Dime building. But I don't ever remember there being a Five and Dime. It was just that that was what the building was referred to. There was a beauty shop underneath and then you walked down the street a little bit, there was a staircase that went down into the basement. I was always afraid to go into the basement. It frightened me....I do remember Hamers and going there on Saturday night. We could get an ice cream sundae for 25 cents. Comes with whipped cream and a cherry. There weren't too many flavors; vanilla, chocolate and strawberry. We could get an ice cream cone for five cents. If we had an extra little bit of money, it was to get two or three scoops of ice cream on that ice cream cone."

-Shirley Ferree Stilgenbauer

"Around the bend from Stockton's there was Yusko's flower shop. And then Stublarac had like a candy store, George Stublarac. There was like an office on the corner. I don't recall what that was. Across the street at the beginning there was Thelma Dreyer's dress shop. Then there was Gladys Miller had that insurance agency. Next from that was John Canigiani's pool hall. And then you made your way up to Bake's Funeral Home on the corner. And going down the other block was Moravek's store, grocery store. Then there was a barber shop at the end of that building. Oh I forgot to mention the two barbers. Doodles was one. His shop was down below the street, sort of not under the bank, but in that area. You had to walk down cement steps. And then McKevitt's had his barber shop right before Kuhns newspaper store. Now he's on the corner of Market Street. There used to be three barbers: Doodle's, McKevitt, and then there was a young barber. That's where I ended up going when I was a teenager to him because he was a younger guy."

-John Vargo

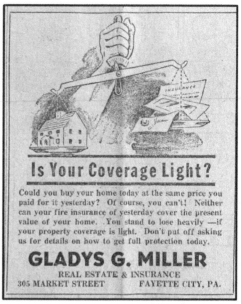

Fayette City Journal
August 2, 1946

Fayette City Journal
December 29, 1944

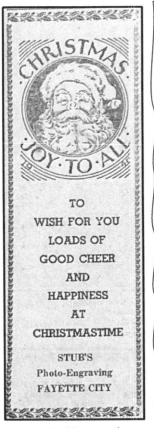

Fayette City Journal
December 20, 1946

"Going up Market Street across from where I lived, was Joe Ciavarra's tailor shop. There was only one tailor shop in town and it was Joe Ciavarra. He actually made the uniforms for the Drum Corps. There was Flo Gator. She had a little millenary store. You could go in there and buy clothing and cards and things. It was a very small store, but that was the only one. Then next to that was Gladys Miller who had a real estate and insurance office. I can remember as a kid, again from the eyes of a child, I didn't know you had to have money in the bank. But my mother would give me a check and I would take it over to Gladys Miller. And she would give me money. I thought she just gave us money if we gave her this piece of paper. Next to that was a little a pool room or billiard parlor, then a couple apartment buildings and then John Bakes funeral home. At the top of the hill was the school. Going down to Main Street, there was Joe Bell's movie theater, which was the only movie theater in town. There was George Miller's pool hall. We called it a pool hall. I can remember walking past there in the summer, and the doors would be open and I could smell the beer. I always wanted to try the beer. Then across the street was Stockton's. A little newspaper store where you could buy candy, I think, was there. I'm not sure if there was a shoe store in town at that time. But then there was a post office at the end of Main Street going up one of the back hills to Back Street. That pretty much was the town. There wasn't much to choose from....There was a drugstore, a movie theater. The bank across the street had already closed. That was pretty much it."

-Shirley Ferree Stilgenbauer

Fayette City Journal
December 22, 1944

"I remember on the corner where McKevitt is when I was a kid there was there was two sisters from Allenport, Flow Gator and Gladys Miller. Where McKevitt is Flo Gator had a millenary shop, where she sold house dresses, better dresses like for church, hats, purses, jewelry. I don't remember slips and bras and that kind of stuff....I remember when I first got married we moved in what years ago Charlie Kuhns lived in the house. There was a beauty shop. Do you remember where Hancock's lived? Across the street, there was a beauty shop connected to the house, which Charlie Kuhns and Dutch lived there. And then there was a little house that was part of their house. Well, that little part was where I moved in when we got married."

-Ella Marie Auther Davis

"There were a lot of stores in town, a lot of bars, a lot of churches....A fellow by the name of George Stublarac had a little candy store, right across, caddy-corner from the school. And I used to go in there and that was right across the street. There used to be Bake's Funeral Home. I don't know if you remember Bakes. Stubby's was right across the street from that....He developed pictures in there too. He had a photography shop in there too. It was a nice place. Nice little store. He was good with kids. He had the world-famous penny candy in there. You've heard stories about all the candies that you can buy for a nickel. You'd get a bag usually."

-Barry Hindmarsh

"Well, I didn't get downtown very much. My parents didn't allow me down there very much because Fayette City, they had a beer garden on every corner. My mother was dead against that. And I wasn't allowed in Canigiani's pool room."

-Willard Jones

"In the 1950s, the main thing I remember was John Canigiani's pool hall. He raised a lot of kids. I started shooting pool in Cani's when I was eleven years old. It was a good place to be. You might learn a couple of bad words...All the kids hung out in John's and Joe Bell's show."

-Jim McKevitt

"Oh, yeah. Now when you when you go in he'd holler "Lady in the House". Then you got your candy and then you went out because those guys used to swear.. We'd go (knocking) can we come in and get candy. Then as we were opening the door he's hollering "Lady" and come back where they shot pool...There was the door on a swing and hinges that you could look underneath and see over the top of that. When we were kids you could see underneath guy's feet...If you were tall enough you could see over, who was in here. But yeah, as soon as you walked in the door he'd holler "Lady in the house".

-Ella Marie Auther Davis

"The pool hall. If you wanted your boyfriend, you had to send somebody in to tell him to send him out. No girls allowed. No girls belonged there. But they went in here and played pool and did whatever else they did. Women didn't know. Gladys Miller's store was along there and Flo Gator, her sister, wasn't they sisters? Glady's Miller was in insurance and Flo Gator had like a little what would you call it? She sold clothes, slips and like night gowns and like ladies underwear, handkerchiefs. From the corner there used to be a grocery store, where McKevitt's is, that used to be a grocery store. And then it was Flo Gators, and Gladys Miller's, Canigiani's, the pool hall and his shoemaker shop. And then Bake's Funeral Home on the corner."

-Eleanor Welsh Owens

"John Canigiani. He had a house next to my uncle John Bake who was a funeral director. When he wasn't busy, he would cut hair. Canigiani live next door. Cani was a cobbler. He had a little shop where he repaired shoes. He would either sew on the replacement soul, or he would put little nails in. He also had a pool room adjacent to his cobbler shop. That's where every boy who was worth his oats learn to shoot pool in Cani's pool room. There was eight of us he dubbed the crazy eight. We were in there all the time. You could spit on the floor. He had a little potbellied stove. A lot of the older Fayette City sages would be in there. And of course, John had a Steeler game or the Pirate game on, had it marked up on a chalkboard. You could also get punch boards where you pay money and you poke holes and maybe you could win some money and things. He had a candy shop and soft drinks. It was a hang out. You could tell someone from Fayette City because they knew how to shoot. Cani was friendly with all the kids. He was a good neighbor. He was good for the town."

-Jack Young

BEST
NEW
YEAR
WISHES
1947

× ×

★ Our earnest hope as we face the coming new year is that we may continue our pleasant relationship with our many patrons and that they, as well as all the folks in our community, enjoy the holiday and the days to follow in peace, contentment and good health.

× ×

JOHN
CANIGIANI

Fayette City Journal
December 27, 1946

Fayette City also had its fair share of service providers including plumbers, barbers, beauticians, and doctors. George Ferris Plumbing was located on Second Street. Barbers Cussy Ingland, Fuzzy Opfar, Doodles, and George Stefnik operated from town hill, Main Street, and Market Street. Beauty shops included Stephanie's Beauty Salon, the Marie Beauty Studio, Mary Ellen's Beauty Shop, and Jerry's Beauty Shoppe.

Multiple doctors served Fayette City thorough out the 1940s. The esteemed Dr. B.L. Stollar died at the beginning of the decade in 1940 at the age of 56. Drs. Aland Dent and Trezise held offices on Main Street. Dr. Dent was practically legendary in the community. He served on multiple boards, gave generously, and lived in the grandest house in town. Dr. Dent shared a practice with Dr. J.R. Connelly later in the decade while Dr. Trezise worked alone. Dr. Uriah Finley Higinbotham provided dental services

Opens Dental Offices Here

Dr. Philip L. Campi announced this week that he is now ready to serve the people of Fayette City and vicinity in the practice of dentistry.

He is a graduate of the University of Pittsburgh Dental School and is a native of Monongahela, Pa.

His offices are located at the corner of Second and Market Streets, which has just been remodeled and modernized in preparation for the opening of the dental offices.

Fayette City Journal
March 7, 1947

"Dr. Dent, Dr. Connelly and Dr. Trezise. When my mother was in the hospital in 1940 having my youngest sister Judy, she had hemorrhaged at home. So they took her by ambulance down at the hospital. And Dr. Dent took care of her. And so when my mother married Jim Hamer, and she was in better financial straits by then in the 1970s, she went up to Dr. Dent, she said, I owe you money for a doctor's bill. She said, "I know when you took care of me in the hospital, that you weren't paid your fee". And he said, "Oh, Martha that was so many years ago, I couldn't even remember, you know, what it was then." And she said, "Well, I know that you were not paid. And, and I want to pay you now." So he said, "Well, how long were you in hospital, Martha?" And she said," I think 30 days." He said, "Well, let's make it $5 a day." So she gave him $150. He was satisfied and she felt better."

-Audrey Tierna Repka

"Fayette City had, when I was growing up, had a lot of nice stores. Doctors, Dr. Dent. We had Dr. Trezise. Way back there was Dr. Stollar. They had their offices there on Main Street."

-Jack Young

"I believe there was a dentist office down on the second floor. We didn't have a dentist a lot. At one time there was Dr. Lazzari. He had lived down on Main Street. He didn't stay very long. And then later on, Dr. Campi came. That's why I don't have teeth because they were so bad. They pulled them."

-Judith Dewar Shearer

"Dr. Trezise was my doctor....He was he was a nice man. We went there and I used to sit and look in his bookcase. He had a bookcase there and he had books that I wanted to read. I wanted to ask him to borrow them but I was I was afraid to. They all looked so interesting.

You didn't go to the doctor for every little thing that happened back then, if your mother could patch it up and you didn't bleed to death."

-Leila Breckenridge Steiner

from his office on the second floor of the Five and Ten Building. Higinbotham was elected Burgess of Fayette City for multiple terms and was also elected Justice of the Peace. The beloved dentist died in 1943 at the age of only 38. Dr. Lazzari had a short run as a dentist in Fayette City in the 1940s. Towards the end of the decade Dr. Philip Campi opened a dentist office at the corner of Second and Market Streets. But he too lasted only a few years.

Wilbur Evans sold potted plants on town hill, about a block from Mount Auburn Cemetery, particularly around Memorial Day when citizens were decorating graves of loved ones for the annual services honoring the town's veterans. Edward Applegate offered his services as Tinner and Roofer. Hawker Coal Company, Hamer Coal Company and Earl M. Opfar offered home coal delivery. These coal operations were small in comparison to mines that preceded them in Fayette City decades earlier. The coal mining industry in and around Fayette City will be discussed in detail in Chapter 5.

Fayette City Journal
June 1, 1945

Fayette City Journal
October 25, 1946

Fayette City Journal
December 28, 1945

Fayette City Journal
April 26, 1946

Fayette City Journal
July 26, 1946

Located at 234 Main Street, in the geographical center of town, Bell Theatre was the heart and soul of Fayette City in the 1940s. The Bell Theatre elicited more fond memories from the narrators than any of the town's other businesses, by far. The Theatre was owned by the Bell family and operated primarily by brother and sister Joe and Isabella Bell. In some ways, Joe and Isabella were as much an attraction to movie goers as the flicks themselves. The short and rotund Joe would walk the aisles trying to prevent kids from disrupting the movie or dating teens from smooching. Isabell would pop popcorn and collect tickets while reading her Bible, talking to herself, and occasionally dozing off in the process.

Television hadn't yet reached Fayette City, so the movies were the primary source of entertainment. For less than a quarter, a kid could enjoy a movie and a bag of popcorn. Serial flicks kept people coming back week after week as did the feature movies. People attended so regularly that they had their own seats, or at least they thought they did. Everyone knew exactly where everyone else sat and wouldn't dare encroach on someone else's seat. The weekly "Bank Night" event was an attraction for young and old alike and is best described by the narrators in the following pages.

The layout of the Bell Theatre was a little unusual. The patron entering from the street would see the projector room at the rear of the Theater and would need to turn around to see the screen at the front. Seating was in a single section with aisles on either side. Bell Theatre had stiff competition from multiple, larger and more elegant theatres in neighboring Belle Vernon, Brownsville and Charleroi. Nevertheless, it survived until 1959 when it was subsequently converted to a duckpin bowling alley. But the Bell Theatre will always be remembered as "the movie theatre" by everyone who lived in Fayette City in the 1940s.

BELL THEATRE

FRIDAY- SATURDAY
DEC. 8-9
"WATERLOO BRIDGE"
starring Robert Taylor and Vivien Leigh
Cartoon and Black Arrow 3

SUNDAY - MONDAY
DEC. 10-11
"SEVENTH CROSS"
starring Spencer Tracy, Signe Hasso and Hume Cronyn

WEDNESDAY - THURSDAY
DEC. 13-14
"THE FALCON OUT WEST"
starring Tom Conway and Barbara Hale
Second Feature
"SAILORS HOLIDAY"
starring Arthur Lake, Jane Lawrence and Bob Haymes

Fayette City Journal
December 8, 1944

BELL THEATRE

FRIDAY - SATURDAY
OCT. 3-4
"Butch" Jenkins in
"Little Mr. Jim"
with James Craig & Frances Gifford

SUNDAY - MONDAY
OCT. 5-6
"The Red House"
with Lon McCallister, Edward G. Robinson, Judith Andrson and Ona Munson

WEDNESDAY - THURSDAY
OCT. 8-9
Olivia DeHavilland, Lew Ayres and Thomas Mitchell in
"The Dark Mirror"

FRIDAY - SATURDAY
OCT. 10-11
Van Johnson in MGM's
"The Romance of Rosy Ridge"
with Thomas Mitchell, Selena Royle and introducing Janet Leigh.

Fayette City Journal
October 3, 1947

"Oh yes, Joe and Isabella Bell. Yeah, 12 cents to get in there. And that was interesting. Joe was interesting character himself, you know. I can remember him walking up and down the aisles and watching us smoochers and that sort of stuff. He tried to keep order in there, but it was fun."

-June Winters Baldwin Jaquette

"Oh, Joe Bell's...There was the Marine Bar, then Joe Bell's....I remember as a kid, his sister worked in the where you paid your money. And then she took care of the popcorn too. Now this is a shame. She used to talk to herself a lot out loud. And which isn't right now, thinking about it, but as a kid we used to laugh. But it was fun because if my mother knew what I did when the reel would break, and it would, you know, take the picture off the screen. Us kids used to go... stomp our feet until it come back on. One time, Mrs. Pegg, she lived where, well the station's torn down and now the other part of the lot that belongs to the Christian Church where Reverend Boring is, that's where Mrs. Pegg used to live. She had a son they called Booner. His right name was Oliver. Well, we had gone to the show one night. I don't know how old I was, me and Mary Jo. I had put on this, this cologne or whatever it was. Now mind you I was maybe 10 maybe 11, I'm not sure. We sat in front of Mrs. Pegg and she made me move because that cologne was so strong, it stunk. She said you got to move. She said I can't stand that smell. She said I don't know what you put on but it smells horrible. So we were laughing about that. But yeah, when the movie reel, when something would go wrong or whatever, we'd all stomp our feet, making a sound like a bunch of cattle. And one night a week, I only think that was one night, Joe had what they called Bank Night. And he had this big barrel that he would roll and put, when they gave you a ticket, they ripped up one half and put the other half in this thing. I can't remember if you won money or if he gave you passes to get into the show. He'd get up there and roll that thing around and pull out a ticket. It was called Bank Night."

-Ella Marie Auther Davis

"We always said the Joe Bell must have loved mothers because every Christmas he would have a cartoon fest and show a first run movie. And it was free....When I started going there it was 12 cents for children to get in and 10 cents for a bag of popcorn....Joe was, he owned the theater. He ran the films and his sister Isabella was in charge of the booth where you paid to get in....The back two rows in Joe Bell's theater was where all the lovers sat. Every once in a while, just for the fun of it, somebody would take a pop bottle and roll it down through the aisle. Of course, this made Mr. Bell really unhappy. The next thing you know he'd stopped the movie and he come out to see who was doing what."

-Grace Martin Hough

"The big thing I remember living across the street from Bell theater, the movie changed three times a week. Back then for kids initially it was 10 cents to get in the movie. And then they started taxing that it was 12 cents. The popcorn was 10 cents. So if you had that 22 cents to go to the movies, you were really living high on the hog. And then there was old Mr. Bell, and they lived in the house, right down on the wharf on the corner there. I remember when the old Bell family lived there. That was before Joe and Isabella. Joe finally got married. I remember old Mr. Bell, they gave him the job of punching holes in the popcorn bags because he would say "All those kids say they pop up" because the kids would blow the bags up, and, you know, make a big pop in the middle of the movie. And every now and then the screen would go off and the kids, we would pound our feet on the floor, you know. Oh, Bank Night, on Wednesday nights was the big night for the adults. I don't know how he funded that, if that was funding all week. But he had a big rolling barrel and they put a ticket in. There was a certain amount of money and I can remember, you know my grandmother would always go "Who won the money?" That was a big thing for the adults who would win the money at the theater. It was called Bank Night. So Wednesday night, that was once a week. That was kind of probably a promotion to get people to come to the movies. That was before television."

-Georgia Nicholson Slezak

51

"We went every Sunday, Wednesday and Friday. We could get in as a child for 12 cents. Adults was a quarter. You could buy a bag of popcorn for 10 cents. Everybody sat in the same seats. You always knew who was sitting where. He didn't always have good movies, but there was not much else to do. So I remember going in, paying our money, buying a little bag of popcorn. Friday night was what we called a cliffhanger and I think it was a Batman series. And they literally left us hanging till the next Friday. We had to go back to see what happened. When we finished our popcorn, we would blow the bags up and let them pop. Joe Bell would get after us. Then finally he figured out if he put holes in the bags, you can't blow them up anymore. We would buy our penny candy at the drugstore. Then in the back of the movie theater, there was this big exit with these big doors that opened and there was a peep hole. The kids would stand and watch the movie in the peep hole. Joe Bell would come chasing around and chase them away. But he never did fix the peep hole. I don't ever remember him fixing the peep hole. He would patrol the aisles, made sure everybody was behaving themselves. But that was a big time. There was not much else to do. And like I said, it didn't matter what the movie was. It was something to do."

-Shirley Ferree Stilgenbauer

"Well, the biggest thing of the movie theatre, I always remember this. The guy who owned it was Joe Bell. His sister would collect the tickets, Isabella. She was always saying the Rosary. There's times that my dad would give me a quarter and say I could go to the show. It was 13 cents. Popcorn was a dime. Then I had two cents I could go across across to Kuhns, over there, and get two cents worth of candy. But some days when I was being a chiseler, I would tell Isabella that I wanted to go in and tell my mother and dad something. They're in that movie. She'd be sitting, and go like that. Well that would save me 13 cents. Then I had more to get candy with. But you don't put that in there. But it's true, it's true. But can you imagine that though. And then I think it was Wednesday nights, they always had a drawing like a bank, they called it Bank Night. Everyone would go there because they put your name, the adults put your name in and they took like his big wheel on a stage up there. They'd crank that and pull somebody's name out. What it was like in there and you could probably imagine this, the regular people went there. They had like saved seats. If you sat in their seat, they told you to move and stuff like that, the kids you know, like the older people they had, and always said, wonder whose seat this is. Pretty soon someone would come in a say, well that's my seat. Well, there was no reserved seat but that's just the way the show was. It was just amazing, amazing. It was a big thrill to get to go to a movie in them days. Didn't have no TVs, no TVs till about the 50s."

-Jack Gargan

"There was Joe Bell's Theater that opened on Back Street. In the summertime they had no air conditioning. They'd open the back doors. We as kids used to sit up there and watch the movie for free. Everybody went every time it changed. It would change three times a week. My brother Bob popped popcorn."

-Joan Cunningham Manetta

BELL THEATRE

FRIDAY - SATURDAY

OCT. 27-28

Alice Faye, Carmen Mranda, James Ellison, Benny Goodman and His Orchestra in

"THE GANG'S ALL HERE"

SUNDAY - MONDAY

OCT. 29-30

"THE SULLIVANS"

starring Anne Baxter, Trudy Marshall, Thomas Mitchell and Selena Royle

WEDNESDAY - THURSDAY

NOV. 1-2

"THE RAINS CAME"

starring Tyrone Power, Myrna Loy and George Brent

Fayette City Journal
October 27, 1944

"Well, the movie changed three times a week. It was Sunday and Monday where we had like cowboy pictures or B-rated pictures. Tuesday he was closed. Wednesday was a little bit better rated movies and Friday and Saturday would be the best ones. There would be two showings a night. One starting at seven and then again, one at nine. We used to pay a dime to get into the movie. But when we got to be 12 years old, we had to start paying 25 cents and we thought that was terrible. Thursday Night was drawing night. During the break between the two showings, Joe would draw numbers out of a barrel tumbler. I can remember Joe's mother, who was really quite old at the time, sat at the lobby booth and sold the movie tickets. And after she passed away, Isabella, Joe's sister, took over. When Gone with the Wind was released, Joe was able to get a copy. And because of all the hype over the movie, everybody in town wanted to see it. So in order to accommodate the crowd, he had a first ever Sunday matinee. In fact, there were two matinees that day plus two regular evening shows. You had to sign up or buy tickets in advance. I'm not sure which, for the show if you wanted to attend. We got tickets for the second matinee, and that's how we got to see Gone with the Wind."

-Nancy Ferree Johnson

"Now, Joe Bell's theater was just two doors away from me. That's where I spent my time, was in those movies. They changed three times a week. I went every time the movie changed, and I saw them all. Sometimes if I liked them all, I'd go see it twice. We sometimes would get popcorn. And oh they said somebody else had popcorn. I remember Paul Moats was the one that made the popcorn when I remember.... Well, when you went in the screen was really up above this way, the projection room was in the back. So you, when you went in you're facing the seats. The seats were facing this way and you went in and the kids usually sat pretty much up front and Joe would be in the back. Although they said his dad, his dad did run a crank. He did run the projection once in a while. But I only remember Joe doing it. I remember sometimes he fell asleep, and the thing would turn, and we'd all stamp or feet. Joe would wake up and he'd fix the projector."

-Judith Dewar Shearer

"My cousin Leonard and I went almost every Friday. We would look at the marquis that they'd put up new. We decided, you know, we were coming down to see that. So it was Friday night, we would go. Then we'd walk home in the dark. Your parents didn't chauffer you around. We would run from street light to street light (in Navoo Hollow) sometimes, especially around that Red Onion because that was a scary building. It was just something and then we were afraid somebody was hiding in the creek and they would come up. We would sort of run from streetlight. I lived on the hill. Leonard was afraid of that graveyard. He would wait until I got into the house before he went in his house. He was just fearful that maybe a dead person would grab me."

-John Vargo

"Yeah, I used to sneak into the movies. Isabella would fall asleep in the booth and we would pretend we were looking at the features on the pictures in the lobby and when she'd fall asleep we'd run through, run in the door. The movie was only 10 cents then. You know it was. What are you going to do? Oh, she'd fall asleep and she'd be talking to herself. Then she would fall asleep. She was, I remember, she read the Bible a lot. She'd be reading and then she'd fall asleep and we'd go, we'd run in them doors. Or in the back, sometimes we would open the back doors and let the big guys in."

-Joe Vargo

"Oh that was wonderful. We never missed, they had Sunday and Monday shows. They didn't have any on Tuesday. Wednesday and Thursday was double featured night. Friday and Saturday was musicals. Wednesday was Bank Night. I don't think I ever missed a show. Of course we didn't have television in those days or anything. Isabella sold the tickets. It was a big deal when they got a popcorn machine. But you paid 14 cents, when before you were I think over 12 you had to pay 35 cents, but before that it was 12 or 14 cents and 10 cents for a bag of popcorn. So you can go the movie and get a bag of popcorn for a quarter. I don't know if that... I don't even think you can get a bag of popcorn for $1 and a quarter now. Times have changed but.... It had only, it had rows of seats. They had aisles on each side. That was it. I would imagine you could probably get 20 maybe 15 to 20 across a row. I don't remember. But it was funny because people had their certain seats. If you went in, if you were sitting in their seat, they all would stand there and stare you down. Sometimes the film would break and instead of fixing it, Joe Bell would come down and yell at the people cause they we're stamping their feet. But you know what, it was fun. We saw a good movies. It was at the entrance. You had to walk up about 10 feet and turn around to see the screen. And then you could, you know, sit where you wanted to. The projector room was in the back. That was if you went out the back door, you almost were at the school house. In fact a couple times you could stand back there and look, peep through a hole and see what was on the movie. We didn't do that very often. Everything was different."

-Kathleen Walton Stimmell

"Well, Joe Bell and his wife, Isabella, no his sister Isabella and the father had the theater there in Fayette City on Main Street. And kids would sit in the front and raise hell. The adults would sit in the back. The projector was in the back. Joe Bell, who's short and kind of chubby, he would be back there running the film. We'd raise hell in the front, and he'd come running down there and everybody would duck down. I remember, if you had to go to the bathroom, you had to go out to where the tickets were sold and ask for the key from Isabella. There was one commode down in the basement, almost like a coal cellar. And then you'd come back up and give give the key back to Isabella. And we had Bank Night. Do you know what Bank Night was? Every Wednesday and Thursday, Joe Bell would, I don't know how much it would be maybe $20 or $30 or something. If he went to the movies on Wednesday night, you would sign a log with your name. And then on Thursday night, people would come, they'd be sitting in the movie, and they would have their names, seemed like a bingo thing. Joe Bell after the main attraction before everybody left, he would crank that bingo type thing and pull people's names out of there. If you were there you got the money. If you weren't there Thursday night, he would check his ledger to see if you had been there on Wednesday night. A lot of people went to the movies."

-Jack Young

"Oh, yeah. We used to go to the show. I think it was like, it wasn't much at all, maybe 14 cents, something like that. Then we'd go into the, you know, we'd go into the show. Isabella Bell would be popping popcorn or she would be taking the money. She'd run back and forth. When the kids from Gillespie, they would all come down in a car to go to the show. I guess when the parents up there, the Veselys, would get a carload of kids, and they'd all come down and go to the show. And then he (Joe Bell) had that where he would draw tickets or money. They'd have Bank Night where he would draw, you know, they put the lights on after the movie was over, or animation, and he put the lights on. He'd get up there and get the big wheel. It was a big container, like a bingo thing, I mean huge, bigger. He'd twirl it around, and then he'd draw."

-Georgia Jean Arrow

"Saturday night movies. They always had a cowboys matinee on Saturday afternoon. That old Joe Bell, you know, he went big time, put that big screen in before they closed up. They did a pretty good business in there. The theatre usually on the weekend was loaded up. What else was there to do? TV was just coming in and there wasn't much on TV."

-Jim Eley

After the Bell Theatre, the business that generated the most memories from the narrators was the indispensable ferry that connected Fayette City and Allenport. Owned by the Jacob's family in Allenport, the ferry provided convenient transport for mill workers on their way to the Allenport mill and shoppers and students on their way to Charleroi. In an era when most people were yet to own their own automobile, the ferry was vital means of transportation.

"First of all, my dad was from Allenport. His family continued to live in Allenport. So that means my grandparents, on that side, were in Allenport. I was on that ferry more times than I'd care to count. From the time I was a little kid, they would babysit me some Saturday nights and I'd just take the ferry over myself. I was on that ferry a lot. I can remember when they had to get a new engine for it and repair the one that was there. That was quite a thing.

The ferry would handle two cars, three if you were daring. The cars in those days were a lot bigger than they are today. The ferry was a big deal. It was right down the street from our house too.

One of the most adventurous things I did as a kid was ride that ferry to my grandmother's place one Saturday morning when there was the flood. Because of the flood, the ferry was taken out of action. They just had a big skiff, a big rowboat that they were taking people across in. I rode over to my grandparents. I got there. My dad who was there taking his lunch hour from his job just beat the hell out of me for doing that because it was dangerous.

Remember what I told you they named my dog? (Mike.) Occasionally he'd like to move around. He was an outdoor dog, indoor and outdoor. But occasionally he'd disappear for three or four days. But he always showed up again. Well, there was this one time he disappeared. The whole week went by and we never saw Mike the dog. We had about given up on him. I was delivering the papers one day down on Water Street, right at the river, the railroad track. I'm getting the paper out of the bag and I look up and there's this damn dog on the other side of the river. He took the ferry and he took the ferry back. I yelled his name. He picked his head up and looked at me, and this is the width of the River and the River is pretty wide. I called his name and he went right over to the ferry, got on it, and rode over."

-Mike Hancock

"Speaking of the mill, I can remember all the men coming down, walking down, and getting on the ferry and then walking up to Allenport Mill. My uncle Jesse lived up in Brownstown. He would walk all the way down the hill, get on the ferry and then walk over, get to work, and do his job at the mill. Then at the end of the shift, they do the reverse. Come back, get on the ferry and walk all the way up to Brownstown. They would run a canoe (during floods). One time, my Aunt Mary Jane worked for Mr. Strawn. She had to get some papers to him. So she got me to take these papers over to him in Allenport. I had to ride in that canoe in the flooded River. I was scared to death. I was really frightened. One time a man fell off the ferry and drowned. I don't know if he thought he was on the shore or what, but he walked off the ferry and drowned"

-Audrey Tiernan Repka

The Jacobs family acquired the ferry in 1891 for a sum of $4,000 from William Huggins and operated it until it closed for good in 1964. During the 1940s, the ferry named "Eleanor" transported passengers and vehicles across the River throughout the day and night with Andy Liviskie at the helm. The ferry could be hailed from Allenport by clanging the large metal ring attached wharf wall. The arrival of the ferry on the shores of Fayette City was always an occasion for excitement. The local kids would welcome the passengers, play on the ferry's ramp, and occasionally hitch a ride across the River.

Operating the ferry was usually a straightforward task since Allenport is directly across the River from Fayette City. However, the occasion flood, as the Monongahela River was known to experience, provided a particularly difficult time for the ferry, so difficult, in fact, that owners of the ferry had to resort to transporting riders by skiff. The fast moving and high water added an element of excitement for everyone involved.

Even in the best of conditions, accidents did occur on crossing. One particularly devasting accident occurred on the evening of June 22, 1945, when James E. Miller drowned after being shoved from the ferry by an unsecured automobile on the ferry deck. Miller, who was on his way to work at the Allenport mill, left behind his wife Viola and five children. Suit was brought against the J.A. Jacobs estate by Mrs. Miller and almost three years later in April of 1948 she was awarded a sum of $35,000 for her loss.

The Jacobs family (top) and Andy Liviskie (bottom) in 1949. Photos courtesy of Vanessa Moskala Pugh.

"Well that was the only way to get from one side of the River to the other was to use the ferry. The ferry ran all the time with workers from the mill and teachers. I knew some teachers who went somewhere to teach, but they crossed on the very first. Speaking of the ferry, here's the most exciting person, two people, that crossed the ferry every day. They lived in Allenport, and they were Flo Gator and Gladys Miller....They were interesting. No matter what the weather was like, Flo had her hat on. Yeah, she did. She had the cutest little hole in wall shop, you know. I always wanted to do something like that, but that didn't work out."

-June Winters Baldwin Jaquette

"Oh, I rode the ferry because it was so much fun. Carl France was one of the ferry boat guys that went back and forth. When we were kids, we weren't allowed to do this, but we did it in anyway. We would stand like, the ferry was straight, but there was a slant for when the cars used to come up on it, you know. They would have three cars at a time going across here. I don't think there was four. I think there was three. That was scary. If you were in a car going across there, even as a kid, I was scared to death. But anyhow, they had that slant. So we used to ask him, can we jump off at the end after you pull out? Well, you better make sure you jumped and didn't land in water. But the one time I landed in the water. I was all wet and I had to come home. Boy did my mother give me heck. Oh my goodness did she gave me heck because we weren't allowed to do it. But we did it. There was like maybe five kids, we each did that. It was something to do. Yeah, it was a lot of fun."

-Ella Marie Davis

"If we had an extra nickel, we would ride the ferry across to Allenport. That was a big treat. It could take one car at a time. Then we would ride back. We did that for fun. The men would go to the steel mills over in Allenport. They would ride the ferry across."

-Shirley Ferree Stilgenbauer

56

"I remember when it was only cables. Then later on they had like a diesel engine on there. I believe the family's name was Jacobs. I think they lived in Allenport. I took music lessons when I was in high school. So I would have to cross the ferry, get on a streetcar, and travel to Pittsburgh. The streetcar travel was about two hours each way without the ferry. Then I remember when there was flooding or in bad weather, sometimes they ran what they called a skiff. I remember going with Gladys Miller in that skiff over to visit over at her house. They lived in Allenport."

-Georgia Nicholson Slezak

"We was always taught we didn't use somebody's first name if they was older than you. But his name was Mr. Liviskie. I can remember him. He was an older guy. He ran the ferry. Then Thurman Smith come on the ferry after that. I remember we used to book the ferry. It was only five cents. We booked the ferry. We didn't have a nickel to go across the River. That's how bad things was. Things wasn't easy."

-Joe Vargo

"We were in the River all the time. The river and playing on the ferry. The ferry guy was across the River. He ran the ferry from across the River when we were young. Of course we would go down there and jump off the ferry when it started. We weren't allowed to do that. But we did. I had to go in after my brother one time to get him out of the water."

-June Cramer Yevincy

"The streetcars would come up on the Allenport side from Charleroi and then to Allenport. The ferry was the capability to get back to Fayette City. The ferry ran regularly unless it was flood stage. Then the owner of the ferry offered to take people across in a schooner with paddles. It was interesting when the water was high and running fast. So if you got in that boat he would row to the south up toward Sisleytown, toward the Allenport mill, go up along close into the land, and then leave when he got high enough, further up the River. Then he would go out into the river and dash across and try to hit the ferry slot on the Fayette City side. It could get dicey sometimes. I remember the ferry was the way to get around. Probably 10, 5 cents a person or 15 or 20 cents a car. You could only get three or four cars on there. But that was the way to get from Allenport."

-Jack Young

Connie and Larry Moskala posing on the ramp of the "Eleanor" (top) and a view of Allenport from the ferry (bottom). Photos courtesy of Vanessa Moskala Pugh.

"My grandfather run the ferry for years,. Mr. Liviskie. He run it for the Jacobs family. After he quit, after the feed store closed, he went to work on the ferry over there for Mr. Jacobs."

-Jim Eley

With optimism brought on by the end of the War, a number of new businesses opened up in Fayette City in the second half of the 1940s. Stub's Photo-Engraving Shop and Dr. Campi's dentist office were mentioned previously. Figel's gas station at the north end of town opened in September of 1945. Johnson's Photography on town hill opened in 1946. In October of 1947, Thomas Emelo opened a watch repair shop on Main Street between Kuhns Confectionery and the bank building.

Open Watch Repair Shop Here

Fayette City's growing list of business houses was increased this week with the announcement that Thomas C. Emelo will open a watch repair shop next door to Kuhns News Stand.

The opening is set for Saturday Sept. 13, from 10 a. m. to 9 p. m. Besides repairing watches, Mr. Emelo will specialize in gift items and pottery. The public is invited to attend the opening and inspect the business house.

Fayette City Journal
September 12, 1947

Fayette City Journal
September 28, 1945

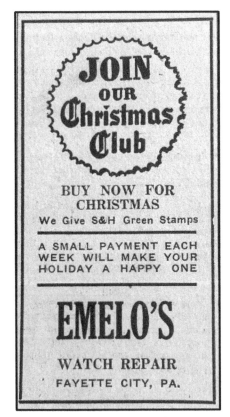

Fayette City Journal
October 10, 1947

NEW BUSINESS OPENS ON MAIN STREET THIS WEEK

A new name was added to the list of Fayette City business establishments this week with the announcement by the Bircsak Flour and Feed Supply that they are now open for business.

During the latter part of December Andrew Bircsak purchased the property that formerly housed the National Flour and Feed Co. from Herman Greenstein and Milton Klein. The two large brick and cement feed stores are located in the southern end of town with one building facing on Main Street and the other on Second Street.

Mr. Bircsak, who was born at Fairbanks, Pennsylvania, is well known in this district, having lived at Charleroi for several years before his going to Newark, New Jersey in 1927. He married a local girl, the former Iva Povlish, who is also well known in this territory. She taught school in Washington Township and just recently was an employee of the War Department at their Newark, New Jersey office of Dependency Benefits.

Mr. E. K. Brown, well know in this territory as the feed man will be manager of Mr. Brown has perience in this

Fayette City Journal
January 17, 1947

Earlier in 1947, Andrew Bircsak purchased the National Flour and Feed Company with buildings on Main Street and Second Street from Herman Greenstein and Milton Klein and renamed it Bircsak Flour and Feed Supply. Just a week prior to the Bircsak announcement, the Fayette Feed Company on the corner of Cook and Front (or Water) Streets publicly denied it was going out of business. Unfortunately, it was not destined to survive the decade.

OPEN FOR BUSINESS

WE ARE PREPARED TO SERVE YOU WITH A COMPLETE LINE OF

PRATTS & OHIO FEEDS
For Poultry And Live Stock

King Midas Flours
For Household Purposes

Headquarters for Farm Supplies

AND A COMPLETE LINE OF PRATTS REMEDIES AND DOG FEED

Courteous Service - Prompt Delivery Guaranteed

BIRCSAK FLOUR & FEED SUPPLY

E. K. Brown, Mgr.   Phone 7780-R-I-2
Main Street   Fayette City, Pa.

Fayette City Journal
February 21, 1947

Fayette City Journal
March 19, 1948

The Craft (sometimes spelled Kraft) family launched a much-needed taxi service in 1948. The taxi stand was a little cubby nestled between Emelo's Watch Repair and Hamer's Dairy Bar on Main Street. The Crafts later sold the taxi service to Margie Mosko who operated the business in the 1950s.

Taxi Service Promised In Boro Soon

Taxicab service will become a reality in Fayette City Borough within the next few days following approval by the Public Utility Commission at Harrisburg.

Sherman W. Craft and sons are at present awaiting the certificate from Harrisburg giving them the franchise for this area. They state that within the next two weeks they will open a cab stand at the room between Hamer's Dairy Bar and Emelo's Jewelry Store.

Fayette City Journal
April 16, 1948

"I do know they (the Craft family) had the taxi service. It was working out pretty good. Then they sold it to,....Margie Mosko. They sold it to her. She run it for a few years before she closed it down. Hauled people up and down the hill. It's a pretty steep hill to walk up."

-Willard Jones

"The taxi service. Let me tell you this about it. A lot of people might go on Facebook or make remarks about Margie Mosko. Some that I've seen, they would just say things about her. Often every time I'd see them I'd say something. I would remark back. I would tell them, you know, Margie Mosko, she was a nice lady. She really was. Anyway, I remember going up, walking, mind you we had no car, in the wintertime, walking up to Brownstown to Donna Mae Traversari's house, which was past the cemetery, past the church up there. I was up there playing and everything. It's cold and it's snowing and it was time for them to eat dinner. So I left. Here I am walking. I had a coat on and a hat. I'm walking by the cemetery and here comes this car, Fancy Cab, it was Margie Mosko. She stopped and she said, Georgia Jean, what are you doing? I said I'm walking home. She says get in. I don't have money to pay you. She said I don't need money, get in, I'll take you home. That lady went and took me clear down home, pulled in front of my house on Water Street and dropped me off. She was good like that. She was a nice person."

-Georgia Arrow

"Margie Mosco's taxi was right next to, just a cubby hole taxi place, between the bank, between Hamer's Dairy Bar and I think a clothing store there. They had that little clothing store there. Back in the 50s they had St. Edwards Park (in Johnson Hollow). The church had a picnic place up in Johnson Hollow. Me and my wife used to walk up there and dance and drink. We would walk up the Hollow and at about 9:30 at night we'd call up Margie Mosko taxi. For 50 cents she'd ride us back down home. We didn't want to walk back."

-Jim McKevitt

"She had that little hole in the wall, as much as it was, down there between Kuhns and Hamers. There was just the door. It went straight through. You'd sit in there and wait on a taxi and she took you. She had that taxi service for a long time."

-Eleanor Welsh Owens

In 1948 Andrew Stefanik opened an Esso gas station at the north end of Fayette City on the road to Belle Vernon. The building had to be reconstructed a few years later when the road was widened to four lanes. After opening the gas station, the entrepreneurial Stefanik opened the iconic Crystal Pool directly behind the gas station. Piles of dirt from the excavation of the pool can be seen in the bottom photograph. During excavation, the adjacent baseball field was rotated 180 degrees to its current orientation.

Local Man Opens Esso Station Here

Announcement was made this week of the addition of another business in Fayette City as Andrew Stefanick opened his newly-erected service station to the general public.

Mr. Stefanick, who is employed at the Allenport Plant of Pittsburgh Steel Company, several months ago purchased property at the north end of the borough line and proceeded to erect a gasoline service station.

The new business will specialize in grease jobs and will dispense Standard Oil Company products recognized by the trade name of Esso. Hours have been set temporarily at 8 a. m. until 12 midnight. Mr. Stefanick will welcome your patronage.

Fayette City Journal
March 12, 1948

"Four gas stations. Can you believe there were four gas stations and they were all busy? Vargo's had an Atlantic Station at the end of town going up to Gillespie. Back down the other way Figel's had a Gulf station. Freshwaters had an ESSO station, no Amoco station. Andy Stefanick had the ESSO station. He also had Crystal Pool."

-Raymond Moody

Esso Station at north end of Fayette City.
Photos courtesy of Eddy Stefanick.

Beauty shops seemed to either change hands or suddenly spring up at the end of the decade. Stephanie's at 200 Market Street was sold to Mary Kay Marinak in October 1946 and renamed Mary Kay's Beauty Shop. The Marie Beauty Studio at Second and Union Streets opened in May 1947 with Marie Rice Proprietor. Just a few months later, Mary Ellen's Beauty Shop opened on town hill with Mary Ellen McCurdy proprietor.

Despite the successful opening of numerous small businesses in the latter half of the 1940s, local merchants felt the need to organize a Board of Trade to do more to make Fayette City an attractive destination for new businesses and shoppers alike. The Board was led by Howard McCrory and was comprised of several prominent business leaders including John Bake, Andrew Bircsak, Joe Ciavarra, Charles Kuhns, and Dr. Campi. The Board held its first meeting in July 1948. Items high on the agenda were a bank (a persistent need since 1927), a public parking lot, and parking meters.

Name McCrory President Of Business Group

A Board of Trade was organized last Friday evening by a group of local merchants with Howard Mc-Crory being named president and Robert Premoshis being named secretary-treasurer.

Meeting at the borough building with aproximately 15 businessmen being present, the group discussed the advantages of having such an organization here and with every-one being in favor, it was decided that temporary officers be named.

A committee on constitution and by-laws composed of R. B. Weightman, Joseph Ciavarra and Charles Kuhns was selected.

The aim of the newly-formed Board of Trade will be to promote better business relations in Fayette City and also to make for better trade facilities for the public in general.

Any businessman in the borough is eligible for membership and will be welcome at the next meeting to be held June 28.

It has been several years since a Board of Trade has operated in Fayette City and from reports that were given the Fayette City Board of Trade was one of the best that ever functioned in this area. It is hoped that the present organization can function as well and if so, the community can expect a revival in business here.

Fayette City Journal
October 17, 1947

Fayette City Journal
May 23, 1947

Fayette City Journal
November 3, 1944

Fayette City Journal
June 18, 1948

Bars

Fayette City had perhaps more than its fair share of bars, seven to be exact. In fact, Fayette City was widely known as the town with seven bars and seven churches. Judging from its reputation for rowdyism, Fayette City could have perhaps used more churches, or fewer bars. Identifying the bars, or beer gardens as they were often called, could be a tricky endeavor as they often changed names or owners, or simply went out of

GRAND
OPENING

OF THE

Newly Remodeled

LIVI'S
RESTAURANT

224 MAIN ST.

Friday, March 19

Open -:- 9 A.M. till 2 A.M.

Fayette City Journal
March 19, 1948

business. To complicate things further, a couple of the bars, the Eagles and the American Legion, were private clubs and not public businesses. To be sure, however, the bars were every bit a part of the community as any of the other town's businesses, or churches for that matter.

"Oh boy let me see. I'll come down, Janeri's had one. Marine bar. Then down the street was the Legion and then come back up there was, Matt's was on the corner of Main and Market. Then you go up a little bit further, it was Livi's and there was a club on Second Street and I'm trying to remember the name of it. It will come to me, I was never in that, that place. The Eagles. I was never in there. That was six, I think. There was a club up Navoo Hollow. The people up there, they called it the hunky club. Everybody called it the hunky club, it seemed like, I guess. And then there was going up the Hollow there was..... Norman Humphries. Humphries had a tavern there. That would make it seven."

-Raymond Moody

"I know Fayette City had a lot of beer gardens because I think my dad visited them all. On payday, he couldn't, he worked on a railroad. He came home from work. He got his supper and got dressed. He took his little cut of whatever, and went to town. I don't know to this day how he ever made it home, up around that hill, that road to get home, up to Sisleytown from all those beer gardens downtown."

-Eleanor Welsh Owens

"We had a lot of bars. Livi's had a bar and they also had like a dairy bar. In fact, I worked in Livi's dairy bar. They sold the Pittsburgh Press. One thing going in there, you were allowed to have ice cream, you're allowed to have some ice cream, which you didn't have to pay for. There was, Joe Janeri had a bar. In fact, when I was in second grade up in where they had the minstrel shows and things. They had the canteen they started that too. He was showing me how to dance at one point. But he had a bar. There was the Marine Bar. There was Matt's Grill down on the corner. George Miller had, it was a bar, you can get good hamburgers there. Minnie Natola worked, you said that was your grandmother, Minnie work there because I can remember watching her pat the hamburgers out. Now they had a bar and my dad said I was about two years old. I don't know if they had a jukebox then, they had some kind of music in there. He would take me up on the bar and I would they would play music and this baby would dance to the music. But I remember going there to get the hamburgers. She made really really good hamburgers. Do you remember that bar's name? It was George Miller's. It was like a bar, and I think that later became the Marine Bar. I don't know if he had anything to do with that when there was the Marine Bar or not. In Navoo Hollow, that was Humphries. To my knowledge, people probably drank, but I don't think anybody, probably somebody, had an alcohol problem for a bit. That wasn't something we focused on."

-Georgia Nicholson Slezak

Most of the bars were located on Main Street. Livi's, the Riverview Grill, the Marine Club, and the Union Grill were located in the 200 block of Main while the American Legion was (and still is) located in the 100 block. The Eagles was located on Second Street. Humphries and the Red Onion were in Navoo Hollow. The Marine Club was originally owned by George Miller. Ernie and Sophie Presock purchased the bar from Miller, renamed it the Marine Club, and remodeled it in 1947. Riverview Grill, with its uniquely angled front door, was owned by the Markish family. Livi's was operated by Alderio Livi who, along with his family also ran a small confectionary/restaurant/dairy bar adjacent to the bar. The Union Grill was located across the street from Livi's on the ground floor of the Odd Fellows Building. In 1945, the Union Grill was renamed Janeri's, and then Johnny's Place in late 1946. Humphries was a tiny establishment tucked in between the hillside and Navoo Hollow Road just beyond the entrance to the Hollow. The bar was later renamed the Lamplight. About a hundred yards further up the Hollow and on the other side of the road was the Red Onion. The original Red Onion, named after its exterior hue, was part of a block of dilapidated wooden apartments usually occupied by Russians, Slavs, and other eastern Europeans who worked in the neighboring coal mines. The Red Onion was also known as the "Hunky Club" because of its primary clientele. The original Red Onion was later razed and replaced by a cinder block building, also painted red, placed further back from the road.

"Oh my, Livi's. The Beach Club but it was the Marine Bar then. The Presocks owned it there. And then on a corner I don't know if you remember, was it...The Riverview Grill. My brother Tom worked for him for his wife. Oh my, he used to do house cleaning, everything for her, cause she was always in the bar. Livi's and the Marine Bar. Before that, I forget who owned that. They come from Detroit or somewhere and bought that place. Ernie and Sophie Presock owned that bar, and then John Heinz bought the bar off of them. They moved back to Detroit, I think. Well, we always had the Slovak club. That was where, right up from Humphries on the opposite side of the road. There was a little house there. That's where they started, I think somebody said they started the Slovak Club down Fayette City underneath the post office. And they moved up to that little house across, I'd say caddy-corner from Humphries bar. They stayed there for a while and then they built a place up the road a little bit, maybe 100 yards, 200 yards on the same side, a brick building. Well before that, that's where the Red Onion was. It was a row of houses. There was about four different families that lived in that big long row of houses. And they called that the Red Onion. I remember that real good. Then they moved from that little house to the end housing project, the housing end of the Red Onion was the Slovak Club in there. And then when they ripped the Red Onion down they built that brick building that's there now.

When school was over, we got home. We always had a job to do. You got to keep living. I mean, you had to try to make a dollar like I was telling you. We passed the shoeshine box down in the family. Then Friday and Saturday, we'd go into Fayette City. You couldn't walk on the sidewalk. That's how many people were in town. It was crowded. I could remember when I was a kid, it was crowded. And then we had a shoeshine box. We'd go into the bars and try to get, you know, shoe shines was 10 cents then. Some of them old coal miners would give you a quarter or 50 cents. You was a millionaire. There was some good ones like Sam Hamer. He had a little coal mine. That was a different Hamer. Jim Hamer. Jim Hamer, that's where my dad worked in the coal mine for Jim Hamer. Because Sam always had, he worked in a coal mine. He always had a little coal mine. He had a little bit more than the rest of the people. But he was he was a good-hearted soul."

-Joe Vargo

"Fayette City, we had a lot of churches, but we had equal amount if not more, beer gardens. We had Livi's, Janeri's. You had the American Legion, I think a place called Toth's, a lot of beer gardens. My dad, my family, my mother and her family, she had six sisters. They all married to local guys. That whole Stark family was teetotalers. No swearing. No smoking. No drinking. I didn't have a full can of beer until I was a lieutenant in the Navy. I sort of followed my mother's rules when it came to that. But yeah, a lot of beer gardens. My grandpa Young after he worked all weekend in the coal mines, he would be known to go down downtown and have a little bit too much whiskey before getting back up to his house."

-Jack Young

Marine Bar on Main Street.
Photo courtesy of Doris Moskala Breckenridge.

Fayette City Journal
December 21, 1945

"A lot of men would spit on the sidewalk. When you were walking on a sidewalk, you'd have to look down so that you didn't step in the spit, the tobacco juice, you know. There were a lot of bars. That was the Marine Bar then. But I remember the hotel on the corner. Do you remember the hotel? It was a hotel on the corner of Main Street and Market Street."

-Audrey Tiernan Repka

"Well, their names changed so often. There was Livi's bar. It was one. They also had a convenience store and a service stand there at Livi's beside the bar and sold vegetables. I can't think of anything because it kept changing so often. Across the street from Livi's beer hall was another one. (Janeri's) Yeah, that was Janeri's before Janeri's left. Janeri's, that was it. There was one down by the theater, right between Joe Bell's theater and the drugstore. (Marine.) Yep, something like that. The guy who ran it was a friend of mine. We'd go fishing once in a while. Then there was a Humphries Tavern up Navoo Hollow. You had the Eagles. You had the Legion. You had the Slovak Club. There was another club there. There was quite a bit of things to do."

-Bill Williamson

"I remember he and his friends, a big thing on Saturday night was their night off and they would go to Matt's Grill at the corner of Market and Main streets. I think it was a family named Markish owned that thing. That was their big night out to go and have a few beers with the other boys. So that I remember."

-Georgia Nicholson Slezak

"Humphries tavern, right before that bridge. It was built against that hill. When we would walk down (Navoo Hollow) you could smell that it was a tavern. And then up the road, there was a building called the Red Onion. It had three living units. The end unit was the hunky club, which is now a building all to itself."

-John Vargo

Union Grill on Main Street.
Photo courtesy of Georgia Jean Arrow.

Fayette City Journal
February 23, 1945

Fayette City Journal
May 21, 1948

Main Street looking south with Riverview Grill on the right.
Photo courtesy of Vanessa Moskala Pugh.

"On the corner, where the bank lot is, there was what they call the Riverview Grill. It was owned by Frank Markish and his wife. I can't remember her name. Frank senior had the bar. Frank Jr. married Marie when she was a Rice before she got married. But the Riverview Grill was owned by Frank's dad and his name was Frank. I wish I could remember his wife's name. Anyhow they had the Riverview Grill there on the corner. There was a window that went around like this, but they had like a railing that went this way and they had curtains there that you couldn't see in. But yeah, I remember that. When we were kids you ran a lot in your bare feet. I shouldn't even say this, those old men would come out of the bar and it had a rounded step around and it was about this thick, round piece of concrete. But it was like black or whatever. Those old men would come out and they used to go (spitting sound). Oh, God, we had to watch when we were kids so we didn't tramp in them hawkers. Most of the time we'd just go around, you know, not go through, we'd go out around on the road and get up on the other part of the sidewalk."

-Ella Marie Auther Davis

HERE'S TO
YOUR
HAPPINESS

1947

Your friendship
and our success are
closely interwoven.
We hope, in 1947,
to strengthen still
further these bonds
of friendship.

**HAPPY NEW YEAR
TO ALL**

RIVERVIEW
GRILL

Fayette City Journal
December 27, 1946

One type of business that was conspicuously absent from Fayette City during the 1940s was a financial institution, specifically a bank. In fact, Fayette City had been without a bank since 1927 and wasn't destined to get another bank until 1957. The reason for the absence of a bank over this 30 year period is linked to what was undoubtedly the biggest scandal to ever hit Fayette City and perhaps even Fayette County for that matter. At the risk of boring the reader, the details of the sordid affair will be recounted here.

The Fayette City National Bank opened in 1903 and was assigned charter number 6800. A capital of $75,000 was posted by J. Audley Black, Louis Cope, Philip R. Luce Joseph Swartz, Andrew Brown and George W. Spalter. The bank printed $1,223,920 dollars between 1903 and 1927 when it closed. The Bank issued ten different types and denominations of national currency including the 5, 10, 20, 50, and 100 dollar bills with both red and blue seals.

ANDREW BROWN, President
LOUIS COPE, Vice President
GUY W. BROWN, Cashier
JESSE R. BROWN, Assistant Cashier

Fayette City National Bank
FAYETTE CITY, PA.

Capital	$75,000.00
Surplus and Profits	$68,000.00
Deposits	$650,000.00

The Evening Standard (Uniontown, PA)
October 21, 1913

In 1913, Andrew Brown, Louis Cope, Guy W. Brown and Jesse R. Brown were listed as President, Vice President, Cashier, and Assistant Cashier, respectively, for the Bank. A few years later, in 1916, the Bank's board of directors were listed as Andrew Brown, Louis Cope, G.W. Spalter, James Patterson H.E. Barnum, Guy W. Brown and J.L. Krepps.

Guy Watson Brown
Pennsylvania State Senator 1923-1926

The success of the Bank in the ensuing years gave encouragement to one of its directors to run for public office. In April of 1923, Guy Watson Brown announced his candidacy for the thirty-second senatorial district of Pennsylvania as a Republican. In his announcement, the 40-year old Brown said "The great problems confronting our State are principally of business character. Its affairs should be systematized and conducted with the same careful consideration that the most efficient business organization give to the administration of their own affairs, in order that the State might receive full value for every dollar expended and that undue taxes shall not be extracted from the people." After winning the primary, Brown went on to win by a big majority over his Democratic opponent, Harry Cotton of Brownsville. A delegation of Fayette City folk accompanied Watson to Harrisburg for the opening session of the Senate. Hopes were high for the young State Senator.

Brown served as State Senator through 1926 and then returned to a private life in banking. In July of 1927, in a shocking turn of events, voluntary petitions in bankruptcy were filed in the US District Court by Guy W. Brown of Uniontown and Jesse Brown of Fayette City and receivers for the two estates were appointed. The Fayette City National Bank was closed on July 6 and was placed in the hands of a bank examiner. During the subsequent trial of the brothers in December of the same year, Jesse refused to answer the majority of the questions posed to him. With other questions he claimed his memory failed him. Guy Brown also refused to answer certain questions claiming his constitutional rights and requested more time to analyze disputed checks which he had issued prior to the bankruptcy. More than 3000 depositors were holding out hope that the bank would reorganize. The following January, a receiver was appointed for the Fayette Construction Company, an entity of the Bank. Its president, John Cope, was held under $10,000 bond on charges of embezzlement. Investors in Cope's company included holders of small savings accounts and local farmers. At the same January proceedings, Guy Brown, under examination, admitted that Peter Zemo, Brown's chauffer, borrowed $20,000 from the bank in 1926 and the proceeds were deposited to Brown's account. Brown then pleaded his constitutional rights, and the questioning was terminated.

By July of 1928, a total of $345,000 was recovered from the Bank by the examiners. Depositors of the Fayette City National Bank received 15% of their total deposits. The First National Bank of Webster, also managed by Guy Brown, was forced to close as well because of its affiliation with the Fayette City Bank. Its depositors were also paid a fraction of their total deposits.

"It was way before my time. But you know, the town talked about that. It seemed like I can remember people still talking about it. It would come up occasionally. They would say "Oh, Guy Brown stole our money, took our money." We didn't have the bank after that. There was no bank in Fayette City. I don't know where people banked. But there was none in Fayette City because we didn't have one. They closed the bank. But I remember saying, hearing people say "Oh, Guy Brown stole all our money, took our money.""

-Nancy Johnson Ferree

"My grandfather owned a couple mines or at least owned a share in a couple mines and had a good bit of money invested in the mines through the bank. The bank in 1927 went broke. This is two years before the crash of the Depression. So it wasn't the Depression that did it. The bank just went broke and closed up and declared bankruptcy. My grandfather and a number of other people got absolutely nothing out of it. Except they lost, you know, it could have been a small fortune. Guy Brown, that's the guy is I'm talking about. My grandfather lost all his money. That was one of the reasons they bumped around in places where they lived after that. But he never acted bitter about it. He wouldn't talk to me about it. He never acted bitter, although I would have been as bitter as hell. But my grandfather went out there and got a job as a calligrapher on the railroad, the P&LE railroad."

-Mike Hancock

The following September, a federal grand jury indicted Guy Brown on 33 counts of embezzlement totaling $137,596. In the newspaper article announcing the indictment, Guy Brown was described as a former state senator, banker and *church treasurer*. Jesse Brown was indited on 4 counts. The total bills attributed to Guy Brown included the following:

- Defalcation of $120,121 from the Fayette City National Bank which included $2,200 belonging to the Home Mission Fund and the Benevolent Fund of the Redstone Presbytery.
- Falsifying the credit of two mining corporations.
- Embezzling $10,000 worth of bonds of the Fayette City Water Company.
- Defalcation of $7,475 from the Webster National Bank.

Guy and Jesse posted bail of $10,000 and $5,000, respectively. At the ensuing trial, several of the former directors of the Bank, including J.L. Krepps, George M. Boyd, and A.P. Barrum, were called as witnesses by the government. None of the men could recall the details of their approvals of dubious notes totaling thousands of dollars. The men claimed that they approved the notes at the recommendation of Guy Brown without knowing the identity and financial standing of the individuals. The specific notes in question were as follows:

- Peter Zemo for $200,000
- D.M Fleichert for $2,500 and $12,000
- A.M. Young for $8,500
- Alfred N. White for $5,000
- C.M. Swift for $5,000
- D.R. Wilson for $9,000

The government charged that all the names were fictitious except for Zemo, Brown's chauffer. Zemo testified that he had signed a blank note which he gave to Brown with the understanding that he was buying stock in a mining corporation owned by Brown. Zemo also testified that he never received the stock.

In November of 1928, in the midst of the court proceedings, Andrew Brown, the Bank's president, passed away. Approximately three years prior to his death, Andrew Brown suffered a stroke of paralysis which made him an invalid. Curiously, Andrew Brown purchased 100 shares of stock in the Bank at $15 per share in May of 1927 just weeks before beginning of the affair.

In February of 1929, a year and a half after the Fayette City National Bank was forced to close, Guy Brown was convicted on 26 counts of embezzlement. Jesse Brown pleaded no defense a few days later after his brother was found guilty, claiming that he was under the influence and control of his brother. Guy Brown was sentenced to serve three years in the Federal penitentiary in Atlanta, GA. Jesse Brown was paroled for three years. Guy Brown requested and then withdrew an appeal. Guy Brown served two years less 24 days for work done at Camp Lee, VA and was released in August 1931.

Brown was married to Cora Patterson and the couple had five children. Newspapers related stories of the marriages of his children in the 1940s. Brown died in 1978. A burial location was not identified.

John Cope, for his part in the matter, was sentenced to serve not less than two years and not more than four in the Allegheny County workhouse. In trying to secure early release from his sentence, Cope claimed he was under the influence of Guy Brown and had not benefitted materially from the embezzlement. Further, his wife Ella claimed that her husband had no money to pay the $500 fine imposed on him. Wooda Carr, the counsel for the Fayette Construction Company, suggested that John and Ella had a clandestine affair before they got married in 1927 while both had spouses by a former marriage and had not been divorced. Carr claimed that Cope's inability to pay the fine was due to the affair.

Shortly after Guy Brown started his sentence in the Atlanta penitentiary, several citizens of Fayette City including William Gaskill, Dr. C.R. Huston and Haryey Barker, met in Gaskill's Hardware Store to discuss plans to organize a new bank. The lack of community interest scuttled the plans, but Dr. Huston remained optimistic saying "There is no doubt we will have a bank here within a comparatively short time. However, interest is lacking now."

In the 1940s, several attempts were made to form or attract a bank. In 1941, Burgess U.F. Higinbotham, George Miller, Elmer Renstrom, Herman Greenstein, Milton Kline and other prominent citizens set a goal of raising $60,000 for the endeavor. Once again, the effort failed. In 1946, Robert Premoshis appealed to the Fayette City Lion's Club for its endorsement of a drive to establish a bank without success. In 1948, Burgess James Thirkield headed a committee to prepare petitions of residents in the borough who were willing to open accounts in support of a new bank. Fifty petitions were circulated with the goal of enticing the National Bank of Uniontown to open a branch in town. This attempt too failed. It wasn't until 1957, a good thirty years after the Fayette City National Bank was forced to close, that another bank opened in Fayette City. On April 7, 1957, more than 2,500 persons showed up to celebrate the opening of the Gallatin National Bank in the old bank building on Main Street. The devastating effects of Guy Brown's misdeeds had finally been overcome.

FAYETTE CITY HAS FIRST BANK SINCE 1927

In a dual celebration last Saturday more than 2,500 persons from Fayette City and the surrounding area marked establishment of the first "home town" banking service since 1927 for Fayette City.

"Open house" was held at the new Fayette City office of the Gallatin National Bank throughout the afternoon and evening, and up the street in the borough's community center the financial institution was welcomed with a reception which included music by Slim Bryant and his Wildcats,

dancing and refreshments for all. A number of the community's residents also joined in, with large signs of welcome on their establishments.

John Canigiani, Sr., extreme right, a member of the Fayette City borough council for the past 20 years, and its present president, officially opened the bank office at 1 p.m. by cutting the ribbon across the new front doors. He was assisted in the ribbon cutting ceremony by Paul Malone, Gallatin National President, center, and Louis DeMay, assistant cashier, who will be in charge of the new office at the left.

The Daily Courier (Connellsville, PA)
April 8, 1957

REFERENCES

Paglia, Ron (2012, August 7) Focus on theaters rings a Bell about reel-life adventure. *The Valley Independent.*

CHAPTER 4 World War II

"I remember the day that Pearl Harbor was bombed. My mother and I and my uncle John Nicholson were standing in our kitchen. We had the radio on. They had announced that Pearl Harbor had just been bombed. I was very, very frightened. I was afraid that we were going to be bombed and kept looking out the window. If I heard an airplane go over, I was afraid. I remember that day so distinctly."

-Shirley Ferree Stilgenbauer

"Well, I'm not sure when the town got news of the bombing of Pearl Harbor. But I remember the day after. We'd gone to school that Monday morning and went home for lunch. I remember the radio was on. President Roosevelt was giving his famous speech declaring war on Japan. I remember that."

-Nancy Ferree Johnson

"I can remember the day Pearl Harbor was bombed. Everybody was so upset. We lived in the bank building right on Main Street which was right across from Bell Theater. We lived on the third floor of that building and there was a flat roof which we had. That was where we hang hung clothes. There were no clothes dryers back at that time. Monday was always wash day. We didn't have automatic washers or anything. We had to carry the water. There was a hallway between the two apartments. We had these big metal wash tubs and we did have a ringer washer. But wash day you started on Sunday night filling like the wash tubs and everything. Then you would have to climb up on a stool and get out this window where the clothes were hung. But the day Pearl Harbor was bombed I remember going out on that roof and being so frightened because I thought maybe Pearl Harbor was across the River where Allenport was. I remember being so frightened because all the grownups were very, very upset."

-Georgia Nicholson Slezak

"Well, I was I was born in 34. So in 41, I was seven. I remember being in the car with my mother and dad and brother, somewhere on town hill. We pulled over up on town hill and somebody said Japan attacked Pearl Harbor. I remember them saying that because I didn't know what that meant."

-Jack Young

"On Sunday, December 7, 1941 in the afternoon, probably wrong. I'm just guessing around four or five o'clock in the afternoon, maybe six o'clock in the yard of Hindmarsh's neighbor, Barry Hindmarsh's neighbor, Barry was just a little boy then, real little. I was watching three or four older boys determined to build an airplane out of strips of wood. I was standing there amazed that they could build that plane when all of a sudden a mother came out of the house and shouted to the boys that Japan had just bombed Pearl Harbor and it probably meant war. I heard two of the boys say that they were going to enlist the next day, the eighth. That partially built skeleton of a plane sat in that yard for what seemed like years. I was just amazed that they had enough originality to even think that they could build a plane out of just strips of wood that were used for plastering. It's just how young people thought back then. Your mind was open to everything."

-Bill Williamson

Soldiers at War

Citizens of Fayette City have a long history of serving their county in the military. One hundred and one men served during World War I, with four giving their lives in the effort. Fayette City's American Legion Brightwell-Dougherty Post 484 was named after two of those fallen soldiers. A complete listing of the men who served in World War I is provided in Appendix III.

Two hundred thirty-six men and nine women from Fayette City served in the military during World War II, more than double the number who served in World War I. A complete listing of these soldiers is provided in Appendix IV. By 1942, registration for the military's Selective Service was required for males from age 18 to 45. Given that Fayette City's population during this time was approximately 1500 and assuming that half of that number were male, it is reasonable to believe that nearly all of the men of draft age served in the military. The impact of losing this vital segment of the population on the town must have been profound in a multitude of ways. The once lively baseball games at ball field at the north end of town were shutout. Fayette City's renowned Trojan Drum and Bugle Corps was silenced. The cemeteries on town hill became overgrown due to lack of manpower. Women were placed in positions previously held only by men. The list goes on.

Needless to say, those who remained home during the War closely followed the soldiers' activities. The Fayette City Journal posted weekly updates in its column entitled "Among Those in Service", routinely announced any commendations received by the men and women, and published letters received from the soldiers abroad. Not all the news was serious though. The Journal even provided a lighthearted update on horseshoe champion Don Evans's participation in the Pacific Olympic Horseshoe Tournament.

Among Those In Service

★ ★ ★ ★ ★   ★ ★ ★ ★ ★

STEPHEN KOVATCH

Stephen Kovatch, a member of Uncle Sam's Navy, who is stationed in Philadelphia is visiting with his wife and little son, Stephen Ray.

WILLIAM CRAFT

William Craft, serving with the U. S. Navy recently visited here with his parents, Mr. and Mrs. Sherman Craft of Connellsville Street. He is stationed at Little Creek, Virginia.

JACK BEATTIE

Pfc. Jack Beattie, son of Mrs. Fred Renstrom of Main St. spent a few hours last weekend visiting here. He is stationed in Phiadelphia.

SAMUEL HICKS

Samuel Hicks, son of Mr. and Mrs. Samuel Hicks has returned to duty in California after having spent several weeks visiting here with friends and relatives. This was the first time Samuel had been home for almost three years.

JAMES E. SKIBO

Pvt. James E. Skibo, son of Mr. and Mrs. Carl Skibo of California Avenue recently wrote home a letter dated October 25, in which he stated he was o. k. and to tell his pals hello. James is serving with General Patton at Metz in the 25th division known as the Yankee Division.

DONALD AND RICHARD BRECKENRIDGE

Pfc. Donald and Cpl. Richard Breckenridge, brothers, are home visiting. They are the sons of Mrs. Rachael Breckenridge of Brownstown. Pfc. Donald is home for nine days and is stationed at Ft. Lewis, Washington. Cpl. Richard, stationed at Ft. Bragg, North Carolina, is here on a three day pass visiting with his wife, who resides with his mother.

CARL RUSSELL

Carl E. Russell, Bkr. 1-c son of Mr. and Mrs. James Russell of Connellsville Street arrived home Friday morning to spend two weeks visiting among friends and relatives. He is serving with the U. S. Navy and has seen a great deal of action since last being home in November 1943. A friend and buddy, Lewis Russell of Gillespie also served on the same ship as a baker. Lewis is the son of Mr. and Mrs. William Russell.

ROBERT B. HAMER

Atlantic City, N. J. — Staff Sgt. Robert B. Hamer of Fayette City, has reported to the AAF Redistribution Sation No. 1 here, after seven months of service overseas in the European theatre of war.

Sgt. Hamer was a gunner on a B-17 Flying Fortress while overseas. He engaged in twenty-nine combat missions. He wears the Distinquished Flying Cross and the Air Medal with three Oak Leaf clusters.

LOCAL PILOT RECEIVES FRENCH MEDAL

At A Mediterranean Bomber Base — The 12th Air Force B-26 Marauder group of 1st Lt., Edward D. Steinman, 104 2nd St., Fayette City, Pa. has been awarded the Croix de Guerre with palm by the French government for precision attacks on bridges in support of the French ground forces in Italy.

Oldest medium bomber outfit in the Mediterranean theatre, the group was cited in an order by General Charles De Gaulle commending an entire Marauder wing. It is the only AAF unit to be decorated in this war by both the United States and French governments, having previously been cited twice by President Roosevelt for the accuracy of its attacks on Rome and Florence rail yards.

Fayette City Journal
November 10, 1944

Fayette City Journal
November 17, 1944

Awarded Bronze Star With Citation

Pfc. George Arrow has been awarded the Bronze Star Medal with Citation for heroic service in connection with military operations in the European Theatre of Operations.

The citation was recently received by his wife, the former Anna Usher of Fayette City. The citation reads as follows:

"Private First Class George Arrow, Field Artillery, Battery B 212th Armored Field Artillery Battalion, U. S. Army. For heroic service in connection with military operations in France, Belgium, Luxemburg and Germany during the period 29 July 1944 to 8 May 1945. As machine gunner, he has displayed outstanding courage, efficiency and skill in the performance of his duties. Despite heavy enemy fire encountered on many occasions he has always remained cool and calm. Entered the military service from Pennsylvania.

Fayette City Journal
August 31, 1945

Local Soldier Wounded

A telegram from the War Department was received here by Mrs. Marian Gill on Friday, February 9, informing her that her husband, Pvt. Ralph Gill had ben wounded. The telegram read as follows: "Regret to inform you, your husband, Pvt. Ralph Gill was slightly wounded in action, twenty three, January in Belgium. Mail address of hospital will follow." Ulio, The Adjutant General.

Fayette City Journal
February 16, 1946

Among Those In Service
★ ★ ★ ★ ★   ★ ★ ★ ★ ★

SARAH J. EVANS

Sarah J. Evans, 25 years of age, formerly Yoeman Second Class in the U. S. Coast Guard as a member of the Spar's, has been released from the service and is now at her home on 301 Connellsville St. She is the daughter of Mr. and Mrs. William J. Evans and has served 34 months in the service.

FRED COVER OWENS

Aboard the U. S. S. Tabora, Wakayama, Japan (Delayed) Fred Cover Owens, fireman first class, Route 1, Fayette City, Pa., helped land occupation troops assigned to the inland cities of Kobe and Osaka while serving with the crew of this cargo attack ship. The Tabora served with the ships of Amphibious Group Eight in occupation assignment. Crewmen of the Tabora previously had seen action from Guadalcanal to Okinawa.

DELORES S. McGEE

Delores S. McGee, H. A. First Class, 23 years of age is now home here in Fayette City, after having received an honorable discharge from the Waves of the U. S. Navy. She is the daughter of Mr. Martin Schroyer and received her training at Hunter College, Long Beach, U. S. N. Hospital Bremerton, Washington and Pasco Naval Air Hospital. All her navy work has been hospital duty and she spent several months in Surgery. Her husband, Pfc. Edward McGee has served almost three years overseas in the European Theatre of Operations but is expected home soon.

FREDERICK DREYER

Sergeant Frederick Dreyer, son of Mr. and Mrs. Frederck Dreyer, Sr., recently received an honorable discharge from the Army. Sgt. Dreyer arrived home last Wednesday evening after serving 25 months overseas in the European Theatre of Operations. A graduate of the local high school, he served three years in the U. S. Army.

ROBERT L. McFEELY

Robert L. McFeely, son of Mr. and Mrs. R. L. McFeely was recently promoted to the rank of Sergeant. Robert has been serving for the past year and a half overseas, stationed in the Philippines. The McFeely family were former local residents, but now reside in Canton, Ohio. Sgt. McFeely is expected home in the very near future.

JACK A. WILSON

Aboard the Aircraft Carrier Boxer, Tokyo Bay (Delayed) Jack A. Wilson, Seaman Second Class, U. S. N. R. and other crewmen of this ship got their first look at Yokosuka when they were permitted to go ashore while the big vessel rode at anchor in Tokyo Bay as part of the occupation forces.

GEORGE V. DOHAN

Pearl Harbor, R. H. Tech. 4 George Dohan, Fayette City, Pa., is now on his way home. Dohan is one of more than 1,100 high point Army and Navy veterans whom

Fayette City Journal
November 16, 1945

Local G. I. In Pacific Tournament

Merry Christmas Greetings received in the form of a telegram arrived Christmas Day from Staff Sergeant Don Evans to his thrilled parents, Mr. and Mrs. Wilbur Evans of Connellsville Street.

Also contained in the telegram was the news that he was in Manila where he would participate in the Pacific Olympic Horseshoe Tournament.

Don has been serving overseas for a period of one year, the last six months of which he has spent on the island of Okinawa. While there, four young men of the Armed Forces were selected to go to Manila for the Tournament and Sergeant Evans was one of them.

He is a graduate of the local high school and took an active part in athletics, especially horseshoe tournaments. His brother, Randall recently received his honorable discharge, having served in the European Theatre of Operations.

Fayette City Journal
December 28, 1945

Andy Turick Wounded

A telegram was recently received by Mr. and Mrs. John Turick from the War Department informing them that their son, Andrew has been slightly wounded. The telegram reads as follows: We regret to inform you, your son, S-Sgt. Andrew E. Turick was slightly wounded in action, sixteen September 1944 in Holland. You will be advised as reports of condition are received.

J. A. Ullo,
Adj. General

Fayette City Journal
October 13, 1944

Local Pfc. Missing In Action

A telegram was received here Tuesday afternoon by Mrs. Mae Cope, rom the War Department, stating that her son, Pfc. Quentin Cope has been missing in action since 20th of December in Germany.

Pfc. Cope entered the service three years ago, along with Lt. Edward D. Steinman, Jr., and has served overseas for several months.

He is a graduate of the local high school, son of Mr. and Mrs. Oliver Cope of Middle Street and the husband of Mrs. Gloria Cope who is employed in New Jersey. Ufc. Cope has two sisters, Mrs. Imogene Wilson and Mrs. Anita Stockton, both of Fayette City.

Fayette City Journal
January 19, 1945

LETTERS FROM THE BOYS-GIRLS

Somewhere in Germany,
Dear Editor:

Here I sit somewhere in Germany and have been for the past two weeks having a ringside seat. I am in excellent health and sure wishing you are all likewise. We are here doing our particular job and doing good. I have had the opportunity already to visit some steel and textile mills. From these and this experience I see now why the war has continued as far as it has. Their machinery and stock on hand at towns taken by our armies was really remarkable. They had plenty of steel and raw materials on hand.

The American Army sure does a nice job and believe you me, the destruction by our air forces and army is terrific. You have to see it to believe it. They have asked for it and they sure are getting it. We do not fraternize with the German civilians and its a good thing, you have to be careful.

Well, I shall close and say good night and best of luck to you all.
Charles Yetsconish, Jr.

Fayette City Journal
April 13, 1945

Cheered By Son's Note

Mr. and Mrs. R. L. Makepeace of Uniontown, Route 3, former local residents are cheered by the knowledge that their son, Pfc. Ralph L. Makepeace, Jr., although a prisoner of war, fared well over the holiday season.

Each one in the continent received special Christmas parcels from the American Red Cross containing canned boneless turkey, deviled ham, Vienna sausages, mixed candy, salted peanuts, four packs of chewing gum, pipe, tobacco, can of Royal Ann cherries, boxed dates, tea, playing cards, two fruit bars, one can cheese, one can butter one can jam one can honey, plum pudding, three packages of cigarets and a wash cloth.

Although it was good to know they were not forgotten, Pfc. Makepeace adds that their thoughts were all of home and wondering if their loved ones were having a white Christmas.

He was taken captive January 30, 1944, while fighting with the First Battalion Rangers on Anzio Beachhead.

Fayette City Journal
March 3, 1945

The Fayette City Journal also had the unfortunate responsibility to inform the town of any soldiers taken prisoner of war, such as the one described here for a soldier whose surname seems appropriate for wartime.

Of course, the Journal reported extensively on those soldiers who were lost in battle. Fayette City, like so many other cities and towns across the nation, lost some of their brightest lights. Families were often notified of the tragedy in person by a representative of the military forces. During the War, there weren't many cars on the streets of Fayette City. Taxi cabs were even more rare. So when a taxi was spotted in town, it often meant bad news for an unfortunate family. Neighbors would watch with bated breath to see where taxi stopped. Families of seven young men received notifications that their son or husband would not be returning home alive. Brief biographies of those soldiers are offered here, in alphabetical order.

Prisoner Home

Ralph Leonard Makepeace Sr., a former local resident, now residing near Uniontown, celebrated his birthday recently with great joy, because on that day he received the most wonderful gift of any year. The gift was a telegram from the War Department informing him that his son, T 5-G Ralph L. Makepeace Jr., had been returned to military control after being held prisoner sixteen months in Stalag 2B prison camp in Germany. He is a member of the First Battalion Rangers, Co. C, and was fighting on Anzio Beachhead when taken captive on January 30, 1944.

Adding to the good news was a message from Sergeant Harold Caldwell who told the parents, that he had talked to their son in Germany the day after his liberation and he was then awaiting transportation home on a C-47 transport plane.

Since that time, the young man has arrived home from Boston, Mass., and is now visiting relatives and friends.

Fayette City Journal
June 22, 1945

"There was no TV in those days, but everyone had a radio. I don't know if you recall, the large console radios were really popular. We had one of those. It was able to pick up shortwave. I had a cousin who was a little older than me who was in the army. The whole family would write letters to him and he was really good about writing back until it suddenly stopped. For a long time, his parents did not know what might have happened. They hadn't any word from him at all. The family found out about a shortwave program. I'm not sure where it was coming from or from whom. But it came on late at night each night. They would read off names of the military that have been captured or wounded or killed in action. Every night for a long time, my mother, my aunt, my grandmother would huddle around our radio, listening for his name. And finally, one night, his name was announced. That's how we found out that he'd been taken prisoner of war. Ralph Makepeace was his name."

-Nancy Ferree Johnson

Kenneth W. Auther
January 19, 1918 – June 7, 1944

KENNETH AUTHER

Kenneth W. Auther was the son of Mr. and Mrs. Adam Auther, 127 High Street, Fayette City, PA. He attended school at Fayette City. He was known to his friends as "Red". Among his chosen hobbies were hunting and fishing, but every sport was his metre. He was employed by Pittsburgh Steel Company on May 8, 1936, and when he entered military service was a riverman in the Automatic Billet Yard of Allenport Works.

Service Overview:

- Entered service April 16, 1942.
- Trained at Fort Benning, Georgia.
- Participated in the invasions of Sicily, Italy and France.
- Killed in action against the Germans in the invasion of France.
- Paratrooper specialty.
- Attached to the 82nd Airborne Division, 505th Parachute Infantry Regiment.
- Buried/Memorialized at Normandy American Cemetery, France.

Commendations:

- World War II Victory Medal
- Purple Heart
- Combat Infantryman Badge
- Parachutist Badge

- American Campaign Medal
- Army Good Conduct Medal
- European-African-Middle Eastern Campaign

"The only thing, the memory that I have was when….Uncle Kenneth, when he came home, that was when he was on furlough. I might have been six. He bought me a big ball. I was bouncing it out on the road and at that time, I don't know if you remember, we had two railroad tracks. Do you remember that? There were two railroad tracks. That's the only thing I can remember about the war. He said to me, quit bouncing that so high, it's going to go in the River. It's going to go across the tracks and go into River. Why didn't I listen? Well I bounced that over the tracks and then in the River it went. The only other thing I can remember is, like I said my mother worked and my grandmother was watching me, and she was sewing at the time. And a knock come at the door. My uncle Kenneth had got killed. Well, I must have been carrying on. I must not have been listening or whatever. Naturally she was all worked up. She just lost her son. I just remember that she took the scissors and threw them at me. I still have the scar where it hit me there on the on the back of the heel. And then I remember she had the flag stand, it wasn't the American flag, but it was what they call the Gold Star. I think it had the star in the middle. She used to hang in the front window. That's the only thing I remember about the War. Oh, my uncle Kenneth. Yeah. His nickname was Red."

-Ella Marie Auther Davis

"I remember Kenny Auther. Kenny Auther got killed. The Grummer boy, I can't think of his name. His dad's name was Frank and I don't remember what his name was. I just remember seeing a picture of him (Kenny Auther). I was friends with his niece, Ella Marie….I mean, you know, there was Mary Jane and Mary Jo and Ella Marie. Jim Bob Davis. And I just barely remember Kenny, but I remember how devastated naturally his parents were."

-Judith Dewar Shearer

Joseph C. Croushore
June 13, 1924 – November 21, 1944

JOSEPH CROUSHORE

"The other sad thing in that building down on the second floor was a family, the Croushore family. They had three sons. Joe Croushore was the youngest. He was probably 19 or 20 at the time, and he went in. He ended up in the Army Air Corps. Anyway, he was such a good-looking young man. I was five years old and he used to tell me I was his girlfriend. Anyway, he became a gunner on a B25, would that be the one back then? Anyway, he was killed. That was so sad. I remember a Kenneth Auther who was a paratrooper. We had a picture of him. They lived on Water Street. We had a picture of him with his paratrooper boots sitting with his feet over the side of the porch. He was killed. Patsy DeRienzo, the oldest DeRienzo boy was killed. Buzzy Grummer was killed. I remember the oldest, Legg was their last name, they lived in Gillespie. Apparently, I was in the movie theater at Bell Theater that night. Isabella the lady who sold the tickets, the daughter that sold the tickets came and was paging Mrs. Legg. And apparently what had happened, the family had just received a telegram that their son had been killed. But everybody in the town grieved the loss of those boys. That was just, you know, and everybody was so proud."

-Georgia Nicholson Slezak

Service Overview:

- Sergeant.
- US Army Air Corps.
- 450th Bomber Group, Heavy, 885th Bomber Squadron.
- Buried in the Florence American Cemetery and Memorial, Florence, Italy.

Commendations:

- World War II Victory Medal
- Air Medal
- Purple Heart
- American Campaign Medal
- Army Presidential Unit Citation
- Army Good Conduct Medal
- European-African-Middle Eastern Campaign

Sgt. Croushore Missing in Action

A telegram from the War Department was reported received here Monday morning by Mrs. Mary Sisley, informing here that her youngest son, Sgt. Joe Croushore has been missing in action since 21 of November over Yugoslavia.

Joe entered the service of his country in September, 1944 receiving Army Air Force overseas training at Charleston, South Carolina. Prior to his entrance, Joe attended I. S. T. C. and is a graduate of the local high school, class of 1942.

Sgt. Croushore is the son of Mrs. Mary Sisley and the late Joe Croushore, and has two brothers, Richard and Lt. Don Croushore.

Fayette City Journal
December 15, 1944

Patsy P. DeRienzo
July 16, 1920 – February 19, 1945

PATSY P. DeRIENZO

Patsy was the son of Mr. and Mrs. John DeRienzo of Fayette City, PA. He graduated from Fayette City High School with the Class of 1938. He married in October 1943. Patsy began his work with Pittsburgh Steel Company on January 30, 1943, as a laborer in the Cold Draw Department. He was a baseball player of considerable skill and loved the game.

Service Overview:

- Entered service November 28, 1942.
- Trained at Camp Beale, CA.
- Technician Fifth Grade.
- Killed in action against the enemy in Belgium.
- Buried in Belle Vernon Cemetery, Belle Vernon, PA.

Commendations:

- World War II Victory Medal
- Purple Heart
- American Campaign Medal
- Army Presidential Unit Citation
- Army Good Conduct Medal

Sorrow struck at the De Rienzo home on Second Street, when Mrs. Concetta De Rienzo received a telegram from the War Department, Friday, March 9. The telegram informed her that her son, T-5 Patsy De Rienzo, 25 years, had been killed in action in Belgium, February 19, 1945.

He was a graduate of Fayette City High School, class of 1938. Prior to entering the service, Patsy was assoiated with the Truck Company, Coal and Road Business formerly operated by the late Philip De Rienzo. Later Patsy attended Jourden School at Pittsburgh and graduated from there in 1940.

T-5 De Rienzo entered the service on November 28, 1942 and has been serving overseas since July, 1943. While overseas he was with a 3616 Truck Company, who had been hauling supplies from recently captured Belgium ports, to troops pushing into Germany. Among the other places the young doughboy served was, England, Normandy and France.

The last letter from Patsy was received by the family on March 5.

Beside his mother, Mrs. Concetta De Rienzo, he is survived by his wife and widow, Ann De Rienzo of Pricedale, three brothers, Marion, Philip and Umberto and a host of relatives and friends.

Fayette City Journal
March 16, 1945

Raymond H. Grummer
April 19, 1922 – September 20, 1944

RAYMOND GRUMMER

Raymond Grummer was born in Charleroi, PA. He graduated from Fayette City High School, Class of 1941. Prior to his enlistment he was employed at the Pittsburgh Steel Company in Allenport, PA.

Service Overview:

- Private First Class.
- Paratrooper.
- US Army.
- I Company, 504th Parachute Infantry Regiment, 3rd Battalion, 82 Airborne Division.
- Killed in Action at Njimegen, Holland.
- Memorialized at the American War Cemetery Margraten.

Commendations:

- World War II Victory Medal
- Purple Heart
- Combat Infantryman Badge
- Marksmanship Badge
- American Campaign Medal
- Army Presidential Unit Citation
- Army Good Conduct Medal
- European-African-Middle Eastern Campaign

Another Fayette City boy has given his life for his country in the name of Pfc. Raymond Grummer.

A telegram received last Thursday afternoon by Mrs. Anna Grummer, mother of Raymond, from the War Department, informing her that her son Pfc. Raymond Grummer had been killed September 20, 1944 while in action in Holland. Ironically enough this was the date upon which his mother last heard from him.

Pfc. Grummer was a graduate of the local high school class of 1941 and enlisted in the service as a paratrooper, February 25, 1942, serving overseas seventeen months.

A telegram received on December 31, 1943 informed his parents he had been wounded the 11th of December while in Sicily. Again in February of this year, the young paratrooper received additional wounds.

Pfc. Grummer was the first local soldier to be wounded on foreign soil and the first local boy to receive the Purple Heart.

He was entitled to wear the Purple Heart and the Oak Leaf Cluster for wounds received, but medals held no glory for him. He loved friends and their smiles were worth more to him than the gleaming bronze of a medal.

Fayette City Journal
October 20, 1944

Frank H. Huseman
November 29, 1918 – November 24, 1943

Fayette City Journal
February 16, 1945

Service Overview:

- Lieutenant Junior Grade.
- US Navy.
- Declared dead while missing in action.
- Buried/memorialized at Courts of the Missing, National Memorial Cemetery of the Pacific, Honolulu, Hawaii.

Commendations:

- World War II Victory Medal
- Purple Heart
- Combat Action Ribbon
- American Campaign Medal
- Navy Presidential Unit Citation
- Navy Good Conduct Medal
- Asiatic-Pacific Campaign Medal
- Navy Expeditionary Medal

Fayette City Journal
February 9, 1945

Frank McKenna, Jr.
October 17, 1918 – June 30, 1944

Bronze Star Given Parents of Late Captain McKenna

Mr. and Mrs. Frank McKenna, Sr., of Connellsville Street, recently received the Bronze Star Medal posthumously awarded their son, Captain Frank McKenna, Jr., Infantry, for meritorious achievement in military operations against the enemy in France.

Captain McKenna, an only son, died from wounds received June 30, 1944, while in action in France, after two years service overseas. Besides his parents, three sisters, Rose, Kathryn and Jeannine survive.

*Fayette City Journal
December 15, 1944*

Capt. McKenna's Body To Arrive

The United States Army Transport, the "John L. McCarley," is due at New York very shortly with the bodies of 2,169 Americans who died in the struggle for the liberation of Europe, among whom is listed Capt. Frank McKenna, Jr., of Fayette City, Pennsylvania

Virtually all the remains aboard the "McCarley" which is scheduled to arrive from Cherbourg, are being returned from the "D-Day" military cemeteries at Saint-Laurentsur-Mer, Blosville and LaCambe, Normandy.

Next-of-kin were to be notified shortly before arrival of the vessel and prior to publication of the names of the dead aboard the ship.

*Fayette City Journal
April 2, 1948*

Service Overview:

- Captain.
- US Army.
- Served with Company I, 175th Infantry, 29 Division, in France.
- Killed at the Normandy beachhead.
- His remains were return to the US in 1948, four years after he was killed. He is interred in the Mount Auburn Cemetery in Fayette City.

Commendations:

- World War II Victory Medal
- Purple Heart
- American Campaign Medal
- Army Presidential Unit Citation
- Army Good Conduct Medal

"One of my neighbors on town hill - you're bringing bad things back to my mind - Frank McKenna Jr. He was an officer and he was killed. His dad sat on the porch all the time. I'm getting sad. I'd say "Hi, Mr. McKenna". That man never got over it."

-Kathleen Walton Stimmell

"I know I had an uncle that was killed in 1944. He made the landing on D-day on Omaha Beach and that was the first part of June. He was one of the ones who made it and he got promoted. He was a captain. At the end of June, when they were going across Europe, he got killed then. Frank McKenna Jr.. I was over, I was on the other side of the hill playing. I think I was with Don Young at that time. My mother come after me and took me home. But like I say, how, how young was I at the time? I was surprised."

-Raymond Moody

James W. Williams
April 10, 1915 – June 6, 1944

Photo Not Available

Service Overview:

- Corporal.
- US Army.
- Company D, 116th Infantry Regiment, 29th Infantry Division.
- Killed at Omaha Beach, Normandy, France.
- Interred in the Mount Auburn Cemetery, Fayette City, PA.

Commendations:

- Purple Heart
- Combat Infantryman Badge
- Marksmanship Badge
- World War II Victory Medal
- American Campaign Medal
- Army Presidential Unit Citation
- Army Good Conduct Medal
- European-African-Middle Eastern Campaign

IN MEMORIAM

IN LOVING memory of our dear son and brother, Cpl. James W. Williams, who was killed in action on June 6, 1944, on the Normandy beachhead.

When evening, shades are falling
And we sit here all alone;
To our hearts there comes a longing,
If he only could, come home.
Friends may think we have forgotten,
When at times they see us smile,
But they little know the heartache,
That our smiles hide all the while.
There is a Dad, who misses him sadly,
And finds the time long since he went.
We think of him hourly and daily
But try to be brave and content.
We often think of his smiling face
As he bade us his last good-bye,
And left his home forever
In a distant land to die.
To a beautiful life came a sudden end
Jim, died as he lived, everyone's friend.
          Sadly missed by Father, brothers, sisters and families.
6-6-c

Fayette City Journal
June 6, 1947

"I'll tell you one thing I remember about World War Two. I was in Moravek's store and they brought, the taxi cab driver brought the telegrams if something happened, somebody was missing in action or killed or anything. I was standing there buying some groceries for my parents and somebody came in and said the taxi was in town. I'll never forget the look on the people's faces. There was about half a dozen turned around and ran home thinking if they had, you know, sons in the service. But that's how they got the news, the taxi. And when the taxicab was in town, it was a bad moment, you know."

-Kathleen Walton Stimmell

Civilians at Home

Those who remained at home during the War supported the effort in a multitude of ways. Everyone participated in air raid drills. Air raid wardens were assigned to every street and neighborhood and inspected each home during a drill to see if any light escaped its windows. A tap on the offending window would let the inhabitants know to take appropriate action. While technically possible for Japan or Germany to launch bombing attacks on the US homeland, it was unlikely to happen, especially in a small town like Fayette City. But Fayette City was situated directly across the Monongahela River from the Allenport works of the Pittsburgh Steel Company where they had converted equipment for making tubes into facilities for making ammunition shells. So a potential enemy attack was not beyond the stretch of one's imagination and provided the needed incentive for everyone to participate in the drills.

"During World War Two, we had to have blackout blinds on our windows. They had to be pulled down every night. If I heard an airplane go by it frightened me. We had air raid wardens that would patrol the streets. I remember my uncles, two uncles, were air raid wardens and they would patrol the streets and make sure everybody had their black blinds pulled down in case there were any enemy planes above, so we couldn't easily be spotted. There was food rationing. We had ration books. I remember particularly sugar, coffee and butter were very, very hard to come by. We'd go to the store and we were given so many rations, so many little ration coupons and we would trade them. My parent, my mother would trade them with other people. So if we needed or they needed a pound of butter, and they didn't have enough stamps, they would find somebody who did. They would trade them off. I remember the books. And I think they were green. I think they were green books. I remember the blackouts. We had fire drills. It was quite a scary time for a young child. The young men would go off to war. Some of them were killed. Again, off my top of my head, I can't remember their names."

-Shirley Ferree Stilgenbauer

"The only thing I can remember about that is they had air raid drills at the time. They'd blow the fire whistles and all that. I guess I didn't know what it was. I know we had air raids. They blowed the whistles. You were supposed to go in the house and all this. Then, when the war was going on, I know they had to have a sticker to get gas. I know they had a sticker to get gas."

-Willard Jones

"Well, you had to keep the lights nonexistent. You had them so that you couldn't see outside. They walked around and knocked on your doors if a light showed. That was door to door. There was rationing. They had rationing, shoes for kids. The mothers complained because the shoes that they made during the war weren't as good as the ones before. You had stamps to buy shoes. You were only allowed so many pairs of shoes. We saved the grease in cans, took it to the grocery store and they paid you for it."

-Joanne Cunningham Manetta

"They would have a certain time they would have a blackout night. So everyone had to shut off anything that shed any light. My dad was like, well you would call an air raid warden, and not just him but even other guys they would go around Brownstown. You had them in Fayette City too, looking for any light they saw. Then they'd tap on a window, knock on your door, put that light out. Everywhere was a blackout .That was, it was like practice. I remember him doing that. My dad said you know some people don't turn the light out. They'd turned it out and as soon as you walk away, they'd turn it back on. Stuff like that. Yeah, that war thing was something."

-Jack Gargan

"The first activity I remember is the blackout drills in town and the air raids. They called them blackout drills. The air raid drills is what they really were. And then we had the air raid drills in school. Since we were close to the Allenport Mill who made seamless steel pipes it was a possible target for attack. Now we didn't even consider how far away we were from Germany or Japan. They'd never get here. But we took it serious. During the home blackout drills our home had to be covered. All possible sources of interior light had to be blocked from the outside so that the enemy bombers could not attack. We tried our best. It must have taken three tries to finally seal the light coming from the house to the outside. I believe everyone, men and women, participated in some manner in the war effort."

-Bill Williamson

"A couple of my uncles were in, but my dad didn't go. He was the air raid warden. He'd have to go up the Hollow and make people turn their lights out when we'd have an air raid drill."

-Pauline Ann Vargo Baker

The children had opportunities to contribute to the war effort as well. Fayette City schoolteachers took their classes on hikes up Navoo Hollow in search of the ubiquitous milkweed plant. Prior to World War II, life jackets were filled with the floss of the kapok tree. While the kapok tree grows in many places in the tropics, the primary source of the tree was in the East Indies, specifically Java and its tree plantations. When Japan captured the East Indies during the War the supply of the floss was effectively cut off. Fortunately, milkweed floss was quickly identified as an excellent substitute. In the fall of 1944, the United States government urged children to collect the milkweed in support of the War. Mesh onion bags were manufactured specifically for collecting the plant. Two bags of the milkweed floss were sufficient to make one life jacket. Picking and handling guidelines were provided to make the task as efficient and pleasant as possible. Children could earn twenty-five cents per bag depending on the weight of the bag. The search for milkweed didn't always turn out as expected. On at least one occasion, some students from Fayette City found more than just milkweed on their hike, poison ivy to be precise, putting an ignominious end to the activity.

The entire community of Fayette City supported the War efforts through the multitude of drives that were held throughout the years. There were War Campaign Fund drives to support the USO and Red Cross. There were drives to help the Salvation Army. There were drives to collect scrap paper and metal and even the left-over grease from cooking. There were canned food drives and clothing drives after the War ended to support our allies overseas. By 1944, Fayette City had distinguished itself "for its ability to be among the first districts in Western Pennsylvania to go over the top in

Milkweed Funds To Be Shared Soon

Fayette county schools will share in a distribution of $1,065.60 paid by the United States government for bushels of milkweed gathered by pupils and classes in response to the nation-wide appeal for the humble milkweed so necessary in construction of life belts, life jackets and other equipment for fighting men.

The money now is in the hands of Assistant County School Superintendent A. J. McMullen, chairman of the county milkweed drive.

North Union township schools collected the largest amount, 684 bushels, for a return of $135.80. Runner-up were the Georges township schools with 349 bushels, for $69.80.

Fayette City Journal
January 12, 1945

"I remember life jackets and vests were filled with milkweed. There was probably an abundance of it around in the countryside around Fayette City. So one day our teacher took the class on a field trip to collect the milkweed. That morning, everybody carried a bag, a sack, or a box. We hiked a good way out of town and found some milkweed, picked all we could carry and headed home. It was late afternoon, we got back, we were tired, sweaty and itching. For some, the itching was not from the milkweed. It was poison ivy. That put an end to any more milkweed picking"

-Nancy Johnson Ferree

"We were asked to help with the war effort. Do you know what milkweed is? Well, milkweed grows, and in the fall, the pod that grows at the top, there's a pod that looks like it's about maybe four inches. You can open that pod. Inside there's like a feathery white down stuff. I remember going on field trips during the war with little bags, and we went out in fields and collected those pods. They used that for stuffing life jackets. Always impressed me that we were helping the war effort."

-Jack Young

"At the right time of the year, our school classes would go on a field trip picking soap weed used in lifejackets and processed into synthetic rubber used for tires and other former natural rubber products. It's a lot of fun picking those sticky weeds and being out of school. The area had millions of these weeds back in the 1940s."

-Bill Williamson

financial drives. A good example of this spirit of giving is the 1944 War Campaign Fund drive in support of the USO. Fayette City's efforts were led by J.H. Renstrom, the local postmaster, and Joseph Moravek. A goal of $700 was set for the drive. By the time the drive ended a month later, Fayette City had raised at total of $1536.21. Contributions ranged from 25 dollars to 25 cents. The Fayette City Journal used more than an entire column of the paper to publish the names of all the contributors and the amount given.

The most important drives of the War years were, without question, the War Bond Drives. World War II was financed in part by the issuance of bonds. Defense Bonds first went on the market in May 1941 and were renamed War Bonds after the United States entered the War with the bombing of Pearl Harbor in December 1941. Bonds were sold at 75% of face value and in denominations of $25 through $1000. A favorite way to buy a bond, especially by children, was to purchase stamps for 10 cents each. The stamps were collected in special books. When the books were full, they were redeemed for a bond. During World War II, the United States held eight War Loan Drives:

- First War Loan Drive   November/December 1942
- Second War Loan Drive   April/May 1943
- Third War Loan Drive   September/October 1943
- Fourth War Loan Drive   January/February 1944
- Fifth War Loan Drive   June/July 1944
- Sixth War Loan Drive   November/December 1944
- Seventh War Loan Drive   May/June 1945
- Victory Loan Drive   October/December 1945

By the time of the Sixth War Loan Drive, Fayette City had become a well-oiled machine when it came organizing the town's efforts. The Sixth War Loan Drive was coordinated by the Lions Club. Edwin Hindmarsh was named chairman of the drive. (The Lions Club, which had been formed in April of 1944, also organized the Fifth War Loan Drive.) With military precision, Fayette City was divided into nine zones covering every home and business in town. A chairman and supporting coworker were named for each zone. Zone 1 was between Fording and Market Streets including part of Johnson Hollow and Connellsville St. Zone 2 was between Market and Union Streets. Zone 3 was between Union and Cook Streets. Zone 4 consisted of Navoo Hollow and Sisley Town. Zone 5 consisted of "Business and Professional Men". Zone 6 contained California and High Streets (both sides) on the left side of Connellsville Street. Zone 7 contained Lower Street to the Cemetery on the left side of Connellsville Street. Zone 8 consisted of South High to Lower Streets on the right side of Connellsville Street. Zone 9 consisted of Lower Street to the Cemetery on the right side of Connellsville Street. Using this detail plan, Fayette City was able to raise more than $12,000 and nearly double its goal.

Fayette City Journal
November 24, 1944

As the smoke has cleared from the Seventh War Loan Drive and the results have been recorded, Fayette City emerges as the top district in Zone 3 "E" Bond Sales.

Although no quota was set the local district leads all other Post Offices in Zone 3 with a total of $30,468.75 sold in war bonds. The closest post office in this district was Brownsville with $25,837.50 in bond sales.

Following is a list of the post offices in Zone 3 and the amount of sales they recorded:

Allison	$ 743.50
Belle Vernon	11,325.00
Brownsville	25,837.50
Chestnut Ridge	1,350.00
East Millsboro	3,393.75
Fairbank	3,768.75
FAYETTE CITY	30,468.75
Grindstone	3,000.00
Hiller	2,344.00
LaBelle	3,112.50
Merrittstown	14,606.25
Newell	6,843.75
Republic	13,005.75

Fayette City Journal
August 10, 1945

This spirit of giving extended to the Seventh War Loan Drive when Fayette City emerged as the top district in Zone 3, outpacing larger metropolises such as Brownsville and Belle Vernon.

The school children participated in the bond drives as well. Each month, all the classes, grades 1 through 12, competed to see who could raise the most money towards the purchase of a bond. The teachers creatively linked the bond drives to specific pieces of military equipment allowing the kids to visualize exactly what their nickels, dimes and quarters could purchase. Like their parents, the children excelled at giving, often exceeding their monthly goals.

"We had savings bonds and stamps. It was a patriotic thing to buy savings bonds and stamps. The stamps if I recall, were like ten cents and twenty-five cents, and bonds were ten and twenty-five dollars. You could buy a bond right out or you have a book to paste stamps in. So when the book was full, you turned it in for a bond certificate. But then you had to wait a few years before cashing it in if you want the full value. In school we were encouraged to buy those stamps. So every Friday, we would come with our dimes and quarters. Someone from the class would be selected to take the list of the money and go down to the post office and buy stamps. It was a contest each week to see which class bought the most stamps."

-Nancy Johnson Ferree

"In school we gave money every week to buy stamps, to completely fill a savings bond book toward purchasing parts for building military equipment like Jeeps, trucks, rifles, helmets and other war items. There would be a poster, large poster, in each room with a large outline of the product we were contributing to build. In other words, it would be a tank or be a Jeep, or be a rifle or be something like that. When you contributed to buy a bond, most of us gave a dime. That was a lot of money back then. What would happen is you would fill up your savings book until you've got enough to buy a bond. A twenty dollar bond, I think you paid seventeen or eighteen dollars in that range. It matured in ten years or something like that. Anyway, let's say our class had twenty dollars in purchases from everybody contributing ten cents or a quarter or whatever they contributed to buy stamps. Twenty dollars might be enough to buy two fenders for a Jeep for instance. So when we got enough money to buy parts for the equipment, we would take a paper layout of the fender and paste it to the big image of the Jeep until the Jeep was completely filled up with everything, windshield and everything. It was quite interesting. It provided to the effort. We did that on a number of things. I know we built a Jeep or two. I know we built, like helmets and we bought rifles and stuff like that. We ended up getting savings bonds. I don't know how many I got with my mother's money, but I had probably five or ten bonds."

-Bill Williamson

"At school, at Fayette City school, I remember being asked to bring in dimes, and change, for liberty stamps to support the war. One thing that really impressed me was our principal. He would have like a contest for us to do that. In fact, he got an outline of a Jeep, a life size Jeep, put it up on a wall. It was just a blank outline of a Jeep. As we brought money in, maybe we brought enough for a tire. Then they would cut out a tire and put it on that mural. Then maybe we got enough for a windshield or we got enough for whatever. Eventually, we brought enough money to have the whole Jeep come alive. That was a big, big thing."

-Jack Young

In addition to the air raid drills and the plethora of fund drives during the War, rationing affected every citizen in Fayette City, and everywhere else in the country for that matter. Everything from gasoline to canned fruits and vegetables was portioned out according to a family's ration books. Bartering with neighbors for specific food items or combining rations with relatives to make a memorable holiday meal were just a couple of the consequences.

Although the soldiers were thousands of miles away from Fayette City, in Europe and the Pacific, they were never far away from the hearts and minds of those who stayed behind. By early 1945, with the end of the war in sight, the editor of the Fayette City Journal, Allan Keenan, penned this moving editorial.

Main Street would indeed come alive again by the end of the year. All but a few of the soldiers would return to restart their lives with the unbridled gratitude of those who stayed at behind.

> Fayette City's school children are to be commended for the fine report which was submitted this week in regard to the Bond Sales set for January.
>
> A goal of $1000.00 was set for the local school children in January and final returns for the month shows $1,973.10 or almost double of the quota set.
>
> Champion room for the month of January was the sixth grade.
>
> Following is a room by room summary of the sales:
>
> Room 1, $192.80; Room 2, $115.60; Room 3. $141.95; Room 4, $74.40; Room 5, $303.40; Room 6, $440.75; Room 7, $26.85; Room 8, $10.00; Room 9, $45.60; Room 10, $23.75; Room 11, $396.25; Room 12, $201.75.

Fayette City Journal
February 2, 1945

"There was a shortage of butter and sugar and coffee. Gasoline was scarce. Every household was issued a coupon book. Sugar was so many coupons, butter was so many. The coupon books were issued periodically, maybe once a month or so, I'm not sure. We would go to the little shop on the corner of Main and Market Street, the little store that was across from Moravek's grocery store. We'd get new ones. If you used up your coupons before time you were out of luck. We didn't have real butter. It was lard in a pound block with a small packet of yellow coloring to mix in. I remember once my mother, my grandmother, my aunt combined all their coupons so that we could have a nice turkey and a nice Thanksgiving dinner. We had scrap drives, metal for military vehicles was scarce. The town would have scrap drives. Folks would clean up their garages and their basements or whatever. Anything metal that they would like to get rid of or could get rid of would be put on the curb and it would be picked up. There were several of those scrap drives until they got to the point where there was nothing left to give. We used to laugh and tease my grandmother. She did give to the drive. But she had a large metal birdcage that hung on a stand. She didn't want to give it up. So she always held it back each time until very last and she finally gave in. We used to joke that that birdcage was what won the war. She did not want part with it."

-Nancy Ferree Johnson

"Of course, I still have a copy of one of my rationing books. It was my family's. Things were rationed, butter, rubber, all kinds of things. Your family members, depending on how valuable your contributions were to the war. I mean, if you had to drive everywhere, maybe you could get retread tires or some gas. Cars had stickers on the windows to indicate how much gas they could be able to get. Every member of the family would get a rationing book. You would spend those rationing cards along with your money to get what you're able to get during the war….When preparing for this, I thought about that. I was talking to some friends here, where I live now. They were in England, they were Brits during the war, during the bombing of London and everything. We cut out rationing right after the war. In England, they didn't quit all the rationing until 1955, ten years later. But I remember and I do have one of those old empty books. It didn't have any stickers, my own rationing book."

-Jack Young

LETTER TO THE BOYS

The street known in Fayette City as "Main Stret," has gone to war. February 1 was the first tester for the universal "Brownout" for your Main Street along with other chief thoroughfares of other villages and cities.

You Marines in the South Pacific, the G I's in the foxholes of Europe or the Sailors on the high seas will have difficulty picturing the old Main Street as it appears—ghostly — gloomy, in order to preserve coal and fuel.

The attractive, cheery lights in store window displays are but a vague outline against the blackness of the evening sky — with only street lights dotted here and there and the twinkling stars above. The flashing bulbs over the local theatre marquee and the shimmering neon signs are a thing of the past — but a fighting beacon for the future.

The zest and life of Main Street are gone — completely now. Gone with the silk, nylons and new autos. But more ironic of all, the life of Main Street marched away with the local service boys. And yet there is little grumbling — come what may, there is a way to go forward. The "Grit" of Americans.

The gay lights of Main Street are gone — for a while. In their place are the service flags with red, blue, silver and even gold stars shining from windows of homes, telegrams from the war department carrying heart break, the honor roll of the community honoring you brave American youth — a tightening of rationing to insure the best for you boys and girls in the services.

Thats the new spirit of the Home Front. Thats why Main Street has gone to war — until that moment when ablaze with light, laughter and confetti, it will echo again to the footsteps and greetings of you now in the armed forces. Until that time your Main Street has become the "Street of Yesterday."

Fayette City Journal
February 9, 1945

"There was a big celebration down on Market Street where all the townspeople gathered. They were screaming and yelling and singing. I'm not sure if there was a band, but it was a big event. I can remember our back porch of course with the stairs going down faced Market Street. I can remember standing on the porch looking down and hearing all the people celebrate."

-Shirley Ferree Stilgenbauer

"I remember VJ Day, the day that we received news that the war was over. The town went crazy. The school bell was ringing. Church bells were ringing. Horns honking. People gathered in the street, shouting, happy and excited. The Drum and Bugle Corps, without their uniforms, got together and with a fire truck started marching down Main Street. Everyone followed. We all went up to the hill to the cemetery and then back down into downtown. But everybody's still celebrating. It was a day that I'll never forget. We were so happy and so excited. The day I'll never forget."

-Nancy Ferree Johnson

"I was friends with Stockton's daughter Jean. She was my age. They lived over in Long Branch, across the River up in. I don't know what township that was up there. It doesn't matter. But I was friends with Jean. She had asked me to come to their farm. They had a farm, the Stockton's had a farm over there, and come for me to stay all night. So I went over, and I stayed all night. Well, while I'm there and the next morning we found out the war was over. Here I am over at Stockton's farm. I missed all this goings on in Fayette City. They had a parade and my dad, I never knew my dad could play a cornet. But they had a parade, my dad was playing his cornet and they were doing all this and they said you missed it. But the next day, I think that was a Monday, that the war ended, it seemed to stick with me that for some reason Stockton's weren't open on Tuesday. I don't know why. But for some reason, anyway, Jack was still living at home. He was coming back over. So he brought me back home the next day. Everybody said you missed everything. I said oh my heavens. So that was VE day, right? And then VJ Day came later on. That I was around for. So we're right next to the church. Of course, we had keys to the church because we would take care of it. So we went down, my sisters and I were ringing the bell. War's over, the war's over. I remember that so vividly, doing that and celebrating. Now they didn't have a parade like they did for VE day. I don't know why. I mean they could have had a parade when I was there."

-Judith Dewar Shearer

"Mrs. Cameron was my Sunday school teacher. On VJ Day, my cousin Audrey and I, they live next to the church, Presbyterian Church. Her dad, my Uncle Frank said that we could go in and ring the bell cause everybody was ringing the church bell. Audrey and I, we didn't know how to rig a church bell. We pulled it down and that church bell took us about five feet off the ground. We didn't want to ring the bell anymore. But that was a wonderful day when the war was over. I don't know whether they dropped the bomb or something. But anyhow, they announced that it was over and everybody started playing. We heard the church bells and whistles and everything. We said can we go ring the church bell? He said yes, and we did. We still to this day laugh at us, both of us holding on to the rope about three, four foot off the ground. We weren't big enough to bring it back down. But it did. It was it was a great day."

-Kathleen Walton Stimmell

A couple of weeks after V-E day, Fayette City held its annual Memorial Day service at Mount Auburn Cemetery. This Memorial Day was different. What in years past was a colorful, joyful celebration became a reverent and somber service. A month after V-J Day, the community held a "Union Service" at the local Methodist Church to honor the fallen. The service was sponsored by all of Fayette City's churches, both Protestant and Catholic. Private Thomas Marriott Jr. of Fayette City, home on leave from Europe, read the list of names of those who gave their all. The list included the seven soldiers from Fayette City and another thirteen soldiers from surrounding communities.

Fayette City Journal
May 9, 1947

Soldiers soon began to return home, some of them seeing their children for the very first time. One soldier, Nick Turek, returned home with a new wife, Pia, a German girl. In true Fayette City fashion, Pia was welcomed to the community with open arms.

Immediately after V-J day, the Fayette City Journal in an editorial called for a living memorial to honor the veterans who fought in the war. Two years later, after no progress had been made, the Journal published another editorial proposing a new honor roll. Finally, in March of 1948, plans for a new honor roll were initiated. Rules for who was eligible to appear on the honor roll were set and the list of names was finalized in May. A new bronze plaque replaced the old honor roll in front of the schoolhouse. Decades later, the honor roll was moved to a small park at the south end of town where it resides today. The names appearing on the honor roll from World War I and World War II are provided in Appendices III and IV, respectively.

"Well my dad come home. I think I was a couple of years old. My dear mother and dad, they were married before he was drafted. I was born before he came home. My dad's job in the army was a machine gunner. I remember my dad would have nightmares....He'd have nightmares about the war and what he saw over there. He was under Patton. He brought me back a black stuffed dog home when he returned. I had it for years. After my mother's passing, I found his love letters to her. You never think they're in love, until you find them."

-Georgia Jean Arrow

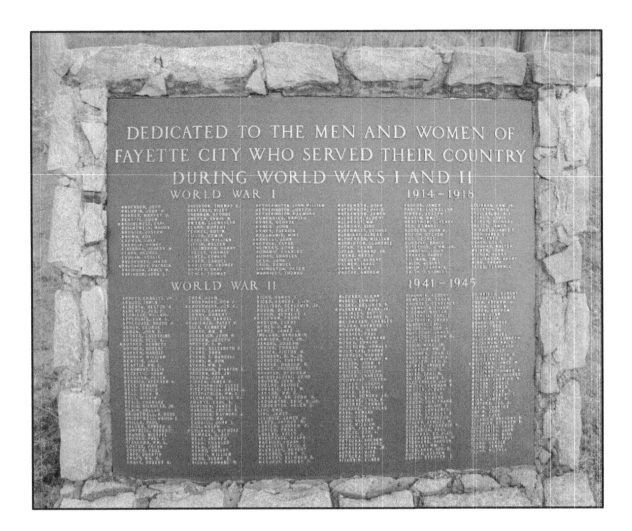

"We had an honor roll. And I'm not sure the year but if I recall correctly, it was early on in the war. The town decided to put up an honor roll for those in the military…I mentioned this large flat cement slab in front of the schoolhouse. It was put there. I believe it showed only the names serving in World War Two…..I don't know if I remember correctly, you only had the names serving in World War Two. A star was placed beside the name of those who were killed. There were some that were killed in an action. Years later I think the Honor Roll was taken down and moved downtown to an empty field across from McCrory's funeral home at the end of Main Street. I think that's where it's at now."

-Nancy Ferree Johnson

REFERENCES

Fayette City World War II Memorial Program provided by Ella Marie Davis.

Conscription, World War II | Encyclopedia.com
https://www.encyclopedia.com/defense/energy-government-and-defense-magazines/conscription-world-war-ii

Honor States
https://www.honorstates.org

Milkweed During World War II - grace grits and gardening (gracegritsgarden.com)
https://gracegritsgarden.com/2020/10/milkweed-world-war-ii.html

World War II War Bonds (sarahsundin.com)
https://www.sarahsundin.com/world-war-ii-war-bonds

CHAPTER 5 King Coal, Queen Coke and Princess Steel

The phrase "King Coal, Queen Coke and Princess Steel" was a well-known moniker for the Monongahela River Valley and the coal fields of Fayette County during the late 1800s and early 1900s. The Pittsburgh coal seam which runs through the region was quickly recognized as being physically and chemically suited for the production of high-quality coke. Coke is produced by the "distillation" or baking of coal under controlled conditions to remove unwanted volatile material including gases, tars, and oils. The resulting product is a hard, porous residue with a dull metallic luster and high carbon content. The high-quality coke produced from the region's coal was ideally suited for the iron and steel blast furnaces in and around Pittsburgh. For several decades, Fayette City, like its neighbors, shared in the prosperity enabled by this triumvirate of coal, coke and steel.

King Coal

From its beginning Fayette City, with its vast natural resources, rich soil, and abundant water resources, had a thriving agrarian economy. Boat construction was also prominent, just as it was in neighboring Brownsville and Belle Vernon. By the middle 1800s, glass factories employed dozens of men in Navoo Hollow and Sisleytown. Coal mining was relegated to small, easily accessible mines in Gillespie just outside of Fayette City to the south. The output of these mines was minimal but proved to be a harbinger of things to come.

"Both of my grandparents were coal miners. George Stark came from Scotland and worked in mines out around Brownstown and other areas. I don't know exactly. In fact, he died one year before I was born. My grandfather James Young, my dad had three brothers, Wilford, Jim, and Gib Young. The uncle, my grandpa James Young, he took me into the coal mines with him when I was, I think, in seventh or eighth grade. It scared the hell out of me. I told him later I'm going to come back in here, grandpap, when they have windows. In fact, I didn't like the idea of being underground. I had seen movies, where miners were trapped and killed. That scared the devil out of me. In fact, when I went into the Navy, I turned down opportunities to be in the submarine force because I didn't like the idea of being underwater. So I wasn't a big enthusiast to go cave hunting like some people are.

The only mine that I remember a name for was Hamer mine. I think my grandpa Young and his brother-in-law Sandy Park, they both live in the same place about halfway up town hill. They went into the Hamer mine. I remember they would come back at the end of the day and there would be this scrub basin and step outside. First they had to get most of the soot and everything else off of them, stripped down about halfway and then they'd go into the basement and take some sort of a shower or a bath of sorts. That was a tough life.

I thought it was interesting that my grandfathers were coal miners. They had sons but none of the sons went into mining. The mines were starting to sort of lose some of their luster. My dad had three brothers. None of the sons, of the four, went into the mines. My grandpap Stark only had the one grandson and he was involved with football and things. I remember reading about cave ins and mine disasters like Naomi. I remember John Lewis leading those big strikes for the coal miners was a big thing. All the miners would have their lunch buckets and thermoses. There were rats in the mines. I remember that. That wasn't always bad because if the rats were dying then something is going wrong at that time."

-Jack Young

The last 20 years of the 19th century saw dramatic growth in the coal industry in and around Fayette City. Little Redstone Mine, the Fayette City (formerly Connecticut) Mine, and the Apollo Mine, all in Sisleytown and Gillespie, opened around 1880 to 1890. The first Arnold Mine opened in 1895 and coincided with the opening of the railroad in Fayette City. Within the next decade, the Arnold No.2 and No.3 Mines, the Marine Mine, and the Naomi Mine started production. All of these mines were within a mile to a mile and a half of Fayette City. The Tremont Mine on the Monongahela River, just beyond the Naomi Mine to the north, was also in full operation at this time. The booming coal mining business attracted an influx of immigrants mostly from central and eastern Europe and caused Fayette City's population to double from about 1000 people in 1880 to slightly more than 2000 by 1900. Coal production and the associated employment in these mines surrounding Fayette City peaked around 1910 and then experienced a devastating decline in the 1920s. By the mid-1920s, the Fayette City Mine, the Apollo Mine, the Arnold No.1 and No.3 Mines, and the Marine Mine were worked out and ceased production. One of the few bright spots in the area was the Fayette Mine owned by the Lowber Gas Coal Company and located just beyond Gillespie to the south. Lowber's Fayette Mine opened in 1919 while the mines nearest to Fayette City were in decline.

Fayette Mine
(¹Lowber, ²Hillman, ³Hawker)

Year	Tonnage	Employees
1919[1]	148063	205
1920[1]	235291	296
1921[1]	67964	263
1922[1]	265850	489
1923[1]	441526	400
1924[1]	62625	429
1925[1]	31538	415
1926[1]	244635	639
1927[1]	idle	idle
1928[1]	idle	idle
1929[1]	idle	idle
1930[1]	idle	idle
1931[1]	Idle	Idle
1932[1]	Idle	idle
1933[1]	161475	558
1934[1]	38556	493
1935[1]	4299	65
1936[1]	231129	513
1937[1]	312605	519
1938[1]	102458	148
1939[1]	140472	345
1940[1]	174605	234
1941[1]	404057	369
1941[2]	73751	322
1942[2]	287768	255
1943[2]	closed	closed
1944[3]	19641	8
1946[3]	≈17000	28
1947[3]	19529	18

The bituminous coal strike in western Pennsylvania in 1927 and the onset of the Great Depression brought further devasting blows to the mining industry in and around Fayette City. Several of the remaining mines were idle at some time between 1927 and the early 1930s. Lowber's Fayette Mine, the Tremont Mine, Arnold No.2, and the Naomi Mine each experienced some idle time during this period. The fortunes of each of these mines will be discussed in turn.

Lowber's Fayette Mine was idle from 1927 until about 1932. It resumed production around 1933 and then in 1941 was acquired by the Hillman Coal and Coke Company. Hillman operated the Mine for two years before closing the Mine in 1942. The Fayette Mine was reopened in 1944 by the O'Neil Hawker Coal Company with only one or two dozen employees. The Fayette Mine employed hundreds of miners under its previous owners. The Hawker Coal Company operated for most of the rest of the decade and provided home delivery for run-of-mine coal from the remnants of the worked-out mine.

Fayette City Journal
April 26, 1946

Run-of-Mine
Definition: Coal that is not graded according to quality or size

The Tremont Mine, owned by the behemoth Pittsburgh Coal Company (PPC), was idle in 1927 and then sold to the newly established Tremont Coal Company a year or two later. The Tremont Coal Company continued to operate the Tremont Mine, although with far fewer employees than it had under PPC ownership, into the 1940s. It also operated two mines, Tremont 2 and 3, in Gillespie beginning in the early 1940s and continuing through the decade. These two mines employed slightly more than one hundred workers.

The huge, PPC-owned Arnold No.2 Mine, situated at the end of Johnson Hollow and underneath the patch town of Arnold City was idle in 1930 and most of 1931 affecting hundreds of employees. It resumed production in 1932 and was ultimately closed by the PPC in 1942. The newly-formed Arnold City Coal Company resumed production at or near the mine in 1944, but with only a dozen or so employees. The mines went by the names Arnold No.20 and No.21 and typically produced less than 20,000 tons per year.

Arnold No.2 Mine		
Year	Tonnage	Employees
1930	idle	idle
1931	0	12
1932	36865	330
1933	118509	208
1934	273059	272
1935	287689	272
1936	294758	250
1937	250653	245
1938	258033	237
1939	248106	215
1940	239324	147
1941	46075	136
1942	closed	closed

The Naomi Mine began production in 1902. In 1907 it experienced one of the worst mining disasters in history when 34 miners were killed in an explosion of firedamp (i.e. methane). In 1927 the Naomi mine was acquired by the Hillman Coal and Coke Company, the same company that bought Lowber's Fayette Mine. The Mine was mostly idle from 1930 to 1932, although not for economic reasons. In July 1930 the Mine's tipple was destroyed in a spectacular fire causing more than $100,000 in damage. The fire was believed to have been started by an ember from a passing P&LE railroad engine. Fire companies from Fayette City, North Belle Vernon, Charleroi, Monessen, and Donora battled the blaze for more than four hours. The economic conditions of the time were not conducive to an immediate reconstruction of the tipple. It wasn't until August of 1933 and the beginning of Roosevelt's New Deal that construction of a new tipple was initiated. The new steel tipple was completed in March of the following year at a cost of $200,000. The start-of-the-art tipple included coal washing capabilities and a five-truck loading facility. The uncommon washing capabilities of the new tipple were leveraged as part of the Hillman's marketing of the coal produced at the mine. Fayette City resident Alfred Makepeace was named superintendent of the Mine. Makepeace was also the superintendent of the nearby Black Diamond Mine. By 1942 it was clear that the Naomi Mine was near the end of its life. Production became limited to the recovery of pillars left standing in past years. The Naomi Mine would eventually close for good in 1943 after forty years of providing jobs for hundreds of miners in the region. The tipple which was so proudly touted as the most modern in the region at its time of construction came crashing down while being dismantled in October of 1946, disrupting traffic on the road between Fayette City and Belle Vernon but injuring no one.

REBUILD TIPPLE AT NAOMI MINE

The Naomi coal tipple of the Hillman Coal Company, near Belle Vernon, which was destroyed by fire three years ago, is being rebuilt and actual work on the structure will begin today. It is expected the job will be completed within three months.

Its rebuilding is an indication that operators are confident the coal industry is in for a long period of activity in this district.

Alfred Makepeace, assistant to the late Thomas J. Branch, superintendent of the Naomi mine, has been placed in charge of the mine.

The Daily Republican
August 28, 1933

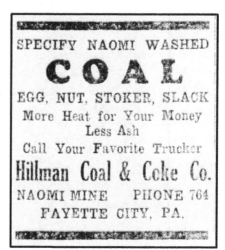

The Daily Republican
December 13, 1937

Pictures Of Tipp'e Crash At Naomi

The Fayette City Journal
October 18, 1946

Naomi Mine		
Year	Tonnage	Employees
1927	107711	329
1928	NA	NA
1929	353168	274
1930	idle	idle
1931	Idle	Idle
1932	Idle	Idle
1933	36218	148
1934	103200	318
1935	229765	319
1936	312292	261
1937	210024	170
1938	175283	257
1939	156396	165
1940	198097	189
1941	196854	170
1942	190237	131
1943	15214	146

"I had a great uncle. I think he was Superintendent of one of the mines there. He also played baseball for a Fayette City team at one time. His name was, they were twins, it was Albert and Alfred. His name was Alfred Makepeace. Ralph Makepeace, if that's who you're referring to, would have been his nephew. The Makepeace family, my great, my grandmother, my great grandmother, my uncle, it would be my great uncle worked in the Naomi mine, my grandfather, great grandfather and my uncle worked in the Naomi mine. As far as I know, the only one they worked in was the Naomi mine. That's the reason they came to Fayette City. They went around you know wherever the mines were, that's where they found work. They were all miners. They came from England. They found work. It was always in the mines. They would go around wherever the mines were mining at that time. I remember during my lifetime that they worked at the Naomi mine. My great uncle would come home at night from the mine covered with dirt. He'd be black from coal dirt. My grandmother would not let him in the house until he'd scrub some of that dirt off. Then he could come into the house, then he could get his bath."

-Nancy Ferree Johnson

"When they were born, my mother was born in Elco, up the river, down the river, whichever, south of us. Eventually they lived right in Fayette City. Mom was born in Elco and her father built a raft and took the children and family possessions down the River to Naomi to work on the new, work at the new coal mine down there, for more pay and a company home down there. The Elco mine was closing so they had to go find a new place to work. So he built a raft and loaded everything on it and down the River they went. Then he moved to Fayette City after living in Naomi for quite a few years. Then in 1918, the pandemic they had back then, my mother lost five brothers and sisters from that pandemic back in 1918. The last one that died, she was holding the baby. Never got over it."

-Bill Williamson

Alfred Makepeace died in 1945 at the relatively young age of 59, just a couple of years after the closing of the Naomi Mine. The Fayette City Journal offered a frontpage obituary of Makepeace describing him as a well-known and liked local resident. Makepeace served as president of the Fayette City School Board and was a member of the Fayette City Methodist Church, the Gummert Lodge No. 252 of the Free and Accepted Masons, and the Lions Club. As was the custom then, the Makepeace family expressed their appreciation to friends and neighbors for the outpouring of support with a Card of Thanks in the Journal.

The last mine of interest in the Fayette City area in the 1940s was the mine owned and operated by James E. (Jim) Hamer. Hamer was well-known in the Monongahela Valley for multiple reasons. He was a successful businessman, a referee for the National Football League, President of the Lions Club, superintendent of the Fayette City Water Company, President of the Fayette City and later the Bellmarette School Board. He was also appointed by Govenor James Duff of Pennsylvania, to the California State Teachers College Board of Trustees. CTSC, located across the Monongahela River from Fayette City, later named one of their buildings after him.

One of Hamer's business ventures was a coal mining operation in Navoo Hollow in Fayette City. An early mine of his was located near Sisleytown and the beginning of Navoo Hollow, not far from the entrance to the old Fayette City (Connecticut) Mine which had closed decades earlier. The first output from the early Hamer Mine was recorded in 1941. Before long, this mine experienced a squeeze and was forced to close. Hamer then opened a second mine about 500 yards further down Navoo Hollow. The mine's tipple, the stables for the horses working in the mine, and housing for some of the miners were located at the intersection of Navoo Hollow Road and Hill Street which connects with Brownstown. The coal was removed from the Hollow by truck. Very little of the coal was used locally. Hamer operated the Mines from 1941 until 1954 and typically employed two or three dozen workers a year. Two workers were killed over the lifespan of the Mine. The first worker to die in the Hamer Mine was Steven Kovatch. Kovatch died on December 28, 1946. An autopsy showed that the cause of death was electrocution. His death was mourned by his wife Gladys and his infant son Sonny, as well as by the entire community of Fayette City. The second death occurred in 1949. Thomas Hamer, perhaps a relative of Jim's, from neighboring Belle Vernon was electrocuted while repairing a motor that powered the mine's water pumps.

> **Squeeze**
> Definition: Settling (without breaking) of the roof and the gradual rising of the floor of the mine, with the possibility of the two eventually meeting.

Coroner Reports On Local Death

The Fayette County Coroner's office reported this week that an autopsy performed on the body of Steven Kovatch proves that his death was due to electrocution.

Kovatch who was a veteran of World War II was killed on December 28, 1946 at 10:30 a. m. in the Hamer Mine. He was formerly employed by the Pittsburgh Steel Company before entering the mining trade the second week in July. Funeral services were held last week.

Fayette City Journal
January 10, 1946

Hamer Mine		
Year	Tonnage	Employees
1941	34832	36
1942	51226	32
1943	43289	26
1944	32725	18
1945	29150	22
1946	26112	31
1947	56560	47
1948	40404	22
1949	8633	17
1950	29597	22
1951	31284	24
1952	16600	15
1953	31505	19
1954	6057	15
1955	closed	closed

John Vargo and Georgia Arrow with the Hamer Mine tipple in the background.
Photo courtesy of Georgia Jean Arrow.

"My family didn't work in the coal mines. Jim Hamer had a coal mine up the Hollow."

-Jim McKevitt

"Jim Hamer was one of the big operators of one of the coal companies. Hamer had a mine right up the Hollow there. He had two mines in the Hollow. One right up there above where Ritarchicks lived. Then another one on out further, above where Vargos lived originally there back then. Back down in the hillside there he had two big mines there at one time."

-Jim Eley

"Jim Hamer had a mine down there. Let me think where else were mines. There was mines, there was mines in Arnold City. There was mines down the River there, down past the tipple, the Naomi mine. And my uncle used to work in the Pricedale mine, Sommers. I remember I had to go and pick him up from work from the mine. That's about what I remember of it. I always remember they had them dilly tracks that hauled the coals out of the mine. There used to be down at Fayette City when you start up past toward Andy (Stefanick) there used to be two trestles went across, like a little tunnel sort of thing. And these railroad cars would haul that coal back in the day across them. I remember that trestle. I don't remember them hauling across. Yeah, but I remember I used to go down and cut down over the corner while I was going down the ball field to go across one of those things and walk up to the ball. There was two of them down there."

-Jack Gargan

"Well my dad was a coal miner and he worked in the coal mine for fifty years. The only thing he got out of there was black lung. That's the only thing. If you wasn't on strike you was working. He worked at a lot of different mines. He ended up in the Hamer Mine up in the Hollow, Navoo Hollow. But he definitely worked at Pricedale. He worked for Hamers.

Hamer, he had a coal mine down by Humphries bar. There was a squeeze on and they come up the Hollow to by where I lived. I would say maybe 500 or 600 yards from Humphries bar. He opened another coal mine and had a big tipple there and horses. Horses and stable, of course. I think there was probably four horses in that stable. They would go work, one worked daylight, the other one of course would work night shift. I guess they always had to have a spare.

They had what they call a squeeze. They couldn't get any, the coal shifted or what I don't know. They called it a squeeze. I was just a kid you know. But I remember a squeeze. Then he had to open another mine up the Hollow where I lived. I would say probably...500 yards, 600 yards from where Humphries were."

-Joe Vargo

"At the Navoo Hollow mine, around four o'clock, around the entrance because around that time, you can hear the bell and all the mules running out and they'd go to the stable. If you were anywhere near there, you were just trampled to death, right on the corner where Vargos used to live up in Navoo Hollow at the sharp turn. That sharp turn, to the right of that sharp turn, maybe 50 yards, that's where the mine entrance was. And before you got to the sharp turn, that's where the stables were on that same side. So they would run back right to the stables every day around four o'clock. So we would play there. Helas lived across the street. We played there. We always had to wait for that bell. As soon as you would hear that bell go off, you knew here comes the mules. They would storm out and go right for it."

-Harry Applegate

"My dad was born in Arona, which is near Greensburg. Then they moved to ....Lowber. He worked there, then they eventually moved to Fayette City. When my dad was in eighth grade, my grandfather told him tomorrow you go into the mines. You've had enough education to be a professor. Tomorrow into the mines. But according to my dad, that didn't last too long. There was some kind of an accident in the mine. My dad never went back.

They lived in one of the company houses that Jim Hamer owned. He owned those two houses that are still there, but they were double houses back then.

So my other grandfather lived in Arnold city. They had to buy everything in the company store, which was at the bottom of the hill. As you come down from Fayette City before you go up to Marion school, there was a big, large company store. That's where they used to buy their foods and that.

Right across the road, I remember it was very noisy when they dumped that. Well when the cars would go up the track, you would hear that belt click, click, click and then they would dump the coal into the waiting trucks below. That was noisy. And then the trucks would drive down the road. We would be walking to school and you had to step off the road to get out of the way, which would not work today.

I think it was only one horse that worked a shift at a time. Uncle Andy sometimes would get their horse ready and walk it into the mine. They were tied in their stalls. They could not lie down. There were four stalls. There were so many flies at those two double houses because of that barn. As kids, we would go in there and give them extra grain which you should not do because I had a horse for 17 years and you just don't give them extra grain as we did. There was a huge wooden grain box. We would even jump down into it. And of course, there were rats. It was upstairs where they kept the hay. Sometimes the blacksmith would come and he would tie the horse to the pear tree outside and shoe them trim their feet and reshoe them. Occasionally a horse would get loose in the night and we'd hear it running through the yards because they were the draft horses. Once there was a black horse, I think he was frustrated a lot of the time because he would kick the wall. There was something, he had a health issue and they put him outside and we heard him carrying on. In the morning we went down and he was dead. The tipple was across from our house. That weigh station, that was so interesting. It was across from Grazini's house where the trucks would drive and on these wooden whatever big, thick wooden boards and they would be weighed. Jim Hammer had his office in there. We would play softball in that empty lot between the barn and the stable and the weigh station. Mrs. Yetsconish would always yell at us that we were making too much noise because they would sit on the porch a lot back then. You sat out on your porch in the evenings. That's when we would play. She would always be hollering at us. Making too much noise, go home, so on and so forth."

-John Vargo

"He (Jim Hamer) had a big one up Navoo Hollow, a coal mine. Yeah, right there. My grandfather worked in there. There was a mine out in Gillespie. There was a mine at Naomi too."

-Tom Jolly

With the demise of the Hamer Mine in 1954 the coal industry in the immediate vicinity of Fayette City had effectively been put to bed. Fayette City clearly benefitted tremendously form the coal industry for many decades. However, there were some negative aspects too. Strikes over wages, working conditions, safety, and the length of the work week were all too frequent. Workers could easily be out of work for months at a time. Violence between the striking miners and the dreaded Coal and Iron Police, or "Cossacks" and "Yellow Dogs" as they were sometimes called, was often inescapable.

By mid-century, additional drawbacks of decades of mining were also becoming evident. In 1931 a petition was circulated asking that mining operation beneath the streets of town hill be terminated to prevent a possible cave-in. Indeed, the Catholic Church at the end of South High Street had already suffered damage. Four homes in Brownstown developed cracked walls and separated foundations in 1948, purportedly from mine subsidence below. By the end of the 1940s, Fayette City enacted an ordinance charging a $500 monthly fee for mining coal within the borough limits. Believing that the town was "mined out" except for stumps and that the removal of the stumps would cause cave-ins, the town council reportedly adopted the ordinance to prevent any further mining within the Borough. A 1930 government survey of the Monongahela Valley district from Elrama, PA to Fayette City predicting that the great coal deposits of the Pittsburgh vein were sufficient for more than forty years of steady mining was proven to be overly optimistic.

> "The borough building? That would be just going up in Hollow right after Gulyas. There was an alley there. My uncle, my dad's uncle Martin, was his name, the coal and iron police drove him back in that alley and killed him. My dad used to tell me all the time about his uncle Martin. He said they say the coal and iron police killed him. They drove him back. They was on horses. They drove him back in that alley. Like I said, I don't know if they shot him or just beat him to death. He said they killed him."
>
> -Joe Vargo

Catfish, Carp Caught In Monongahela River

In less than two hours, Narney Sells, who lives near Naomi mine, caught two catfish and a carp in the Monongahela river, while fish-ink from a skiff below Fayette City Friday. The catch discredits the legend of recent years that pollution has become so great in the river than nothing can exist in the water.

The Daily Republican
June 20, 1932

One final unwelcome consequence of decades of coal mining (and steel manufacturing later) was the unchecked pollution in the Monongahela River and the streams feeding into it. It was common for the children of Fayette City to swim in the River and for young and old alike to fish in the River even though the contamination was so obvious and visible that the primary daily newspaper of the region felt compelled to celebrate the catch of two catfish and a carp nearby!

Queen Coke

Unlike the plethora of patch towns in the Connellsville District of Fayette County, Fayette City produced no coke. The patches were constructed in the late 1800s and early 1900s with the goal of mining coal, converting it to coke, and then shipping it to the iron and steel mills in and around Pittsburgh. Fayette City, of course, was founded long before coke became a precious commodity. The lack of suitable land in Fayette City for constructing the ubiquitous beehive ovens used to convert coal to coke most likely contributed to the absence of any coke ovens. The coal mined in the vicinity of Fayette City instead was shipped by rail or by barge downstream to plants such as the Clairton Coke Works for processing.

Interestingly, coke ovens were also nonexistent in Arnold City, the closest patch town to Fayette City. The nearest coke ovens were a couple of miles away on the River road to Belle Vernon. Originally constructed by S.M. Speers, the battery of about sixty beehive coke ovens operated until about 1945. The Biggie Coal Company announced intentions to reopen the ovens in 1947. It is not known if the ovens were ever reopened as announced; however, their remnants are still visible today from across the Monongahela River.

REOPEN COKE OVENS NEAR BELLE VERNON

Workmen are remodeling and preparing the string of coke ovens on the Fayette City road, near Belle Vernon, for firing.

It is understood that the Biggie Coal Company, headed by Stephen Frederick of Belle Vernon, will operate the battery of approximately 60 ovens.

These were originally started and operated by S. M. Speers of Lynnwood until about two years ago. The ovens there are the last remaining in operating condition in this section of the valley. Further details on the operation will be announced later.

Fayette City Journal
March 7, 1947

Princess Steel

As mentioned earlier, employment in the coal industry in the vicinity of Fayette City reached its peak between 1910 and 1915. Fortuitously, contemporaneous developments at Fayette City's cross-river neighbor Allenport help to offset the declining job market for miners.

The world-famous U.S. Steel Corporation was created in 1901 when a group headed by Elbert H. Gary and J.P. Morgan bought Andrew Carnegie's steel company and combined it with their own holdings in the Federal Steel Company. That same year, the independent, locally owned Pittsburgh Steel Company (PSC) was formed. The PSC purchased a sixty-acre tract at Monessen, PA located about thirty miles south of Pittsburgh on the Monongahela River. Monessen offered prime, flat land along the River, plentiful natural resources such as coal, coke and gas, an abundant water supply, slack-water transportation, and excellent railroad connections to Pittsburgh. PSC grew rapidly and enjoyed boom conditions during World War I when the demand for steel skyrocketed. After the War, business naturally declined creating an imbalance between steel making capabilities and finishing capabilities. With space running out in Monessen, PSC addressed this imbalance by constructing a new seamless pipe mill at Allenport, PA, about six miles to the south.

Rumors had started in late 1916 that a large company had purchased 320 acres along the River between Allenport and Stockdale boroughs. Those rumors were confirmed the next year when surveyors working for the Pittsburgh Steel Products Company (PSPC), a subsidiary of PSC, began work at the sight. By 1920, the new steel mill at Allenport consisted of a two-stand, seven pass continuous rolling mill, a piercing mill, a coal-fired piercing mill furnace, cold draw benches, a pickling house, annealing furnaces, and gas producers at a reported cost of $300,000 to $400,000.

The sale has been completed, but the deeds have not been delivered for an 80-acre tract of land suitable for mill or by-products plant in Dunlevy borough. This news leaked out today, but neither the name of the purchasing concern, a large steel company, nor the price paid could be learned. Houses located on the tract are being sold and moved away. However nothing will be done toward utilizing the site until the first of the year.

A little farther south, a subsidiary company of the United States Steel corporation has purchased approximately 320 acres of land between Allenport and Stockdale boroughs, and it is believed will utilize this location next year.

All the Dunlevy purchase is located between the railroad and the river, taking in the bottom land there. The idea that the Pittsburgh Steel company is the purchaser of the bottom land still sticks, though it has been impossible to verify it.

The Daily Republican
August 10, 1916

"I used to go down every night when my dad come home from work because he rode the ferry back and forth. He worked at Allenport. He would go down in the morning, walk up the railroad tracks to the mill. At night, whenever he was coming home, we would go down, throw stones in the river until he came home and we walked up the hill. When we walked up the hill, he was right ahead of us and we'd put our finger, or I did, put my fingers in his back pocket so he could pull me. We walked down until we've got our driver's license. Then we got to drive down and pick him up."

-Willard Jones

"My father went to work for Pittsburgh Steel in Allenport when he was a teenager because his father wasn't around. He supported the family. He was the water boy or something. He didn't work in the mill. But he worked there. So he worked all his life there. That's what happened to the Valley. Everything left and there's no place to work there anymore. Is there?....It was in the 30s...So like I say, he was only fourteen. He was a water boy. He took water around for the workers when it was a break. They evidently didn't have drinking problems or anything like that. Then after that he worked, you know, worked in the mill and he worked there all his life. That was the main employment in the area, the Allenport and Monessen mills."

-Kathleen Walton Stimmell

The new mill attracted workers from all over the region. Most of the men in Fayette City worked for the PSC either at the Allenport mill or the Monessen mill. Men from Fayette City had a particularly easy trek to the Allenport mill. They would typically cross the River using the ferry, which had connected both sides of the River for decades, and then walk about a half-mile to the mill. Workers from Brownstown had the option to ride a bus which crossed the River at Belle Vernon in route to Allenport.

The mill was closed for most of 1921, reopening in December with a workforce of 600 men. The discovery of large amounts of oil in Texas and Oklahoma after the World War I created an increased demand for steel tubing to

Military officials visiting Allenport mill during World War II. Mill worker pictured on left is James E. Miller who died in a ferry accident in 1945 on his way to work. Photo courtesy of Lauri Miller Thompson.

transport the oil. Seeking to take advantage of this lucrative opportunity, PSC took over PSPC and renamed it the Tubular Division. A $3,000,000 investment was made in the Allenport mill making it possible to now manufacture tubing up to twelve inches in diameter.

The onset of the Depression in 1930 affected the PSC just as it did every other company. Downtime in the mill was not uncommon. However, by 1931 PSC, believing in an upturn in the demand for seamless tubing, announced an addition to the plant at Allenport.

Business was booming by the end of the 1930s. In October of 1939, the PSC announced its largest payroll in two years. A total of $346,000 was distributed at its plants in Monessen and Allenport. The Allenport mill was reportedly operating at 100%. A year later, both plants were operating at near capacity with 4,000 workers at Monessen and another 2,000 at Allenport.

The onset of World War II brought still more demand for steel, particularly of the tubing variety. A $10,000,000 government-financed addition was made to the Allenport Plant in 1942. The biggest challenge facing the PSC at the time was finding enough workers to run the plant!

Although all of the workers at the mill clearly supported the War efforts, they still went out on strike when they felt the need. In 1944, during the throes of the War, 2300 men at the mill were made idle when 180 men in the cold drawn department and another 50 cranemen staged a "sit-down" over a wage dispute. The tubing produced at Allenport was so critical to the War effort that Army and Navy labor relations officers and the U.S. Conciliation Service stepped in to help resolve the dispute. Another brief strike in July of 1945 idled between 800 and 900 men. Nevertheless, the War period represented a high-tide in labor management relations, and the years from 1939 to 1946 were some of the most profitable ever for the Pittsburgh Steel Company. By 1947 the Allenport employed 2500 workers and 3000 a year later.

"My dad told me a story about the mill when instead of making tube, they converted to shells during the war. He said a man worked there who was very quiet, but when he spoke, he had an unusual accent (different than the Slavs). There were government men who would come in and inspect the factory and observe the workers. A short time after one of these inspections, this guy didn't show up for work. Come to find out he was being watched, and when the officials went to where he lived, everything was gone! The word was he was a spy watching how these shells were being made! Again, this is the story my dad told me and I have looked for information about this with no avail."

-Frank Jacobs

The more than 1600 PSC employees who had served in the armed forces eventually returned home from the War. Jobs were plentiful and the outlook bright as the decade of the 1940s came to a close.

REFERENCES

Brestensky, D.F., Hovanec, E.A., Skorma, A.N. *Patch/Work Voices: The Culture and Lore of a Mining People*. Patch/Work Voices Publishing, 2003.

Coode, T.H. *Bugdust and Blackdamp, Life and Work in the Old Coal Patch*. Comart Press, 1986.

DiCiccio, C. *Coal and Coke in Pennsylvania*. Commonwealth of Pennsylvania, Harrisburg, 1996.

Enman, J.A. *Another Time Another World: Pennsylvania Bituminous Coal, Coke, and Communities*. Patch/Work Voices Publishing, 2010.

Heberling, J.A., Kudlik, J.J., Carlisle, R.C., Heberling, S.D. *Contextual Essays on the Monongahela River Navigation System*. U.S. Army Corps of Engineers, Pittsburgh District, Pittsburgh, 2012.

Moskala, E.J. *From Freeport to Fayette City: A History of a Small Town in Southwestern Pennsylvania from Its Founding in 1800 to Its Zenith in the 1920s*. Amazon Publishing, 2019.

Pittsburgh Steel Company Monessen Works, Monessen Pennsylvania (historic-structures.com)

Reports of the Department of Mines of Pennsylvania. Harrisburg, PA, Various Years.

Soroka, Mark (2016, December 12) Small Town Life: Life goes in in Allenport despite economic downturn. *The Herald Standard*.

CHAPTER 6 The Big News Stories of the 1940s

World War II obviously dominated the headlines during the first half of the 1940s, and rightfully so. The end of the decade was capped with the Sesquicentennial, the biggest celebration Fayette City had ever seen. Chapter 10 is dedicated to that wonderful, weeklong event. In between the War and the Sesquicentennial there were a handful of news stories that merited big, bold headlines in the Fayette City Journal. A couple of these events had a very positive impact on the town. Other events, while seemingly minor on the surface, were portents of things to come in later decades. The first event discussed here, however, is notable as much for its rarity as it is for its brutality. For the sake of historical context and continuity, these events will be discussed in chronological order.

The Sunshine Girl

Fayette City Journal
September 7, 1945

Anna Elizabeth Dreyer was known as the "Sunshine Girl' to her friends because of an exercise program and "sun-bathing" regiment she undertook after falling ill with a "rheumatic heart". To her friends, Anna was always cheerful and a picture of health afterwards. On Saturday, September 1, 1945, Anna was reported missing by her parents, Mr. and Mrs. Fred Dreyer of the Sisleytown neighborhood of Fayette City. Anna was last seen leaving her job as a waitress at a Monessen restaurant with a young man who had offered her a ride. She never made it home that evening.

On Thursday, September 6, an intensive search of the area on the Fayette City-Connellsville Road about six miles from Fayette City turned up parts of Anna's clothing including her blouse, brassiere, part of a slip, and purse. Her body was found a short time later in a clump of bushes about 2000 yards from where the clothing was found. A leather strap was pulled tightly around her neck. Police believed that Anna was slain a few hours after leaving her job. Her mostly nude, dead body was then hidden in a clump of bushes surrounded by high weeds near the highway. Police believed that the body had been moved there from another location. After a coroner's autopsy, the body was transferred to the Bake Funeral Home in Fayette City for services.

A 19-year-old Monessen War veteran told police that he had offered Anna a ride from her place of work that evening and left her off about 100 yards from her home. After the body was found, state police issued an alert for the apprehension of ex-sailor Frederick E. Hauser for questioning. Apparently Hauser had already fled along with a friend who was believed to have been along on the ride. The husky, freckle-faced Hauser known as "Red" was soon apprehended two days later near Imperial, PA. On September 11, the same day as his nineteenth birthday, Hauser was charged with murdering Anna Elizabeth Dreyer.

Hauser cooperated with police and took them on a 27-mile route he admitted to taking after Anna accepted his offer for a ride. Hauser confessed to beating and strangling her after she backed out of a promise to pet. The beating occurred at a barren slag pile outside of Vanderbilt, PA. Hauser stated that he then threw her nude body down an embankment with the leather strap still pulled around her neck.

In November District Attorney H. Vance Cottom sought a murder indictment against Hauser on the charge of murdering Anna Elizabeth Dreyer. The case came up for trial the following month. After previously confessing to the murder, Hauser left a note in his jail cell after an attempted jailbreak that said he knew the name of the person who killed the girl.

The trial began in early December. After a day and a half of unsuccessful jury selection, a recess was called by the defense. After a brief meeting with presiding Judge W. Russell Carr, Hauser changed his plea to guilty.

On December 10th, 19-year-old ex-sailor Frederick E. "Red" Hauser began a sentence of life imprisonment at the Western Penitentiary in Pittsburgh. Red's brother, Sergeant Gus Hauser who had been wounded in Europe during the War, reportedly told District Attorney Vance Cottom "You had your duty." Cottom, a Democrat, was elected Judge to Fayette County's Court of Common Pleas just one month prior to Hauser beginning his sentence.

As one might imagine, the gruesome murder of Anna Dreyer had a devastating effect on the community. Practically everyone in Fayette City knew her and her family. People waited in line for hours at the Bake Funeral Home to mourn the loss of the pretty russet-haired waitress known as the "Sunshine Girl."

> This week a climax to the murder case which brought sorrow to Fayette City was reached when, ex-sailor Frederick Hauser pleaded guilty.
>
> After a day and a half of trying to select jurors for the trial of Hauser, without one person being acceptable by both counsels, a recess was called at the request of the defense and after a short conference, followed by a conference with Judge Carr, Hauser changed his plea to guilty.
>
> Hauser's fate now rests with the President Judge W. Russell Carr, who pass sentence on the youth. Upon Judge Carr rests the decision of the confessed killer's fate.
>
> Standing before the court for the second time on Tuesday, the six foot, curly-haired Hauser, his trembling hand raised, changed his plea and said "Guilty" when asked by Clerk Joseph Sansone: "How do you plead, guilty or not guilty."
>
> As the youth made his answer his mother broke the silence with her sobs as Defense Counsel Attorney David H. Weiss attempted to console her.
>
> Commonwealth witnesses Tuesday detailed events leading up to the crime and the discovery of the waitress' body in a clump of bushes near a highway.

Fayette City Journal
December 7, 1945

> This past week brought an end to the murder case which will be long remembered by Fayette City residents as Frederick E. (Red) Hauser, was sentenced for the rest of his natural life in Western Penitentiary.
>
> Hauser, who is now number "B-9474" began paying his debt to society on Monday, when he was taken to the Penitentiary.
>
> The young murderer who was termed a "psycho-epileptic" during his trial, went into jail determined to win parole at the earliest moment by becoming a model prisoner.
>
> Warden Stanley Ashe greeted him with "How are you, Red?"
>
> The red-haired youth replied with a cherry "hello."
>
> His calm broke down when prison officials asked him "How much time did you get?"
>
> The word "life" seemed to stick in his throat.
>
> He immediately donned the number B-9474 and began the life sentence for the murder.
>
> Wearng a GI khaki shirt and slacks, handcuffed and escorted by Fayette County Deputy Sheriff J. Wendell Byers and a state policeman, the 19-year-old youth showed no emotion as the heavy gates of the prison clicked.
>
> Hauser was sentenced Saturday by Judge W. Russell Carr in Uniontown on his plea of guilty. He had previously confessed he beat and stranguled Anna Elizabeth Dreyer.

Fayette City Journal
December 14, 1945

Hauser was released from prison in 1963 after serving eighteen years of his sentence. In 1972 he was killed when a 10-ton road roller, which he had been operating, accidentally rolled over him.

Fredrick E. Hauser (left) reads a transcript of the statement he made to the police of Fayette County in connection with the death of Anna Elizabeth Dreyer, Fayette City's "Sunshine Girl". District Attorney H. Vance Cottom (right) is with Hauser. Photo from author's collection.

"Yeah, I remember her. Her aunt lived across the hall from us in the apartment. She had one of the apartments right across the hall from us. The Dreyers, Chris Dreyer, his wife's name was Thelma, Thelma Dreyer, Chris and Thelma Dryer. Her name was Anna, Anna Elizabeth Dryer used to come and visit. It was always, my sister and I would always go over and bother her, wanting her to play with us. So I do remember her and when she was murdered. It just, you know, it just terrified us. We were just scared to death. It was a shock. It was a shock to us. It was a shock to everybody in town. And he (Hauser) had a brother who lived somewhere, Fairhope or somewhere, Arnold City or somewhere. We used to say, "Oh, we got to be careful because Hauser's brother will get us." We were scared to death. We were always afraid the brother was going to come get us.

I remember the funeral. She was buried in Bake's Funeral Home. I remember the day of the funeral. People had tried to get into that funeral home and they were standing out on the street. I remember that very well."

-Nancy Ferree Johnson

"Anna Dreyer. We bought the Dreyer house….it was during World War Two or something. And there were no houses to buy. We bought it. My dad fixed it up. I haven't seen it lately. But that, they call that Sisleytown. Yeah, I remember. That was terrible. It was devastating to the family. But she made, you know, the wrong, I don't know, whether that was a boyfriend or something. But he went to prison.

But I remember she was she was a nice girl. Anna Elizabeth Dreyer had red hair and kind of tough, you know. But she was in that group of the high school where they had the May Day and everything. Yeah, I remember. It was very devastating for the family. Ruth Dreyer, her sister was married to Howard McCroy, the undertaker. It was a very tragic thing."

-Kathleen Walton Stimmell

"The only thing I really remember was the name and that she got murdered. But I can't remember, did they ever catch the person that did it? And that was, that was a big, big scary event Things didn't happen much in them days, back then. That was the one that always sticks with me that I can think of."

-Jack Gargan

Fayette City Journal
May 24, 1946

The grand schoolhouse at the head of Market Street was built in 1870 at a cost of $15,000. In its time it was one of the finest school buildings in the area. The adjacent smaller schoolhouse was built around 1905 to accommodate Fayette City's growing population. There were twelve rooms between the two buildings housing grades one through twelve. Enrollment in the Fayette City School naturally varied with the town's population. At the beginning of the 1930s, approximately 440 students were enrolled in the school (or about 37 students per grade). By 1945, only 238 students were enrolled, 65 in the four high school grades and 191 in grades one through eight. A year earlier the school board consisting of Alfred Makepeace, George Hancock, James Hamer, John Cameron and Dr. Aland Dent began discussing the potential consolidation of the local high school with neighboring Marion. Elimination of the high school, however, became the only option after the board reviewed changes to state law. The rational for the elimination of Fayette City's high school and transfer of its students to Marion was that Marion had far more space and equipment with which to operate a high school and could provide a much richer experience for the students. It was noted that there were already eighteen students from Fayette City attending other high schools where they could get a broader education leaving only sixty-five students in the local high school. Before making any final decision on the subject, the school board chose to feel out public opinion.

The 1945-1946 academic school year began with a new principal, Jack F. Hoyes. Any decision to eliminate the high school was put on hold. It was announced in March of 1946 that the High School would produce its first ever annual called the "Fay-View". Ironically it would be just two months later the school board would announce the discontinuation of the high school. Consequently, the first annual for the Fayette City High School also became its last. A few pages from the 1946 Fay-View annual are provide in the following pages. (The annual was provided by the family of Mildred Virginia Welsh Miller, the vice-president of the class of 1946.)

The commencement exercises for the fourteen students in the class of 1946 began with a Processional by Mrs. Wilbur Evans on the organ followed by an Invocation by the Rev. John Bowers of the Christian Church. Jeannie McKenna gave the Salutatory address. Ester Marie Burig, the daughter of the school's former Principal and one of the current teachers, gave the Valedictory. The Fayette City High School Mixed Chorus provided a selection of songs including the School's Alma Mater "Fayette City" with these lyrics:

WILL PRODUCE ANNUAL

The Fayette City High School will produce the first Annual under the combined efforts of the Senior Class and the English instructor, Mr. Jack F. Hoyes. All the material has been sent to the printer and the Annuals will be in the hands of the subscribers as soon as they are returned. This project has been hailed as a huge success, especially since it has provided the financial backing for most of the Seniors contribution to the Annual Junior-Senior Banquet-Prom event. Because of the uncertainty in the minds of the Seniors as to their ability to sell their first Annual, they limited their subscription list and it will not be possible to accept any more orders than have already been taken. The Class wishes to take this opportunity to thank those who have helped them in this matter, the subscribers, advertisers, and members of the community who provided the incentive to make it worthwhile.

Fayette City Journal
March 15, 1946

Fayette City, School of Honor, we are loyal too,
For your future we conspire, every heart is true.
With brave hearts we face the future, Victory we will see,
Proud to call you Alma Mater, Dear and grand F.C.

Victory, Victory, Our hopes are for F.C.
Victory, your school and mine, Our name on land and sea.
Our future days, we'll fill with praise,
Each heart with courage too.
Through smiles and tears of coming years,
Our hearts will be of you.

Dr. I.C. Keller of the California State Teachers College addressed the students and then James Hamer, president of the local Board, presented the Burig Award. Finally, Principal Jack Hoyes distributed the diplomas. The last graduating class from the Fayette City High School consisted of the following students:

- Ester Marie Burig
- Beverly Yvonne Carlson
- Mike Dohanich
- John Fedora
- Leonard Lee Gaskill
- Jeannine McKenna
- Norma Jean Roy
- William Morgan Trezise
- Catherine A. Turek
- Louis Nessley Usher
- Mary J. Vargo
- Mildred Virginia Welsh
- Margaret Grace Whitelaw
- James McGregor Williams

Burig, McKenna and Trezise were listed as the Honor Students while Gaskill and Williams were listed as serving in the Armed Forces. With this class, an era had come to a close.

On Wednesday May 24, 1946, the Fayette City School Board voted unanimously to discontinue operation of the local High School. According to the Board, a new state law which would allocate funds on a per pupil basis instead of on a teacher basis would make it prohibitively expense to continue operation of the High School, particularly since only forty high school students were expected for the 1946-47 term. The Board further decided that Mr. Hoyes would stay on as principal for the remaining grades.

With the elimination of the High School in Fayette City, the students were given a choice. They could attend either Marion High School or Charleroi High School. The following year, nine Fayette City students elected to attend Marion while only four chose to attend Charleroi. Those electing Charleroi had to spend ninth grade at their junior high school before attending the high school as they were in different buildings. When the 1946-47 school year started, students attending Marion High School were offered a short bus ride from the steps of the Fayette City schoolhouse to Marion.

"I went to Fayette City elementary school, through seventh grade. Back then, the school, hard to believe in that little space up there, it was 12 years of schooling. But they merged with surrounding school districts the year I was in seventh grade. And then from eighth grade, we went to a different school. The Fayette City school was just for kindergarten through sixth grade. And then those of us who were above sixth grade, went to Marion, Washington Township, junior high school and then high school. So that's where I went. The high school was called Bellmar, short for Belle Vernon and Marion."

-Mike Hancock

"Probably fourth or fifth grade, and sixth grade. I think, seventh grade, we went out to Marion. I was only out in Marion for one year. At that point in time, they sort of dissolved the Fayette City High School, so to speak. At that point, the students who went there had a choice to go on to Charleroi or to Marion for their final, you know, education. So, I went to Charleroi. I wanted to pursue...they had the beauty college course for girls. They also had home economics for girls too. But you could, I went into the beauty college for the hairstyling and all that sort of stuff. It was big at that time, you know."

-June Winters Baldwin Jaquette

"In ninth grade in 1950, we moved to Brownstown on Third. We moved into one of Wilbur Leighton's houses. We rented that house. And then I went to Marion for ninth and tenth. Then the jointure came about during my junior year. It became Bellmar. 1952 would have been the first graduating class from Bellmar. I graduated in 1953, which would have been the second class graduating from Bellmar."

-Georgia Nicholson Slezak

The closure of the Fayette City High School proved to be a harbinger of bigger changes to come. By the late 1940s, Fayette County was seeking to reduce the number of school districts in the County. Shortly after the beginning of the 1950-51 school term, representatives from Fayette City, Belle Vernon, North Belle Vernon, and Washington Township (Marion) began discussions on a possible jointure of the four school districts. Such an action faced one major obstacle in that Fayette City was in Fayette County while the other school districts were in Westmoreland County. The invisible but substantial barrier was eventually overcome and on April 6, 1951, the Bellmarette Joint School District was born. The 1951-1952 school term was the first year for the jointure and the newly named Bellmar High School.

More changes were to come a decade later. In early 1962 plans were being made for the merger of the new Frazier School District in Fayette County with the Bellmarette School District. A few months later, the Bellmarette School District petitioned the State of Pennsylvania to consider a merger between Bellmarette and the Rostraver School District. Once again, Fayette County and Westmorland County were in a battle of the school districts. The merger between Bellmarette and Rostraver was approved in 1964 and took effect at the beginning of the 1966 school year. The new school district was named Belle Vernon Area and remains that today.

The Fayette City Elementary School eventually closed its doors for good at the conclusion of the 1970-71 school term. The changes that started in 1946 with the closure of the Fayette City High School had finally come to a fateful end.

"I wanted to go to Marion because I wanted to play football and baseball with sports. And I played basketball, but I wasn't very tall, not tall enough, not that good. I wanted to go to Marion and my parents were on me trying to get me to go to Charleroi. They talked to some people and George Hancock, who's one of the leaders back then, got me aside. I really like George; he was a nice guy. And he told me some reasons why I should go to Charleroi. I still wanted to go to Marion. Bap Manzini was coaching a year after that at Bellmar. But anyway, so anyway, I went to Charleroi and got along alright. I wasn't on the honor roll because I wasn't planning to go to college at that time.

We had busses back then and tokens for the bus. We used tokens to go (to Charleroi High School). But you had to be there a certain time, and then you had to come back home a certain time. So, I was playing activities, wrestling, and I was playing some sports in junior high and high school. So, it didn't work out too well. So, I started hitchhiking to Charleroi and back at night, because you know, I couldn't get a ride back to Fayette City sometimes when practice was over and stuff. So sometimes I'd ride my bicycle down there and back."

-Bill Williamson

"Fayette City schools, the elementary school was a brick structure to the right. So the main building at one time had a high school in it. I went to elementary school in the smaller building. As you face the front of the eighth grade, there was a smaller brick building, and that's where I started up through grade four. And then we moved over into the bigger building. There was no high school then, just the fifth, sixth, seventh and eighth grade there.

I had a choice of either going to, because Fayette City discontinued having a high school, I could either choose to go to Charleroi High School or to Marion High School. I chose Charleroi because of two counts. One, my brother Bob, who was five years older than me, had gone to Charleroi and studied vocational shop there. My father, Clarence Young, whose family grew up in Fayette City, he worked in Charleroi .... as an automobile mechanic. So he went every morning, he drove into work, and then we'd come back at 5:30. I wanted to have a free ride. By the way, Helen Backstrom, then Helen Scullion, was two years ahead of me, and she rode with my father also to Charleroi in the mornings. Now I didn't take a bus back, or wait for my dad who left at 5:30. All the boys who went to Charleroi like I did, would run down to First Street in Charleroi and hitchhike back to Fayette City. There were regular buses that ran, but we all hitch hiked daily back to Fayette City."

-Jack Young

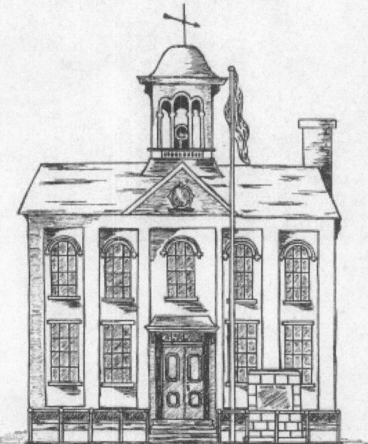

DEDICATED TO YOUTH

WHO GAVE US VICTORY IN 1945

WHO SYMBOLIZE THE NEW ATOMIC AGE

WHO REPRESENT DEMOCRATIC IDEALS

WHO HOLD OUR HOPE FOR FUTURE PEACE

TO YOUTH---WE, THE CLASS OF NINETEEN HUNDRED AND FORTY-SIX,

RESPECTFULLY DEDICATE THIS FIRST EDITION OF OUR SCHOOL

ANNUAL, "FAY-VIEW".

Pages from the Fay-View 1946 Annual.
Courtesy of Becky Miller.

BOARD of EDUCATION

Standing: George Hancock, Secretary; John Cameron, Treasurer; George Hoy, Member

Seated: Dr. Aland Dent, Vice-President; James Haxer, President

In Memoriam
of
Alfred E. Makepeace

Pages from the Fay-View 1946 Annual.
Courtesy of Becky Miller.

PRINCIPAL

Mr. Jack F. Hoyes came to the Fayette City School District as the Supervising Principal in the latter part of the 1944-1945 school year.

His educational background includes eleven years of teaching while serving as teacher, coach and music director. These years were spent at the Washington Township and the North Belle Vernon Borough Schools. His hobbies include sports and music. During the years as a teacher he followed these interests as a Basketball coach and as the Director of Mixed Choruses. At the present time he is furthering his educational background in the study for a Doctor's degree, since he already holds a Bachelor of Science Degree in Education from the California State Teachers College and a Masters Degree in Education from the University of Pittsburgh. While he attended the University of Texas in Austin, Texas, he studied with several educators in the field Advanced Psychology.

Jack F. Hoyes

FACULTY

Standing: Mrs. Feng, Miss H. Nelson, Mrs. I. Wilson, Mr. Underwood, Miss Hoehl, Miss Alkmetter, Miss L. Nelson

Seated: Mrs. Wyatt, Mrs. Hurig, Miss Schwartz, Mrs. Welch Mrs. Williams

Pages from the Fay-View 1946 Annual.
Courtesy of Becky Miller.

Bill Trezise

WILLIAM MORGAN TREZISE

" DOC "

President of the Class (3-4)

Member of Boy's Sports Club (3)

Secretary Boy's Sports Club (4)

Member of Dramatic Club (1-2)

President of the Glee Club (4)

Member of the Dance Club   (4)

Part in High School Play (1-2)

MILDRED VIRGINIA WELSH

" V "

President of the Class   (2)

Vice President of the Class   (4)

President Girl's Sport Club (2-3)

Secretary Girl's Sport Club   (4)

Treasurer of Dramatic Club   (1)

Member of the Library Club   (4)

Member of the Dance Club   (4)

Member of the Glee Club   (2-4)

Took part in May Day   (2-3-4)

Pages from the Fay-View 1946 Annual.
Courtesy of Becky Miller.

The Marine Mine was located just beyond the northern end of Fayette City Borough at the junction of the road to Naomi (current Route 906) and the road to Belle Vernon (current Route 201). The Mine was opened in 1899 and closed not long after that in 1907. Coal was extracted from the mine and sent by dilly tracks over the highway to a tipple on the Monongahela River. The dilly tracks and tipple were torn down not long after the Mine closed.

The flat land along the River made an ideal playing ground for baseball. The original baseball diamond had batters hitting in the direction of the Mine opening. (See map below.) Fayette City had enjoyed decades of success on this field, never giving much thought to the fact that the land on which the field was located did not

Fayette City Journal
October 11, 1946

belong to the Borough. (Fayette City's long and illustrious history of baseball will be discussed in a later Chapter.) The ball field was part of a large tract of land along the River that extended from the Borough's edge into Naomi and belonged to the Marine Mine Company. In October of 1946, the announcement that the Haney R. Worthington Company of Pittsburgh was putting up for sale its holdings in the Marine Mine Company rocked Fayette City. While the headline in the Fayette City Journal didn't use the largest font on the front page, the potential outcome was clear to everyone. "Are we going to lose our cherished ball field?"

The property up for sale included the ball field, nine frame houses on lots measuring 100' x 150', and a century old brick mansion on a 150' x 500' lot. The mansion was listed for $550 and described as an excellent location for a

Victory Gardens during World War II. Future site of Crystal Pool.
Photo courtesy of Eddy Stefanick.

125

tearoom, restaurant or gas station. The land was offered at 2.5 to 3 cents per square foot. The property was offered for sale individually or as a whole.

The land at the border of the Borough had been used as Victory Gardens during World War II. The photograph on the prior page shows the Gardens as viewed from behind the stone house built by the Stefanick family. The Stefanik ESSO gas station was built across the road from this house in 1948. The famous Crystal Pool opened in 1953 on the site of the Victory Gardens.

The baseball field with the cross-river hills in the background.
Photo courtesy of Eddy Stefanick.

Soon after the Worthington announcement a group of concerned citizens met to devise a plan to purchase the baseball field. The group expressed an urgency to move on the purchase before it could be sold to others. The cost of the property was not yet known since a survey had not been completed. One local man summed up the group's feelings when he said, "We should not think of the cost but of the town's future." One week later, John Canigiani was named chairman of the group interested in purchasing the ball field. He expressed plans to call on all local civic, fraternal, and church organizations to explain the project and the details of the fund-raising drive. The price of the 350' x 450' field was initially set at $4,100 but finalized at $4,200, or 2.7 cents a square foot. The drive started in earnest in January of 1947. Employing the same methodical and disciplined approach used for the many drives during the War, volunteers were assigned to canvass Fayette City's neighborhoods. A promise was made to publish the names of the contributors and the amounts given in the Fayette City Journal.

John Canigiani, 1947.
Photo courtesy of
Leila Breckenridge Steiner.

The price of the plot of ground is $4100 and is about two times the size of the present ball field. Mr. Canigiani states that he knows that the price of the field is high but rather than see the community lose it to other interests feels that the purchase must be made now.

Volunteers who will make the canvass have been named by the chairman as follows:

Brownstown— Charles Hough, Gilbert Hamilton and Wilbur Long

Town Hill— John Canigiani and George Hancock.

Downtown Businessmen— Joseph Moravek, J. H. Renstrom and Howard McCrory.

Navoo Hollow— Charles Humphries and Joe Alberta.

Downtown Homes— Pat Hynes, Marion DeRienzo and James Hough.

Contributions can be left with the chairman at any time if you are missed by the solicitors. Anyone who resides out of town and wishes to contribute may do so by sending their money to the chairman, John Canigiani.

Names of those who contribute $5 or more will carried in this paper each week until the drive is complete, so hurry and get your contribution in and be at the top of the list.

Fayette City Journal
December 13, 1946

The agreement to purchase the field was signed in July of 1946. A down payment of $600 left a balance of $3600. The Journal provided a list of all of the initial contributors and contribution amounts, from fifty dollars to fifty cents. The next installment was due the following October. The response to the drive was so good that the funds for the second installment were raised by May. Contributions came from a variety of sources including local citizens and businesses, baseball players and managers, the local Lions Club and American Legion, and even the Allenport Mill where so many Fayette City citizens worked. By September, just nine months since the beginning of the drive, $2,800 had been raised. Another $700 was paid in April of 1948. The final $700 was paid in early 1949 even though the original contract to purchase the ball field called for a 5-year term. With the full support of the community, the field was paid off in just two years. As promised by the drive committee, when the field was paid off, the deed to the property was presented to the community of Fayette City. The remarkable display of community spirit saved the baseball field and united the town as never before.

However, this was not to be the last drive for the baseball lovers in Fayette City. A second drive was initiated later in 1949 to buy a smaller track of land adjacent to the original baseball field. The drive quickly achieved its goal with contributions not only from local citizens, but also from state congressmen, senators, prothonotaries, and even a judge. The purchase of this second piece of land led to an interesting "turn" of events, so to speak. The Stefanick family began excavation for what became Crystal Pool around 1952. Dirt from the project was used to remedy drainage issues with the ball field. At about the same time, the baseball diamond was rotated 180 degrees to its current orientation.

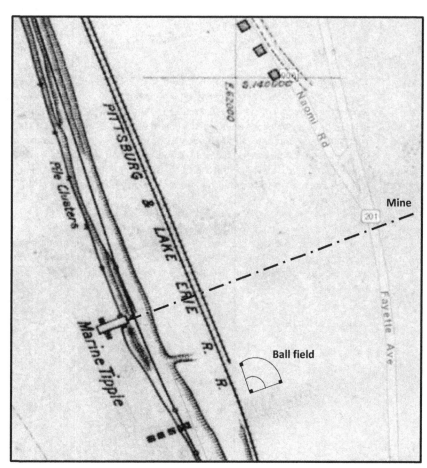

Pennsylvania Mine Map Atlas with overlay showing location of Marine Mine opening and ball field prior to 1952.

"The ball field? A lot of memories there. First of all, my first recollection of it, the ball field was turned 180 degrees the other way. Somewhere around I guess around 1950 they decided to expand the field and make a picnic area and that sort of thing down there. But to do that they had to turn the field around, which they did. That's when it was turned the way it is laid out even today. And I think it's still there. That's the field I most remember. We played on the other one, but I was awfully young then. But the field after it was turned, the second time is what I mostly remember."

-Mike Hancock

"That was naturally before the roads were all put in and everything. McFalls lived in the brick house up there. They had a well. That was what we did for our summer. We either went to the freight station or went to the ball field. And we went to the ball field, like you say it was turned, and we would play and play and walk up to that well. That water was always so cold."

-Raymond Moody

"Dinger (Young) signed as a pitcher with the St. Louis Cardinals and managed a number of Fayette City teams later. He was my best friend ever. We played ball all the time in the back of his yard with the Scrogg's fishpond a home run. We would go to the ball field, we would go to the ball field many times in the mornings, which we helped rebuild with the Russell brothers Carl and Jack and catch and throw, I from third base and Dinger on first base because he was a lefty first baseman when he wasn't pitching. Back then the ballpark was laid out the complete opposite than it is now. The old field had home plate where centerfield is now. Centerfield today is where home plate was then, and vice versa. Centerfield is where home plate is today. The change was made some time between 1950 and 55."

-Bill Williamson

"Before I was big enough to play, I would go down to the field where the older people were playing. And I volunteered to be a bat boy or a water boy carrying water from the field up to McFall's well out in right centerfield. Or I'd be a ball boy chasing balls that were fouled off, sometimes over into coal cars along the back of the playing field, which was located about a half a mile outside of Fayette City toward Belle Vernon."

-Jack Young

Fayette City Journal
December 5, 1947

When Colonel Cook and Joseph Downer laid out Freeport's 51 lots around the year 1800, they made all of the streets 30 feet wide with the exception of Market Street which they made 45 feet wide. Two-way traffic in the days of the occasional horse and carriage could be easily managed. However, the arrival of automobiles, buses, and delivery trucks more than a century later coupled with a fully developed business district eventually made two-way traffic on these narrow streets an all-too-common nightmare.

At the beginning of the 1940s, all traffic passing through Fayette City in both directions, north and south, was funneled through Main Street. Traffic jams were particularly problematic when the many businesses on Main Street were loading or unloaded goods at local businesses. Truckers would often use detours to avoid going through Fayette City all together. The idea to create one-way traffic on Main Street (traveling north) and Second Street (traveling south) was first proposed by the well-known town leader George Miller in 1943. With the help of State Legislator Charles Thrasher, Miller was able to gain approval from the State for the project. However, the project was never undertaken due to a wartime ruling that limited projects to $5,000.

In the summer of 1946, a special session of the Fayette City Borough Council was called by president Edwin Hindmarsh to review a proposal by the State Highway Department to resurface the road in Johnson Hollow Road. The road was in a sorry state of disrepair due since the coal mines in the Hollow closed and the railroad tracks that were used to transport the coal out of the Hollow were no longer needed. The ordinance was passed on first reading. A second proposal to open a roadway through Fayette

"I was going around when they changed the streets and I thought it's about time they did that. It used to be that you would have to pull over, and someone goes through, and pull over. That's where you went through there. I don't think I was driving then, I don't think."

-Jack Gargan

City from Second Street to Sisleytown on the southern end of town was also reviewed and passed. The project would require the construction of two new bridges and a traffic circle permitting traffic to turn in the opposite direction. The new traffic pattern created one-way traffic on Main Street going north and one-way traffic on Second Street going south.

The project was completed in December of the following year. Route 711, as it was known then, went south on Second Street and north on Main Street. "One-Way Do Not Enter" signs were posted at both ends of town to warn any travelers unaware of the changes. Burgess James Thrikield warned the public that 25 mile per hour speed limit signs had been erected and that stop watches were being used to enforce the speed limit. Today's travelers through Fayette City routinely face much more sophisticated measures!

"Well, first of all, there was a period of about a month when there was a large number of accidents because people were accustomed to a different way. It's hard to believe that Main Street had two-way traffic on it plus parking. But it did. I remember when they did that. They put down new pavement and threw out the old pavement. It was a really big deal. My mother, who was a bit of a tomboy, when they were doing this, when they closed Second Street to repave it, the kids adopted it for bicycling and roller skating. Because it was close, it was a great place to do all those things. My mother came out one day and said let me let me give that a try, Mike. Let me have your bike. She did and she got her pant leg caught in the chain. The wheels screeched to a halt and she went flying over the handlebars and knocked her front teeth out. That's the truth. My dad never did get over giving her hell about that. Fortunately, her uncle was a dentist, and he was able to take care of most of it."

-Mike Hancock

Where New Road Is Being Constructed

Pictured above is a view of the land where the new roadway making one-way traffic possible thru here will be built. The photo shows the intersection of Second and Cook Streets. Second Street will be extended to the present highway. Work is expected to get underway immediately on the project which was stopped when inclement weather set in.

Fayette City Journal
March 21, 1947

Second Street between Market and Union Streets during construction.
Photos courtesy of Judith Shearer.

"I can remember Main Street used to be two ways on the same street, one going up and one coming down. Well, then they tore all of that up and put the concrete down. So, they had to do it naturally in sections. So, we used to get our street skates, you know, the ones that you had to slip your shoe on, and the key. And we used to roller skate up on that after they got so much of the section done. Oh, yeah. It was a lot of fun to roller skate on the street where they had fixed. That was in the mid or late 1940s I think."

-Ella Marie Auther Davis

Fayette City Journal
September 3, 1948

When the Pennsylvania and Lake Erie (P&LE) Railroad made its first entrance into Fayette City in 1895, the immense crowd that had gathered to welcome the train could not have envisioned the day when the new train station would close. So many citizens had worked so hard and so long to convince the P&LE to extend the railroad from Belle Vernon. Fayette City was ready for an economic boom that the railroad would surely deliver. Indeed, over the next couple of decades, the population of Fayette City would more than double due in large part to the expansion of the coal industry made possible by the railroad.

The train station was located at the corner of Union and Front Streets. When the train station opened in 1895, riders could catch a train four times a day to Belle Vernon, Monongahela, Elizabeth, Glassport, McKeesport, and Pittsburgh. By the late 1940s, however, passenger traffic on the railroad had become nearly nonexistent. Many people had their own cars by then and no longer had to rely on the train for trips to Belle Vernon, Charleroi, or even Pittsburgh. The train station had become relegated to serving the occasional needs of local farmers and businesses for incoming and outgoing freight. On January 21, 1948, notices were posted throughout the Borough that the P&LE had filed an application with the Public Utility Commission (PUC) to close the freight and passenger station in one month if no protests were filed with the Commission within 30 days of the posting. As they had done before, local citizens swung into action. Petitions against the closing were sent to the PUC and resulted in a delay of any action to close the station. In the following May, the PUC held a hearing in Uniontown, PA to allow signers of the petitions to state their case. Only three people attended the hearing to oppose the station closing. The following week, the editor of the Fayette City Journal penned a scathing editorial asking why so few in the community seemed to care about the closing.

The PUC eventually authorized the P&LE to close its freight and passenger station despite the protestations of the Fayette City Journal, the Fayette City Board of Trade led by Howard McCrory, and a few local citizens. The notice below announcing the closure of the train station on October 1, 1948, was posted at the station in early September. The end of the line had indeed finally come. Not long after its closing, the station became a private residence. It was eventually lost in its entirety in a fire a few decades later.

132

Notice is hereby given that in accordance with Pennsylvania Public Utility Commission Order dated July 26, 1948, Application No. A-71521, the status of the station at Fayette City, Fayette County, Pennsylvania, will be changed from that of an agency passenger, baggage and freight station to that of a non-agency passenger, baggage and freight station, effective October 1, 1948.

Dated August 23, 1948

The Pittsburgh & Lake Erie Railroad Company, C. G. Stewart, General Manager.

Fayette City Journal
September 3, 1948

"I used to go down to the train station and pick up all the, that's where all the stuff would come in for the post office, all the packages and everything. There was a lot of train traffic on this side of the River and the other side. Every once in a while, you would get a passenger line that would come down from West Virginia and Pittsburgh on this side of the River. After a few years they went to Kennywood on the train. The train would pick you up here and drop you off in I think it was Braddock or somewhere. And then you had to go up over the hill to Kennywood. I rode those trains a couple times."

-Jim Eley

"I remember that train station. It was a large, large building. There weren't too many trains that went through. The Fayette City train did go to Pittsburgh. I remember as a very small child, we would, my sister and I would go meet the train every night and meet my father. There was hardly any traffic at all on the streets. But we would cross the street and certain people in town would make sure we got across the street. We walked up the street past the bank building and some houses there. There was another family on the corner where the train came in. They made sure that we were safe there until my father came in on the train. My father always had something for us, either candy or a little toy. And then we would walk back home. That would be one of the highlights of my day."

-Shirley Ferree Stilgenbauer

Fayette City train station around 1930 (top) and around the late 1950s or early 1960s (bottom). Photos from author's collection.

REFERENCES

BVA 'In the Day', SWPA History
https://swpahistory.wordpress.com/pennsylvania/papublicschools/westmoreland-county-school-districts/bvasd/bvaintheday/

Fay-View 1946, Fayette City High School Annual provided by Becky Miller.

Pennsylvania Mine Map Atlas (psu.edu)
https://www.minemaps.psu.edu/

CHAPTER 7 Community Spirit

"Community Spirit" is one of those nebulous terms that can be difficult to define and even more difficult to measure. You just know it when you see it. By whatever means you choose to define and measure community spirit, Fayette City clearly had it in spades in the 1940s. Evidence of Fayette City's community spirit was previously illustrated by the plethora of fund drives during World War II when Fayette City gained a reputation throughout the region for its outsized generosity compared to its larger neighbors. Other examples include the array of civic organizations in Fayette City such as the Lions Club, the Woman's Club, the local American Legion Post, the Volunteer Fire Department, the Free and Accepted Masons, and Fayette City's renown Trojan Drum and Bugle Corps. The younger generation participated in Girls Scouts and Boy Scouts, and the Rainbow Girls for those whose parents were members of the Masons. The town's seven churches were routinely filled with devout worshippers. School activities such plays, the annual May Day celebration, sporting events, and of course, graduation ceremonies, were the center of attention for the entire community. Fayette City's political scene was also active with numerous citizens vying for positions as Burgess, Justice of the Peace, and Borough Councilmen. There was something for everyone and most everyone participated in something for the benefit of the greater good.

> **Community Spirit**
> Definition: Community spirit finds expression in individual or group activities in which members of a community choose to engage for the benefit of that community. These activities may be locally organized, or informal and spontaneous.

Civic Organizations

Lions Clubs International is an international non-political organization founded in 1916 with the motto "We Serve". The Fayette City Lions Club was founded in February of 1944 with the ubiquitous James E. Hamer as its president. One of the Club's earliest activities was leading the Sixth War Loan Drive under the leadership of Edwin Hindmarsh. The Club also lead the Seventh War Loan Drive and the Victory Loan Drive the following year. The Club routinely held their biweekly meetings at the local Methodist Church and invited local pastors from Fayette City's churches to speak.

In line with their motto to serve, the Lions Club was active in identifying community needs such as a movie projector for the school, new Christmas streetlights, rescue boats to help with River drownings, and the persistent need for a local bank. Their biggest accomplishment in the 1940s, by far, had to be the inaugural Fayette City baby parade in 1946 "to honor the babies of this

OFFICERS OF FAYETTE CITY LIONS CLUB

Pictured above are the officers of the Fayette City Lions Club reading left to right: J. H. Renstrom, treasurer; P. Paul Jesick, | past president; Edwin J. Hindmarsh, newly elected president, Jasper Hare, 3rd vice president; George G. Hancock, 2nd vice | president; Allan S. Keenan, secretary. Missing from the picture is William Mascare, 1st vice president.

Fayette City Journal
July 4, 1947

territory". Although the Baby Boom had just started with the end of the War, baby parades were not new to the United States; cities in New York state had already held them for several years. But the concept of a baby parade was something new for Fayette City and the region. It is difficult today to image that a contest whose goal it was to identify the community's prettiest baby, at the expense of those babies who were not, would be good for community spirit. But surprisingly it was. George Hancock was the chairman in charge of the first baby parade. Age limits were set at one day to six years with an entry fee of one dollar. All of the entry fees were planned to be returned as cash prizes with $150 set as the goal. Prizes were given for prettiest babies, the best decorated and unique carriage, and the best decorated and unique float. Members of the local Lions Club were marshals for the parade. Judges were brought in from out-of-town to avoid any appearance of partiality and their names were withheld until parade time. A week prior to the parade a bicycle section was added to give the older youths a chance to compete. Another twenty dollars was added to the prize money to cover the bicycle entries. The list of prizes for the event were as follows:

- Most Unique Float $25.00
- Prettiest Decorated Float $25.00
- Most Unique Carriage $20.00
- Prettiest Decorated Carriage $20.00
- Prettiest Auburn Boy $10.00
- Prettiest Auburn Girl $10.00
- Prettiest Brunette Boy $10.00
- Prettiest Brunette Girl $10.00
- Prettiest Blonde Boy $10.00
- Prettiest Blonde Girl $10.00
- Bicycle – First Prize $10.00
- Bicycle – Second Prize $5.00
- Bicycle – Third Prize $3.00
- Bicycle – Fourth Prize $2.00

The parade started at 6:15 PM on Saturday, September 28 with Howard McCrory as the Grand Marshal. Over two thousand people were on hand for the event. Approximately seventy-five babies from Fayette City, Allenport, Charleroi, Belle Vernon, Lynnwood, Washington, Newell and Speers lined up at the vacant lot at the corner of Main and Cook Streets and marched up Main Street to Market Street and then up Market Street to the schoolhouse. The Fayette City Drum and Bugle Corps kicked off the parade followed by the babies accompanied by their mothers or sisters. The carriages and floats followed the babies and the Marion High School Majorettes and Marion Band brought up the rear.

The prize winners were announced on the steps of the schoolhouse. Billy Shook of Fayette City was named the King of the parade and Kaye Louise Trickett of Belle Vernon was named the Queen. Billy and Kaye were also given the privilege of leading the Second Annual Baby Parade the next year. The 1947 parade had one hundred twenty-four entries, an increase of 65% over the previous year, and was viewed by more than two thousand five hundred people. Annual baby parades continued to be held in Fayette City for the remainder of the 1940s and into the 1950s. A new tradition had begun.

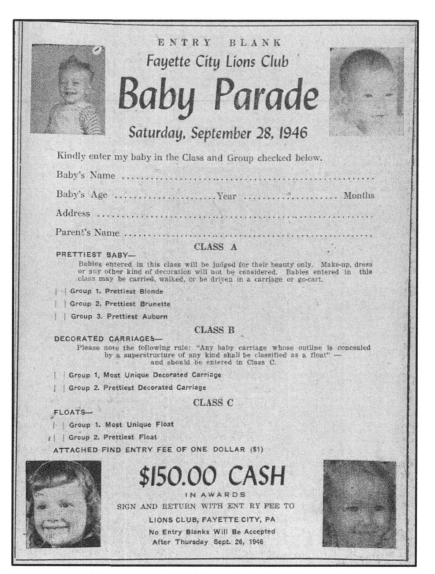

ENTRY BLANK

Fayette City Lions Club

Baby Parade

Saturday, September 28, 1946

Kindly enter my baby in the Class and Group checked below.

Baby's Name ....

Baby's Age ....Year .... Months

Address ....

Parent's Name ....

CLASS A

PRETTIEST BABY—
Babies entered in this class will be judged for their beauty only. Make-up, dress or any other kind of decoration will not be considered. Babies entered in this class may be carried, walked, or be driven in a carriage or go-cart.

| | Group 1. Prettiest Blonde

| | Group 2. Prettiest Brunette

| | Group 3. Prettiest Auburn

CLASS B

DECORATED CARRIAGES—
Please note the following rule: "Any baby carriage whose outline is concealed by a superstructure of any kind shall be classified as a float." — and should be entered in Class C.

| | Group 1. Most Unique Decorated Carriage

| | Group 2. Prettiest Decorated Carriage

CLASS C

FLOATS—
| | Group 1. Most Unique Float

| | Group 2. Prettiest Float

ATTACHED FIND ENTRY FEE OF ONE DOLLAR ($1)

$150.00 CASH

IN AWARDS

SIGN AND RETURN WITH ENTRY FEE TO

LIONS CLUB, FAYETTE CITY, PA

No Entry Blanks Will Be Accepted
After Thursday Sept. 26, 1946

Fayette City Journal
August 23, 1946

"I remember the baby parades. I had a bicycle at that time. They also had along with that a bicycle parade. My sister and I went to the local stationery store. I don't remember what the name of it was. But we bought these big pieces of cardboard and tried to make an elephant out of it. We put it on the bicycle, and we rode down Main Street. One year I remember Tommy Dorcon, I think that was the name, little kid, was one of the winners. Yeah, that was a big event also."

-Shirley Ferree Stilgenbauer

Fayette City Journal
October 4 and 11, 1946
Photos of Fayette City's
First Baby Parade.

Organizations like the Lions Club and the American Legion Post were dominated by men, as was the custom then. The women, seeking to express their own interests in bettering the community, organized the Fayette City Woman's Club in September of 1947. The Club was led by Mrs. Aland Dent, wife of the esteemed Doctor, and within weeks had outlined its program for the next six months. The first regular meeting of the Woman's Club was held in the home of Mrs. W. Glenn Burig, the widow of the recently departed principal of the Fayette City School, Glenn Burig. One of the first activities of the new Club was to raise $100 for curtains for the new school auditorium. The Club grew quickly and had more than sixty members in less than a year. In 1949 the Club landscaped a park at the south end of town in the area that had been created by the new one-way traffic pattern. The Club maintained the park until 1968 when the Borough assumed responsibility.

Another prominent civic organization was the Brightwell-Daugherty Post No. 484 of the American Legion. Post 484 was formed around 1930 and named after two Fayette City residents who were killed in World War I, Carl Brightwell and Partick Daugherty. With the end of World War II, the Post

Woman's Civic Club Organized By Local Women At Meeting

On Monday evening, September 15, a group of civic-minded Fayette City women gathered at the home of Mrs. Aland Dent to discuss the possibilities of organizing a Woman's club. On Monday evening of this week, another similar but more organized meeting was held in the Fayette City school building, and plans were furthered for the new group.

Election of officers was a main feature of this week's meeting, and resulted in Mrs. Dent being chosen as president; Mrs. Glenn Burig, first vice-president; Mrs. John Wilson, second vice-president; Mrs. Miller Boag, corresponding secretary; Mrs. George Troth, recording secretary; Mrs. Howard Opfar, treasurer; and Miss Permelia Bald-win, parliamentarian. In addition to the officers, election was also held for a by-laws committee. This group is composed of Mrs. Lydia Beazell, chairman, Mrs. George Hancock, Mrs. Walter Ridgeway, Mrs. Mildred Janeri and Mrs. George Troth.

The third Monday of each month was designated as the meeting night of the club, although the women plan to meet every Monday evening until fully organized. The roster now is composed of thirty-six members. The name of the group has been chosen as the Fayette City Woman's club and their purpose will be civic improvement and betterment.

At next Monday's meeting, Mrs. Dent will announce her supporting committees for the year.

Fayette City Journal
September 26, 1947

experienced somewhat of a resurgence. In November of 1945 the Post purchased a piece of property on Main Street which it intended to use as its new home (and where it still resides today). A year later Fayette County judge H. Vance Cottom granted the Post a charter making it an official corporation. At that time the Post's assets were approximately $4,000, with $2,400 in liabilities which included $1,500 from remodeling the Post's new home. At the end of 1946 Post 484 initiated a class 300 new members freshly back from the War. The Post had an active American Legion Auxiliary consisting of women who served in the military or were the mother, wife, sister or daughter of someone who did. A Junior Auxiliary was also created for anyone between the ages of 12 and 20 and whose father or brother was a member of the American Legion.

The motto of the American Legion is "We Serve In Peace As In War". True to organization's motto, the Fayette City Post served not only its members but the entire community of Fayette City as well. One of the first post-war activities of the Post was to sponsor an all year round athletic program which included basketball, bowling and most notably baseball. In the spring of 1947, the Legion sponsored its first baseball team with Joe Alberta as manager. This team was destined to become legendary by the end of the decade. The Women's Auxiliary held an annual fundraiser selling poppies that people could wear to show they remember and honor the sacrifice of those who died in battle. The Auxiliary also began to sponsor a Girl Scout Troop in 1947.

The Legion was most well-known, however, for sponsoring the annual Memorial Day exercises and parade. Annual Memorial Church services were usually held on the Sunday prior to Memorial Day. The Union (or joint) Memorial Church services were rotated among Fayette City's seven churches with a Union choir providing special musical selections and the sponsoring Church's pastor providing the message. On Memorial Day, the parade began at the school grounds and then proceed down Main Street and up Connellsville Street to the Cemetery. Members of the Legion would march along with the Fayette City Drum and Bugle Corps and the Marion High School Band. Children would decorate their bikes in a most patriotic fashion and join in the parade.

The ceremony at the Cemetery included the presentation of school awards. Beginning in 1927 the Brightwell-Daugherty Post recognized the outstanding boy and girl from the eighth grade with a medal. Qualifications for the award were scholarship, courage, honor, service, and leadership. (Winners of this award include two of the narrators for this book.) The eight-grade boy was responsible for reciting the Gettysburg Address while the girl would recite "In Flanders Field". The service would conclude with a firing squad and taps performed by members of the Legion.

"Memorial Day, that was always our last day of school. And we had a parade and decorated our bikes up. We went up the hill to the Cemetery and then they had a program up there. That Memorial Day Parade was a pretty big parade for a little town. They shot the guns off at the cemetery there. That's where they gave a pin to the eighth grader who was graduating. They had to recite "In Flanders Field" during the ceremony up there. They had all servicemen up there at the time."

-Willard Jones

"Oh my golly the Memorial Day parades. We got ready for that. And our bicycles, we would get our bicycles ready and get the crepe paper. It came in rolls and you'd weave the crepe paper in around the spokes of the wheels and then we had to push it all the way up on the hill and then ride it down. I said I was a little bit leery of riding down but we got down. They'd have the program every year. The kids got their American Legion award. And they would have to say their poem. Flanders field the poppies blow between the crosses row on row that mark our place. Why would I remember that?"

-Judith Tiernan Shearer

"In my eighth grade, Fayette City American Legion selected a boy and a girl who had been good students who had promise and we were honored at Decoration or Memorial Day in the cemetery in Fayette City. And the selectee, the boy had to recite from memory, the Gettysburg Address in front of the crowd there at the cemetery. The girl had to recite in Flanders Fields, The Poppies Grow.

I remember decorating my bicycle with red, white and blue crepe paper, flags on it. People would start downtown in Fayette City and literally march up town hill and come into the cemetery. People would come for days or weeks in advance to decorate the gravestones and put flags on it. That was a big, big day. And a lot of us boys would get our wagons out and go over the cemeteries as people came from distant places and were going to clean up their grave sites. We would volunteer for a fee to help them do that. We would make some money that way. But Memorial Day or Decoration Day was a very big event."

-Jack Young

"We lived up on the hill right by the cemetery. It was a double house. We lived on one side and Betty Mossberg and her sister and her husband lived on the other side. Now back then before Memorial Day, everybody scrubbed their porch down. You didn't do it with a hose. You did it by hand. The house was painted but that was hard scrubbing that down and the banisters and everything. But that's what everybody did. You scrubbed your porch down. You put your porch furniture out. You got them flags from the Legion and your sidewalk went up like this. You lined your flags up and then their flags up going across here. Every house coming up the hill had flags. Every house. Back years ago like before, they would have a parade for Memorial Day. They had all the school kids march in the parade, march up to the cemetery carrying flags. Then they decorated their bikes and they rode their bikes."

-Ella Maria Auther Davis

"(Memorial Day) always was a big day here in town. I mean, the Legion always had a parade starting in the morning. They ended up at Mount Auburn Cemetery by 11, o'clock. There was usually picnics all over the place, you know. Different families had their reunions. It was just a big holiday here. And of course, there was a lot of veterans. People don't realize the amount of people who served in World War Two here out of this little community."

-Jim Eley

"It was it was a big event. Everyone decorated and everyone, you know, put their flags out, all the flags up the sidewalks. The kids got in the parades. They had the parades downtown and everyone would try to outdo each other decorating their bicycles. It was a big event."

-Jack Gargan

"Well, when I was in eighth grade, I received the American Legion award, which was you know, that was a big thing on Memorial Day. I believe classmates voted on that. I forget how we were picked. But we had to learn the Gettysburg Address and Flanders Field. I can't remember which one. That would have been 1948 I think."

-Georgia Nicholson Slezak

Services Set For Cemetery

Everything is ready for the local Memorial Day services. The program calls for a big parade beginning at 10 a. m. with services at the cemetery following the parade.

All organizations of the borough are invited to participate in the parade which will form at the school grounds at 9:45 and proceed over downtown streets and thence to the cemetery.

Union Memorial Church services were held last Sunday evening at the Christian Church with all local organizations taking part. A fine program was presented with Rev. Bowers, pastor of the church delivering the main address.

The program for the exercises at the cemetery following the parade is as follows:

Invocation — Rev. Wallis

Hymn "America" — Audience.

Band Selection by the Marion High School Band.

Solo — Fred Weightman

Gettysburg Address — Fern Layne.

Band Selection

Duet "America The Beautiful"— Dorothy Salyers, Donna Jean Brewer.

Flanders Field — Erma Jane Smith.

The Answer To Flanders Field— Arlene Roley

Presentation of School Awards — Pat Hynes.

Address — Col. Coldren

Benediction — Rev. Bowers.

Firing Squad

Band Selection

Fayette City Journal
May 30, 1947

The Fayette City Volunteer Fire Department (VFD) was another civic organization that contributed to the community spirit in ways that often went far beyond its obvious firefighting responsibilities. The VFD aided in rescue operations, searched for lost children, cleaned the sewars and streets, pumped water from wells, cisterns, and cellars, and provided entertainment through parades and street fairs.

Fayette City had a long history of fires devastating large swaths of the downtown business district dating as far back as the late 1800s. Oddly enough, an effective fire fighting force was not always a high priority of the community. But by the 1940s, Fayette City had established one of the finest volunteer fire departments in the region. Their firetrucks were always a point of pride. At the beginning of the 1940s, the VFD's truck was only a few years old and was the pride of the community. By the end of the War, however, the truck had become worn out and outmoded. So in February of 1946, less than a year after the end of the War, the Fayette City VFD placed an order for a new truck from the American La France company for a sum of $6,000. Delivery of the new engine was expected in the following Fall. The only problem was how to pay for it. A variety of fund-raising activities were undertaken. Every year the VFD solicited donations from the community to buy new equipment and to keep it up to date. Donations typically ranged from 25 dollars to 50 cents. Just as had been done with so many of the other fund drives in the community, the Fayette City Journal published a list of the contributors and the amount contributed. It was not unusual for these lists to include all the businesses in town along with most all the citizens. The public list no doubt contributed to everyone's generosity. The VFD

Fayette City Journal
May 3, 1946

also held weekly dances and parties at the Odd Fellows Hall to pay for the truck.

The truck was delivered in a railroad boxcar at the local freight yard in August of 1947, almost a year later than planned. When word got around town that all that was needed to unload the truck was a ramp, "all kinds of help was available". The American La France fire engine was driven to the Borough Building at the corner of Cook and Fourth Streets as crowds gathered to admire the dazzling white beauty. Shortly after the new engine was checked out by the VFD, the old engine from the mid-1930s was sold to a volunteer fire department in

Fayette City VFD Fire Truck at the Borough Building circa mid to late 1930s.
Photo courtesy of Nancy Ferree Johnson.

144

Yorkville, OH. The new engine was put on display at the schoolhouse a few weeks later for the entire community to admire. The nearly two-year wait was well worth it. There was one unexpected problem with the new truck, however. It was a tad longer than the previous engine. So the rarely used jail cells at the back of the Fire Hall had to be rearranged to accommodate the extended length!

Fayette City's New Fire Truck

Fayette City Journal
August 22, 1947

Another favorite fund-raising activity of the VFD was the annual, week-long street fair or carnival. Every summer, typically in June, Market Street would be blocked off for the fair. A variety of games including Bingo and penny pitch along with sales of hot dogs and kraut generated funds for the VFD. The highlight of the annual carnival was a parade of firetrucks and marching bands. The parade route would usually begin in Johnson Hollow and proceed down Fording, south on Second Street to Cook Street, up Cook Street to Main Street, and then north on Main Street to Market Street where it would disband. Parades were curtailed during the War years, so the parade in the summer of 1946 was particularly festive. Twenty-six local fire companies participated in

"Big event it (the Fair) was, you know, because there wasn't a lot to do. The one I remember the most is the penny pitch. We used to pitch them pennies. Walter Zelinski, they called him Shindy, he always would be the guy to be raking them off and stuff you know. Well after he see us running out of pennies, he'd say oh, you had a winner and then he'd give you something, just for kids. Kids could do it too. Just throw them pennies on that little board. Do you ever see that? You had them little numbers and if they landed inside the number you get whatever amount it was, four cents, three cents, two cents. That was the biggest. And then food. The food was always good. It was just like a big event. When there's nothing going on, why not go to the carnival, right? That was good. It was good times them days."

-Jack Gargan

"The fireman would give a nice little box of Gene and Boots candy. I remember Mr. George Roy was Santa Claus for many years. As a kid, then, you know, we would go sit on his lap and tell them what we wanted for Christmas and everything. Finally, I kind of figured out that was Mr. Roy when I was a little bit bigger. So for years, I always called him Santa Claus when I would see him. Yeah, Mr. Roy, I remember him."

-Georgia Nicholson Slezak

"They always closed, they always closed the street off and had a big parade. They had the chuck-a-luck wheel. That was always a good time. That was a big event for a week in the summer."

-Raymond Moody

the parade along with the Drum and Bugle Corps from Fayette City and Belle Vernon. A couple of years later, with the War well behind the country, sixty-eight units from 53 fire companies participated in the annual parade. Fireman's parades like these were a common occurrence at the time with awards given for best truck, best band, and so on. With Chief Driver Earl Opfar and Fire Chief Lou Harris at the helm, Fayette City's new truck was entered in a parade in Uniontown just two weeks after the truck was unloaded at the freight yard. In a field of 140 fire departments, the new truck won first prize and a check of $75 and was the envy of Fayette County.

In addition to fighting fires, holding carnivals and participating in parades, the VFD provided another notable service to the community. Every Christmas, the children would gather at the steps of the schoolhouse to meet Santa Claus and receive a treat courtesy of the VFD with support from the community and local merchants. In true Fayette City fashion, the names of the contributors along with the amount of their contributions would be published in the Fayette City Journal. The hundreds of kids who participated in the event during the 1940s received much more than a treat. They also were left with an indelible impression of true community spirit.

"Oh my gosh, the carnivals. The Firemen's parade when all the towns around would bring their fire-trucks and they would have it. Then we'd have the penny pitch. We'd have the wheel. We'd have Bingo. We'd have hot dogs. And even in later years George and Jane (Hancock) would ask us to come on up and we'd sit on their porch. I remember one time playing Bingo. My mother said, "I'm not staying any more Judy. I'm going home." I said, "Well, I'm gonna play some more Bingo. What if I win? What do you want me to bring home?" You know, my mother goes, "Yeah, you're gonna win", you know? Well, she says bring home that that kettle. I need a new kettle. I said, Well, okay. Guess who came home with the kettle. I won Bingo. So I said, I'll take that kettle. I must have only been 9 or 10 at the most. I don't know. My mother said "Oh, for heaven's sake." She couldn't believe it."

-Judith Tiernan Shearer

"Oh, the fireman every summer had a fair and a carnival. That was usually held, they shut down Fourth and Market where Cani's...was. And they had the food stand. They had penny pitch. They had Bingo. Bingo was the big thing. I remember one year I won a baby doll playing Bingo. That was a big thing."

-Georgia Nicholson Slezak

"Well, there was Christmas Eve. At the schoolhouse every Christmas Eve, at six o'clock, the children would go and get treats that were handed out by the firemen. They were the red mesh, very stiff stockings. There was an apple, an orange, a candy cane, and a box of chocolates from Gene and Boots candy store. Gene and Boots was the Godiva of Charleroi and Fayette City. We would go over there every night. My father Guy Ferree would play Santa Claus. For years, I didn't know it was my dad and I could never figure out why he was never at home at six o'clock on Christmas Eve. But he was playing Santa Claus."

-Shirley Ferree Stilgenbauer

"The parades, the fireman's carnival once a year, and they had it right there on Market Street, right in front of our apartment. I remember it would be like a week long, from Monday through Friday. That was a big draw. People come to play bingo. They had a penny pitch. We used to go down in the mornings. We would go early to see if any pennies had fallen on the street to pick up a penny or two every day."

-Nancy Ferree Johnson

If there was one civic group that embodied community spirit, it had to be the Fayette City Drum and Bugle Corps, also known as the Golden Trojans. Fayette City has a long history with community bands dating back to at least the 1880s when the Monongahela Valley Republican newspaper declared that the Fayette City band was 'rapidly winning its way to the best in the valley." The early band often consisted of miners and would perform in support of striking miners in the neighboring patch towns of Fayette County. In the 1920s, the band was aligned with Fayette City's American Legion Post and would entertain parade spectators in their orange jackets and silver helmets. By the late 1930s Fayette City's Drum and Bugle Corps, now well known as the Golden Trojans marched with the

Fayette City Drum and Bugle Corps circa late 1930s.
Photo courtesy of Nancy Ferree Johnson.

Fayette City Volunteer Fire Department. As the decade of the 1940s began, the Trojans had a recurring column called "Notes on the Golden Trojans" with the byline "Pride of the Monongahela Valley" in the Fayette City Journal. The column provided updates on fundraising drives and future performances, along with a healthy serving of good-natured gossip about members of the Corps. Eugene "Ham" Johnson was the President of the Corps following Robert Pivarnik who held the position in 1939. The year 1940 proved to be eventful for the Trojans. They won best drum and bugle corps in the Labor Day celebration and parade sponsored by the Brownsville Industrial Committee and the United Mine Workers of America. The Junior Trojans "kid" unit was a big hit wherever they went. However, the

most memorable event of 1940 for the Trojans was an accidental shooting that sent two members to the hospital. As the story goes, Drill Sergeant Earl Opfar had borrowed a revolver form Fayette City Police Chief John Whitelaw

"They were a big deal after the war...The Drum and Bugle Corps performed at every public function, outside function, in Fayette City. And they weren't too bad. But all the parades they were in, and they were made up mostly of World War II veterans wearing their uniforms, their military uniforms. They did a pretty good job. They attracted a lot of attention, positive attention. Parades were a big thing in Fayette City. I mean the fire department had a parade every year. There was always a Fourth of July parade. There was a parade around Armistice Day. There was a parade around Memorial Day. They were all pretty big parades and the Drum and Bugle Corps performed in all of them."

-Mike Hancock

"Well, they wanted me to join. I played drums. I played drums in high school. I tried to join the Fayette CityDdrum and Bugle Corps and they wouldn't let me. So I joined with Belle Vernon......Fayette City, they were kind of a ragtag bunch. I think I know all the songs that, they only knew about three or four different songs. They had nice costumes though. They had big hats."

-Barry Hindmarsh

to accentuate his appearance in a parade in Port Vu, Pennsylvania near McKeesport. The gun, which Opfar thought to be unloaded, accidentally discharged. One bullet passed through the abdomen of Ralph Clegg, 22, and then the thigh of Jack Beattie, 18. Another bullet ricocheted through the crowd and struck a nearby bank building. Clegg and Beattie were color bearers for the Golden Trojans. Both young men survived the embarrassing incident.

Drum Corps To Purchase New Uniforms

Fayette City's crack drum and Bugle Corps are busy at work pre-paring for the parade season that is just around the corner.

In anticipation of keener competition and of a greater demand for their services, the local corps has just purchased new uniforms from the Exix Co. in the amount of $2,700.

The new uniforms which are of a military style are symbolic of the name Golden Trojans as the jackets are to be of a bright golden hue. A sample of the type of uniform purchasd is on display at Williams Pharmacy.

History of the Trojans goes back to several years before the war when the local corps was much in demand and copped many prizes as they strutted before the public. They hope to once again regain that position as they continue to practice faithfully.

Fayette City Journal
March 12, 1948

The Trojans continued to entertain crowds until the middle of 1942 when the drain on membership caused by the War made it impossible to continue. Soon after V-E Day, an announcement was made that the Drum and Bugle Corps intended to reorganize. By the middle of 1946, the Golden Trojans were once again practicing on a regular basis and preparing for future performances. Although thirty-five men had signed up to play, Fred Dreyer, the new head of the organization, was looking for at least thirty more. In his plea for more members Dreyer said, "It is not necessary that you be able to play an instrument to become a member because the local corps is prepared to teach those who need teaching." It wasn't long until the Trojans were winning prizes again, like the award for best drum and bugle corps at the 1948 Armistice Parade in Monongahela before twenty-five thousand spectators. The Trojans would continue to wow crowds well into the 1950s with Bill Ciavarra leading the 70-member strong band. Although some detractors thought the quality of the Trojan's musical performances was lacking, there was no disputing the effervescent spirit of the group that represented Fayette City with pride.

"When I think of the Drum and Bugle Corps, I think of one person. Bill Ciavarra. That's the guy I always think of. I'm sure I knew other ones. But his name always comes up when I think of the Drum and Bugle Corps because he was like the leader of it. I think he was. Yeah, he did a good job. They were good."

-Jack Gargan

"Oh, well, they were in every parade in Fayette City. Billy Ciavarra really took off. He'd take that baton and swing it, and he would march, you know, to lead the band. It was really nice. I always said he was the best tailor who ever lived, Billy Ciavarra. He was a wonderful tailor. He learned off his dad."

-Audrey Tiernan Repka

"Billy Ciavarra was the head major. They had the most beautiful uniforms. They were black and gold. They had these hats that sort of reminded you of an old Australian hat bent up on the side. On the side that was bent up there was a golden feather plume."

-Grace Hough Martin

"I do remember he (Guy Ferree) was with the Drum and Bugle Corps and he marched with the Corps every time they would go anywhere. He was very involved with that and the fire department and a lot of the activities in Fayette City. But I remember he used to, he would have to babysit. My mother would be going or doing something so he would take us to the parades with him. And he would say to us, "I have to march". He would park us on a corner somewhere or somewhere along the street. And he would say to us "Don't you dare move, you don't go with anybody, you don't do anything. As soon as I get through with our marching, I'll come and pick you up." And he always did."

-Nancy Ferree Johnson

"They (the Trojans) went every place there was a parade, a fireman's parade. Every city had them. I was a majorette and we just, we just traveled here there and everywhere. After the parade, all the guys went to the local bars. And the girls were just, you know, the guys all went and had a beer. We'd march three or four miles in some of those parades. But I remember it was long."

-Joanne Cunningham Manetta

"I was in the Drum and Bugle Corps. Well, I was in the second time around. I wasn't old enough in the first, the first original Corps. But the second Corps, Billy Ciavarra, seems like he was in charge of it. And oh, we had a great time. We had good looking uniforms. We strutted ourselves. We did pretty well too. We did pretty well. It was a good time. We got to go all over to Valley, all over the state actually. It was a good time."

-Raymond Moody

"Well, I remember they had flashy yellow uniforms. For a while they had like silver World War One helmets they wore with him. All the towns whenever they had celebrations, then drum and bugle corps from the different towns would trade back and forth. I remember Fayette City was really proud whenever they were sort of invited and went to Winchester, Virginia for the Apple Blossom Festival. They looked snazzy."

-Jack Young

"I remember the Drum and Bugle Corps. Not too many people could play. They just walked and pretended they were playing. Of course Billy Ciavarra was the head of it. He would parade first and that's about the end of that."

-June Cramer Yevincy

Fayette City Drum and Bugle Corps with Bill Ciavarra child mascot, circa 1928 (Top).
Fayette City Golden Trojans Drum and Bugle Corps with Bill Ciavarra drum major, circa 1950s (Bottom).
Photos courtesy of Stephen Russell.

Anyone passing by Fayette City on the Monongahela River could not help but be impressed with the grand schoolhouse buildings at the head of Market Street directly up from the local dock. Their prominent location and impressive architecture emanated a sense of civic pride. Indeed, Fayette City took great joy in its school system and in the quality of students it produced.

At the beginning of the 1940s, the Fayette City school offered grades one through twelve, which was convenient considering there were only twelve rooms between the two buildings. With the elimination of the high school in 1946, the Fayette City school was left with grades one through eight, and a few extra rooms. In December of 1946, local parent Mrs. Marriott inquired about the possibility of offering a kindergarten like the other neighboring school districts. The school board studied the proposal but ultimately decided there wasn't enough interest in the community to add the new grade. The school board eventually acquiesced, however, and in the Fall of 1949 Fayette City had its first kindergarten class.

Easter Parade of the first kindergarten class in Fayette City.
Photo courtesy of Georga Jean Arrow.

The two school buildings had always suffered from a lack of an auditorium and gymnasium. Plans for adding these facilities were proposed in the late 1930s and early 1940s but were never approved by the Board. Fayette City's basketball team was relegated to playing in the Opera Hall of the Odd Fellows Building on Main Street using the baskets and backboards which had been removed from the YMCA when the St. Eusebius Church took over the building. In 1938 both school buildings were the beneficiary of a W.P.A. project at no cost to the school district. The project added new restrooms in the basement, new fireproof stairs in the big building, new lights in all of the rooms, new paint inside, and a new flagpole. One of the rooms freed up with the elimination of the high school grades in 1946 was soon converted to a small auditorium complete with a stage, curtains and rows of fixed chairs for the audience. The new auditorium was inaugurated in November of 1947 with two sold out performances of the play "Lazy Town".

During the 1940s the school board was populated with some of Fayette City's most prominent community leaders including Alfred Makepeace, James Hamer, George Hancock, John Cameron, Dr. Aland Dent, George Roy and Stephen Figel.

William Glenn Burig was the principal of the Fayette City School at the opening of the 1940s. He was elected principal in 1936 and served in that position until his death from a brief illness on January 14, 1945, which ironically was also his 46th birthday. Burig was survived by his wife, who was a teacher at the school, and two daughters Helen and Ester. The Burig family, like the majority of the school's faculty, resided in town. In fact, the Burigs lived across from the schoolhouse on Fourth Street. For Burig's funeral, Mrs. Burig had him laid out in their living room as though he had fallen asleep reading a book. Students and parents alike filed through the Burig home to pay their respects to the beloved principal. At the end of that school year, the first annual Burig Award was given to Umberto DeRienzo as outstanding graduate of his class. Miss Bess Welch, one of the school's teachers, became acting principal upon Burig's death and served until Jack Hoyes was appointed full-time successor. Hoyes' tenure lasted just two years. Once again, Bess Welch served as acting principal until a permanent successor, this time John

Schoolhouse Auditorium.
Photo courtesy of Linda Russell Nelson.

Wheeler, was named. Wheeler closed out the eventful decade as the school's principal. The teachers in the 1940s included, among others, Mrs. Burig, Mrs. Barker, Mrs. Batwinis (later Yusko), Mrs. Wilson, Mrs. Wheeler, Mrs. Welch, Mrs. Wyatt, and the unmarried Nelson sisters Lucille and Hildred. Almost all the teachers lived within walking distance to the school, which only added to the deep connection between the school and the community. They were not only teachers, they were next door neighbors as well. Many of the teachers had lifelong tenures in the Fayette City school. Indeed, several of the teachers mentioned above continued to teach until the school closed permanently in 1971.

"My cousin Shirley Ferree was 11 months older than me. So when she started to school, especially if I knew they were having a party, I would go and climb up the fire escape on the side of the building and look in, especially if I knew they were having a party. And I would be invited to come in and join. So we kind of laughed, I kind of went to first grade twice because I was kind of a party crasher back then. Then second grade, I had Miss Lucille Nelson for first. I had, she was Mrs. Genevieve Williams, Genevieve Jones, who became Mrs. Genevieve Williams for second grade. And then I believe Lucille Nelson came in. And then Mrs. Williams also had third grade, Mrs. Burig had the fourth grade. That was in the building that set to the far right. Then the other building was the high school. I went to fifth, sixth, seventh and eighth grades there. For fifth grade I had Mrs. Bess Welch. She was very good on geography."

-Georgia Nicholson Slezak

"I remember every teacher. There was no kindergarten at that time. I started first grade, I think about 1939, 1940. Miss Hildred Nelson was the teacher. My mother said that she had had her for a teacher and she taught my daughter. So she was the Mother Superior I think of school teachers. She was wonderful. Second grade I think Lucille Nelson taught. Then I had Mrs. Burig and then her husband, Glenn Burig, at one time was the principal of the school."

-Kathleen Walton Stimmell

"I'll tell you, the teachers was good. Mrs. Barker. Mrs. Welch. Mrs. Burig. They were all good. If you didn't get what they were teaching in the regular hours of school, you stayed after school until you got it. I mean, they were loyal teachers and probably they didn't make a lot of money then either. But they was good teachers."

-Joe Vargo

"My fifth-grade teacher was Mrs. Barker. I was quite wild and independent in fifth grade. You can imagine all the hormones floating around.... I misbehaved sometimes. After I made a fool of myself for taking a dare from a girl, I got two paddlings from Mrs. Barker. The second one changed my outlook on life. I thought why are all of these other students getting on the honor roll and I kept getting in trouble. I believed I was as smart as most of them and I decided I would start concentrating on better performance. Very difficult for me then. From then on, I would reach the honor roll just about anytime I wanted."

-Bill Williamson

LIST HONOR ROLL FOR FIFTH PERIOD

The honor roll for the fifth six weeks period in the Fayette City public schools has just been released by the new supervising principal, Jack Hoyes. Following are the names of those who made the roll:

Seniors
Umberto De Rienzo, Grace L. Brightwell, Betty Rutledge, Lena Steele and Kenneth Evans.

Juniors
Esther Marie Burig, Beverly Yvonne Carlson, Jeannine McKenna, Catherine Alesandra Turek, Mildred Virginia Welsh and William Morgan Trezise.

Sophomores
Nancy Ann Davis, Anna Fedora, Anna Sobek and Olga Yetsconish.

Freshmen
Ruth Ann Rutedge, Shirley Mc-Crory, Gertrude Markish and Oliver Niemala.

Eighth Grade
Jean Auther, Mary Ellen Barker, Betty Dewar, Anna Helga, Eileen Jones and Catherine Russell.

Seventh Grade
Blanche Park, Elizabeth Mae Hamer, Leah Marrioft, Catherine Calcek and James Ridgway.

Sixth Grade
Kathryn Lorinchak, Margaret Allen, Audrey Dewar, Nancy Ferree, Dana Badwin, Violet Martin and Kathleen Walton.

Fifth Grade
Jack Young, Joe Alberta, Rita Erdely, Billy Arrow, June Cramer, Tommy Lee Davis and Shirley Ferree.

Fayette City Journal
May 4, 1945

Before the high school was eliminated in 1946, the Fayette City Journal published regular honor rolls listing the outstanding students from the fifth through twelfth grades. After the elimination of the high school, the honor roll was limited only to the fifth through eighth grades.

"School wasn't my favorite subject. I'd rather been out outside than in school. But you learn. Well, we had Mrs. Welsh, who is a teacher. She made history enjoyable. Then we had the Nelson girls, Lucille and Hildred Nelson that taught school for years. I think every kid in town either having one or the other in first or second grade. If you had problems, they were there and they helped you."

-Jim Eley

"I attended the school from first grade through the eighth because by that time they had done away with the high school. So that would have been like 1939 to 1947.

He (Mr. Burig) was very well liked. Kind of a quiet man. But one thing I do remember when he died, he got sick. When he died, instead of having him in the funeral home, Ruth Burig had him laid out at home on a couch as if he had fallen asleep reading a book. Folks were allowed to go in for the viewing. We were allowed to go in and see him sitting there on the couch. I remember that so well. It just stuck in my mind. That's what she did. Instead of the funeral home she had him laid out at home."

-Nancy Ferree Johnson

"I remember a boy in my fourth-grade class said the word dam one time in school. Mrs. Burig went over and got his head in her arm and stuck a bar of soap in his mouth. She'd be in jail now."

-Audrey Tiernan Repka

"I was in the first kindergarten class at Fayette City School in 1949 to 1950. I went in the afternoon…..There were two kindergarten classes; one in the morning and one in the afternoon. The younger ones that were like four, you know, going to be five, they went in the morning. The older ones went in the afternoon."

-Georgia Jean Arrow

"I had, there was the Nelson sisters, Hildred and Lucille, Mrs. Burig, Mr. Wheeler, Rose Batwinis. She taught kindergarten. And there was another, Bess Welch. That's about all I can remember. Bess Welch was a real good friend of my mother's. In fact, when Bess retired, my mother and she used to go to Florida together. My mother went down there for a couple of months just to get away. That was right after my dad died and all."

-Barry Hindmarsh

"For Lazy Town, I played one of the major roles in that play. So I do remember going over spending time in that auditorium. It was upstairs as far as I could remember. It seemed like the sixth grade was across the hall. And the auditorium was on the other side. And then in that hallway is where they rang the bell, but they never let me ring that bell. I always heard someday I was going to get picked to ring the bell. I remember they would pull that rope, and their little feet would go up in the air as they were ringing that bell. But I didn't get to ring the bell."

-Linda Russell Nelson

"I remember having a lot of music. We would sing. Most of the teachers played the piano. And then we would sing, sing songs which I thought was great. We had the bands, the rhythm bands. There were sticks you could play. There was a triangle. There was a tambourine. We did that. And then we would go outside for recess. I remember staying after school and cleaning the erasers. First grade was Hildred Nelson. Second grade was her sister Lucille Nelson. Third grade was Genevieve Jones Williams. And then I had Mrs. Burig, Ruth Burig for fourth grade. And then fifth and sixth, I had Thelma Barker. And then around that time was when Mr. Wheeler came to Fayette City. I had him for seventh grade. That was upstairs. And then you know, they had made whatever it used to be, they made that into an auditorium. In fact, I have a picture of us having a play in there. Then eighth grade, I had Anna Wyatt."

-Judith Dewar Shearer

"The kids in our class were very close. The teachers took a lot of time with us. It seemed like the people were all, they were all good students. The teachers were all very good to us and like I say we were very, very close. Mrs. Barker was a teacher. She was the, Raymond Barker was the high school principal and Mrs. Barker taught in Fayette City. There was Mrs. Wyatt and Mrs. Welch. John Wheeler was a principal there. I think he taught math too. His wife taught there, Dorothy Wheeler. Hildred and Lucille. I wouldn't have passed them up!"

-Raymond Moody

"First grade was Hildred Nelson. She was just the nicest lady. Second grade was Lucille Nelson who was her sister. They more or less were, I would say, well, they were old maids, or spinsters. They never married. Third grade was Mrs. Burig. She lived on…..Fourth Street. I don't remember who the fourth grade teacher was, but fifth grade was Mrs. Welsh. Mrs. Welsh was also the principal of Fayette City school at the time. Sixth grade was Mrs. Barker."

-Grace Hough Martin

"We were the first kindergarten class. That was 1949 to 1950. We were the first kindergarten class and Rose Batwinis was the teacher. I think originally she taught third grade before that....But anyway, what was unique was she had the four year olds in the morning....And then in the afternoon, she had the five year olds. But that was the only year that she had that because after the War, we had the all the babies being born and enrollment increased. So when I went to second grade, there were then two first grades. When I was in second there were then two third grades, because there were a lot of kids. But we were always the only grade. We were the only second, the only first, the only sixth. But the one grade ahead of us always had two rooms, and the grade behind us had two rooms. Mrs. Batwinis taught kindergarten. She later became Mrs. Yusko.

After kindergarten, we went over to the smaller building for first grade. That was Miss Hildred Nelson. I loved her. She's the one who inspired me to be a teacher. I loved her so much. I wanted to be a teacher. So she was first grade. She never raised her voice. We learn to read with the Sally, Dick and Jane readers...And then second grade, I expected to have her sister Lucille Nelson, who was unmarried also. When I entered the building Hildred Nelson said no John Richard, you go upstairs. Second grade is upstairs, Miss Cookham. So I went upstairs and we had Mrs. Cookham, who was the complete opposite of Miss Nelson. Miss Nelson was soft spoken and never yanked you or shook you or grabbed you. And then we went to Mrs. Jean Cookham. We sat at tables in kindergarten, first and second grade. So when you're at tables you tend to talk. She would bring in these white rags. If you talked, she put it under your chin, up above your head, and tied it. You looked like a rabbit, a white rabbit. You could not do that today to children. Or she would put you out in the hall. There was a landing there with a coat rack. And she would put you in the hall with others and we would do our workbooks. We would do them all together. One day I put my name on my paper before she said put your name on your paper. She put me out in the hall. I was standing there and the door opened down below and who came in but Mr. Wheeler. Everybody was frightened of him. So I hid in the coats and he saw my shoes. He brought me out. He took me into the room and he wanted to know why I was out there. She told him. He told her he will learn more in the room than being in that hall. Third grade was Mrs. Barker, who was a happy teacher. She also inspired me to be a teacher. That was the first time we sat at a desk was in third grade...And that's where Georgia and I became real friendly, in third grade because our desks were together. Then fourth grade with Mrs. Anna Wyatt. She was the opposite of Mrs. Barker. She was loud and she paddled. I was afraid of her. Then fifth grade we went to Mrs. Welch. She taught my father. Mrs. Wyatt taught my dad too....And then in sixth, we went up to Mr. Wheeler, who was also the principal. He inspired me to be a teacher too because he was sort of more modern.

Everybody lived in Fayette City except Mrs. Cookham. Mrs. Cookham lived in lower Belle Vernon. Mrs. Wyatt lived on Second Street in that blonde brick house. Mrs. Welch lived close to where you lived. The two Nelson sisters lived on town hill close to St. Edward's church. Mrs. Barker lived across from the cemetery. Mr. Wheeler lived on town hill, down a house or two from Joan Grados."

-John Vargo

"I attended Fayette City elementary school up through the eighth grade. By the time I got to the eighth grade, there was about 12 people with me. We were with each other for those eight years. We had wonderful teachers, the Nelson sisters, everybody remembers the Nelson sisters, taught first and second grade and had other very, very good teachers.

Fayette City schools, the elementary school was a brick structure to the right of the main building. The main building at one time had a high school in it. I went to elementary school in the smaller building. As you face the front of the eighth grade, there was a smaller brick building, and that's where I started up through grade four. And then we moved over into the bigger building. There was no high school then, just the fifth, sixth, seventh and eighth grade there.

I was good academically. Myself, Joe Alberta, and Rita Erdely, were sort of three top rung people with grades when they came out. And then you had a grade at the bottom for citizenship. I would often have straight A's except in citizenship where I would get a C or a D. I was told I talk too much and asked too many questions and wouldn't shut up when I was supposed to....When I was in eighth grade, I had never gotten a whipping in school. But in our family and a lot of other families where if you got a whipping in school, you would get one when you got home. Well, when I was in eighth grade, I went upstairs in what used to be the high school part of the school. There was a big blackboard up there. I drew a picture of the rear end of a horse. And then I drew an arrow down like he was taking a poop. I just did that. I didn't put my name on it. Now I went back downstairs. And then they found it. And then they found out that I did it. My cousin Doris Wheeler was the assistant principal at Fayette City. So after school that day, she came in, she bent me over the front desk and had that big, big paddle. She laid into me about two or three times. That's the only whipping I ever got in school. But my dad did give me one when I got home that night to keep things honest."

-Jack Young

Fayette City Students

The honor roll for the Fayette City public schools was announced this week by acting principal, Bess Welch and gave the names of those who made the honor roll for the first semester of the 1946-47 term:

GRADE 5 — Regina Erdely, Margaret Falusky, Mary Ann Puskas, Dorothy Zelenski and Mary Elizabeth Layton.

GRADE 6 — Virginia Scullion, Robert Cunningham, Kenneth Karcesky, Georgia Nicholson, Julia Dohanich, Dorothea Yelanich.

GRADE 7 — Jack Young, Keith Stark, Rita Erdely, Joe Alberta, Shirley Tiernan.

GRADE 8 — Audrey Dewar, Kathleen Walton, Margaret Allen, and Dana Baldwin.

Fayette City Journal
February 14, 1947

Gillespie School News

The following pupils from Gillespie School were on the Honor Roll for the second six weeks period.

Grade 1, Willis Gardner, Georgeanna Pudish, Eleanor Hamer; Grade 2, Joseph Summers, Annette Dankowsky, Heisdy Gardner; Grade 3, David Krivda, Barbara Krivda, Jean Parkins; Grade 4, Betty Smider, Patricia Prewett, Eileen Gardner; Grade 5, Melandi Fidnarik, Thomas West; Grade 6, Florence Prewett and Elissa Turek.

Fayette City Journal
December 7, 1945

LOVEJOY SCHOOL HONOR ROLL IS ANNOUNCED

Mrs. Olga Smith, principal and teacher at the Lovejoy school announces the honor roll for the period just ended.

First grade: Harry Jolly, Phyliss Deline, Warren DeMoss, Patricia Rice, and Howard Gage.

Second Grade: Doris Miller and Jack Vargo.

Third grade: Sharron Roley nd Nancy LaRew.

Fourth grade: Kay Jo Butler and Almeda Nichols.

Fifth Grade: Irene Helmken, Sally Ramsey and Polly Ann Vargo.

Fayette City Journal
October 12, 1945

The Journal also printed regular updates on neighboring Marion School (where the Fayette City High School students were sent) and two local elementary schools from Brownstown and Gillespie. The Gillespie Elementary School was located a mile or two outside of Fayette City and had an enrollment of about 50 students in grades one through sixth in the mid-1940s. Brownstown's even smaller Lovejoy Elementary School consisted of two one-room buildings with grades 1-3 in one building and grades 4-6 in the other. When the Bellmarette jointure between Marion, Belle Vernon, and Fayette City was formed in 1951, both elementary schools were closed, and the children were sent to Fayette City. The large schoolhouse in Gillespie was converted into the Slovak Citizens Club which was destroyed in a blaze in 1960.

"What it (Lovejoy) amounted to, there was two school buildings. There was a one building where there was first, second and third grade with one teacher. And then in the other building, there was fourth, fifth and sixth grade with one teacher. It had a potbelly stove; an old potbelly stove was the heating element. The thrill of the day was getting to dust the erasers. If you can make it to be a patrol boy, you had a badge and a thing you put on and you'd stand out there and guide the kids across the street in the mornings. Then later, you'd put the flag up and put it down and stuff like that. That was your, that was your thrill of the day. In the class I was in, there was five and in the other class maybe had a couple more, maybe seven or eight. So we figured five, eight, thirteen. It wouldn't even be 20, I don't think in the whole building."

-Jack Gargan

"My cousins, Polly Ann and her brother Jack, lived above me. They both went to Lovejoy because the line went through our backyard. My parent's house was in the Borough and Uncle Paul's house was in Washington Township. So they went to Lovejoy. It had two rooms. A primary room, an intermediate room for grades four, five and six. There were two outside outhouses, two outside toilets. One for boys, one for girls. The one room was grades 1, 2, 3. And the other room was grades 4, 5, and 6."

-John Vargo

No discussion of the Fayette City School would be complete without mention of the annual May Day celebration. May Day was usually celebrated on May 1st or the first Monday in May. The event marked the traditional first day of summer and involved dancing around the Maypole and crowning the Queen of May. Every grade and almost every student participated in some way in this elaborate annual event.

The 1946 May Day celebration was held on the school grounds for the entire community to attend. Norma Jean Roy was voted May Queen. Her Senior Attendants were Ester Burig and Jeannie McKenna. The Junior Attendants were Florence Sobek and Nancy Ann Davis. The Sophomore Attendants included Ruth Ann Rutledge. The Freshman Attendants were B. Dewar and Eileen Jones. The theme for the event was a Mexican May Fiesta and was designed to offer the community some insight into the manners and customers of their neighbors to the south. The event was described as one of the biggest events ever held by the Fayette City schools and was attended by several hundred local people. Newspapers throughout western Pennsylvania lauded the school's good will gesture in presenting such a program. Little did the students, and the rest of the community for that matter, know that this would be the last May Day celebration for the Fayette City schools. The high school and this event were eliminated the following school year. With this last class, more than one tradition had come to an end.

The Queen and her attendants at the May Day Celebration on May 10, 1946.
Photos courtesy of Audrey Tiernan Repka.

"The most fantastic May Day was probably the last one around 1945. it was held on the school grounds, right at the Fayette City school. It was a Mexican Fiesta. Norma Jean Roy was the beautiful princess with the tiara and I think Billy Trezise was the prince. They had the Mexican hat dance. Every grade had something. Those were big times back then, the May Day. Before they had it at the school, they used to have May Day down on the ball field down there where they played baseball."

-Georgia Nicholson Slezak

"We would go down to the ball field in Fayette City. We learned to do little dances. I know one time we had a little Irish dance. There was a May Queen and her court. They did a gymnastic thing…. I remember that. This was May and most of those young men were going to the army next month. And they did. So that would have been 1942, 41 or something like that. And then after that they discontinued the high school. So it was only up to eighth grade."

-Kathleen Walton Stimmell

"I don't know where the idea originally came from. It's a labor union thing I think, the idea of May Day. But schools all over the country did that in those days. It really wasn't unusual that we did it. It was out in that school yard. I've seen films of that somebody had. But I have no idea where they were or when they would be. But it was a celebration of sorts with hot dogs and you know, that kind of thing. The Maypole was erected in the middle of the schoolyard and the girls would dance around it with these ribbons of cloth that they held. Where it came from, I don't honestly know."

-Mike Hancock

"And every year in May, we would have May Day, which was a big event for the school. All the grades participated. They would have the Maypole. The senior girls would be in their different colored evening gowns and do the Maypole dance. Each grade had a different part in it. I remember one year, the theme was Mexican. I remember doing the Mexican hat dance. My grandmother, Martha Walton, everyone referred to her as mom Walton, would go down to the ball field, sit with her hat, white gloves and umbrella, and watch her grandchildren during their performance."

-Shirley Ferree Stilgenbauer

Churches

Fayette City's seven churches, the counterweight to its seven bars, were the anchor of the community in the 1940s. Four protestant churches, two Catholic churches and a Later Days Saints Church offered a variety of theological doctrines from which to choose. The Protestant churches included the Methodist Church, the Church of Christ, the Presbyterian Church, and Brownstown's Christian and Missionary Alliance (CMA) Tabernacle. The two Catholic Churches included St. Edwards on South High Street and St. Eusebius on Main Street. Except for St. Edwards, all the churches advertised their services in the Fayette City Journal during the 1940s. The Methodist Church in Allenport, the Christian and Missionary Alliance Church in Braznell, and the Christian Science Church in Monongahela also advertised their services in the Journal.

Fayette City Methodist Church circa 1940s.
Photo courtesy of Perry Weightman.

The decade of the 1940s saw numerous changes in the leadership of Fayette City's churches. The Methodist Church, Fayette City's oldest church, was the largest and most active church during the decade. Pastors lasted about two years on average and included A.J. Howes, Louis Wallis, G.L. Smith, E.A. Stephenson, and George L. Bayhs. Pastors at the Church of Christ included Clarence Sloss, J.R. White and John Bowers. Bowers served an unusually long term from 1942 until 1959. The Presbyterian Church was serviced by pastors from the "student supply" (i.e., seminary students) during the entire decade including Russell Hilty, David Molyneaux, D.L Zacharias, Prescott Williams, and H.D. Hough Jr.. Pastors for the CMA Church were Daniel Andresen, A.G. Biggins, and C.R. Ellenberger. Pastors for the LDS Church were Samuel Winship, James Hough, and Arthur Warner.

"The Presbyterian Church and the Methodist Church were very, very conservative Protestant churches. They did a lot of things together. They did musical performances where the two choirs would perform together. They had fundraising dinners, where they would support each other."

-Mike Hancock

The Protestant Churches along with the LDS Church often held joint services for important events such as Memorial Day, Thanksgiving, Easter, and the National Week of Prayer, demonstrating a unified community in its commitment to glorifying God. Their pastors were regular speakers at meetings of the Lions Club. The CMA church held annual missionary conventions for the community. St. Edwards and the Methodist Church sponsored Boy Scout and Girl Scout troops, respectively. These are just a few of the many examples of how Fayette City's seven churches served and brought unity to the community.

Good Friday Services Here

Next Friday, April 19, from 12 noon until 3 p. m. there will be a Community Good Friday service in the local Methodist church, under the sponsorship of the local ministers.

This service is open to the general public. "Words of the Cross" will be the theme for the service. All local ministers will take part in the program, which includes seven speakers.

The afternoon's worship will be so arranged that anyone wishing to, may attend for any part of the service.

Fayette City Journal
April 12, 1946

To Organize Union Choir

An effort is being made by members of the choirs of the various local churches to present a union choir at the Memorial Day services.

All members of the various local choirs are asked to attend the first rehearsal which will be held at the local Methodist Church on Monday evening, May 24, at 8 P. M.

Fayette City Journal
May 21, 1948

"We went to the Presbyterian Church. There was a lot of churches in town, and but except for a few, you were either Presbyterian, Methodist, or Catholic. They were very important. They were like the center of social life. There were women's groups activities and children's programs, holiday parties. Every summer there would be a vacation Bible school. Every church would participate. There would be different activities at different churches. We would march through town singing Onward Christian Soldiers, going from one church to the next to do the next activity."

-Nancy Ferree Johnson

"There was a Presbyterian Church and a Christian Church also. There were two Catholic churches; one down by McCrory's funeral home. He later bought it and had it for storage for his funeral home. There was a Catholic Church up on the crest of town hill that looked over.. I think the one downtown was an Irish Catholic church and on the top of the hill was a Slovak Catholic church because they didn't get along too well sometimes. There were a lot of churches."

-Kathleen Walton Stimmell

To Observe Prayer Week Jan. 5 to 12

National Week of Prayer will be observed in Fayette City January 5 to 12 through a series of union services planned by the local ministers. "Prayer" is the general theme of the services all of which begin at 7:30 p. m.

Sunday and Monday evening's services will be in the Latter Day Saints church; Tuesday in the Christian Church; Wednesday and Thursday the services will be held at the Methodist Church; on Friday the Presbyterian Church will be the host; and on Sunday the Christian Church will again be the scene of the services.

Local ministers will do the speaking for the services and special music will be presented at every service.

The public is invited to attend all these services.

Fayette City Journal
January 3, 1947

Union Church Services Here Next Thursday

Thanksgiving Union Services will be held Thanksgiving morning November 28 at 9 a. m. in the local Methodist Church.

Rev. John Bowers, pastor of the Christian Church will have charge of the program. The invocation will be given by Samuel Winship and the scripture reading by C. R. Ellenberger, pastor of the Brownstown Christian and Missionary Alliance Tabernacle. Special music will be rendered by the Presbyterian Church Choir. Rev. E. A. Stephenson, pastor of the Methodist Church will deliver the sermon and the benediction will be given by Samuel Winship of the Latter Day Saints Church.

An invitation is extended to the community to attend and unite in worship.

Fayette City Journal
November 22, 1946

The two Catholic Churches have a shared history dating back to the beginning of the century. St. Edwards was founded in 1902 as a "mission church" by Saints Cyril and Methodius Catholic Church of Charleroi. After spending a decade in the old Presbyterian Church on South High Street in Fayette City, they constructed a buff-colored, Romanesque church further down the same street. Just prior to construction of the new building, St. Eusebius formed as an offshoot from St. Edwards driven by language differences in the congregations. St. Eusebius purchased the YMCA building on Main Steet in Fayette City and converted it into their sanctuary. St. Eusebius was a "mission church" of the T. Joseph Roman Catholic Church in Roscoe, PA, and catered more to those of English and Irish decent. St. Edwards catered to the Slavonic languages and congregants from Eastern Europe and Russian. St. Eusebius was serviced by supply priests during the 1940s including Rev. J.H Wilhelm from St. Joseph's. St. Edwards was also serviced with supply priests in the 1940s including Revs. John and Valentine Sedlak from Cyril and Methodius who served from 1940 until 1947. In 1947 Rev. Charles W. Ribick was appointed as full-time pastor of St. Edwards. Ribick served the Church through 1957. Eventually differences in the congregations became less an issue and after more than fifty years apart, the two Churches reunited in 1964 as the Holy Spirit Church.

Name Priest To Local Church

The Rt. Rev. Hugh C. Boyle, bishop of the Pittsburgh Diocese has appointed Rev. Charles W. Ribick, as the pastor of the local St. Edwards R. C. Church.

Rev. Ribick comes here from Donora where he served as assistant at St. Dominic's church.

Until the appointment of Father Ribick as resident pastor, St. Edward's was a mission church of the Sts. Cyril and Methodius Church at Charleroi and was served by Fathers John and Valentine Sedlak.

It is reported that the new pastor will move to Fayette City as soon as housing is available.

Fayette City Journal
June 20, 1947

YETSCONISH

Mike Yetsconish, died August 15, 1947, at 11:30 a.m. at his home on Cook Street Extension, due to complications. He was born in Austria on November 19, 1878, and was 68 years of age.

He was a member of the Russian Brotherhood Organization No. 25 of Fayette City, and the Holy Trinity Greek Catholic Church of Charleroi.

Friends were received at the late home until Tuesday, where at 2 p. m., services were held in charge of Rev. Gregor Soroka. Interment followed in the Belle Vernon Cemetery.

He is survived by his wife, Mary Yetsconish, two daughters, Mrs. Martin Markovitch of Fayette City, and Mrs. George Kosiba of Detroit, two sons, Mike of Fayette City and George of Detroit. Nine grandchildren also survive him.

George M. McCrory & Son were the funeral directors in charge.

Fayette City Journal
August 22, 1947

The language differences that resulted in Fayette City's two Catholic Churches can be traced, at least in part, to the residents of Navoo Hollow. The great coal boom in the early 1900s attracted an influx of immigrants from the Slavic and predominately Catholic countries of southern and eastern Europe. Navoo Hollow, with its proximity to the large Fayette City and Apollo Mines in Sisleytown and Gillespie, enticed the miners to live in the company homes. So many of these immigrants lived Navoo Hollow that it became known by the broader Fayette City community as "Hunky" or "Russian" Hollow. In fact, the Hollow even had its own chapter of the Russian Brotherhood Organization. Fayette City's original settlers were of Irish, English and Scottish descent. Consequently, the cultural and linguistic differences, not to mention differences in historical ties or lack thereof to Fayette City, created the need for separated congregations. Navoo Hollow was isolated from the rest of Fayette City not only by geography but by these ethnic differences as well. In the 1940s, many of the grandparents and even parents of the families in Navoo Hollow were first generation Americans. They took great pride in their heritage and traditions as demonstrated in their family recipes and immaculately kept gardens. Nevertheless, they were persistent in encouraging their children to assimilate into this new world of which they were now a part.

"They (the churches) played a big part in the community. There were all kinds of churches. Families, they dressed up on Sundays and went to church or Sunday school. If I played sick because I didn't want to go to church, I wasn't allowed out the rest of the day. I mean, she made me stay in. So now we had to go to church. My dad and I, we both went to classes to join the Presbyterian church together. In fact, I still have the Bible that they gave me. And I even got a mustard seed bracelet they gave me. My mother was already a member of the church before my dad and I joined. They thought it was nice that we joined together."

-Georgia Jean Arrow

"We used to have seven churches and seven bars...I used to know all of the bars and every one of the churches. But I'd have to sit down and try to remember and write them down. But we used to laugh about it. There was only one town with seven churches and seven bars. We had an even number. But the church was very important to everybody back then. You went to Sunday school. I don't remember staying for church after Sunday school. Maybe we just had Sunday school and then just stayed there while you know, our family was in church. Oh my gosh, back then there was so many people in church. It was unreal."

-Ella Marie Auther Davis

"Well, the Catholics, most of them were the Slovaks. Not many Italians. Ukrainians came in and there was a Catholic Church, a large Catholic Church. I remember them ringing the church bells. I forget exactly where in Fayette City it was. It wasn't right in town. But it was a big stone building. And that's where that's where they worshiped. They weren't, they didn't mingle like people do today. Everybody had their church. Everybody had their seats, had the same seat every Sunday."

-Shirley Ferree Stilgenbauer

"When I was in ninth grade we moved down to the Presbyterian Manse, which was right on the corner. Now there's an educational building that used to be Weightman's hardware store. We lived in the manse for probably seven or eight years. I think we moved down there about 1942 or 1943....The Presbyterian Church never had a regular minister. They would send out what they called supply from the seminary in Pittsburgh. During the summer, they would come and either stay at our place or in the Masonic building where the druggist Bob Williams and his wife lived. We called them Uncle Bob and Aunt Molly. They had a separate wing that had a bedroom and a bathroom and all that. And sometimes the minister would stay there."

-Judith Dewar Shearer

"There was a Methodist Church and Presbyterian Church. I remember going every Sunday and we had to be dressed up. We wore a hat and gloves. The church started at 11 o'clock and ended at 12. And then the younger people went into the Sunday school rooms. There were big accordion doors going from the main church into the social room. There was a kitchen behind there. They used to have Christmas and holiday programs where the children all participated....If you were Presbyterian, you shopped at Moravek's grocery store. If you were Methodist you shopped at Stockton's....If you died, you went to John Bakes if you were Methodist. If you were Presbyterian you went to McCrory's. The elder Mr. McCroy had fans that he would leave on the seats for people to use in the summertime. I remember sitting there. It was like an accordion style fan, nice size, with a long wooden handle with his name and phone number on it."

-Shirley Ferree Stilgenbauer

"The Methodist Church, when they had a vacation Bible school, there must have been close to 100 kids there....The Presbyterian Church is the first one I ever attended. H.D. Hough was the minister there. I liked that church. In fact, Mr. Hart lived there. He used to send everybody a postcard on their birthday, of some place. It wasn't necessarily Fayette City. And he signed them. He had a stamp made with a little red heart."

-Audrey Tiernan Repka

"That's the one area where I would say that there were a significant number of first and second generation immigrants in Fayette City. That much I remember when I delivered the paper. But when I delivered the paper, and I was talking to the people who lived there, many of them didn't speak English at all, and others spoke it with a heavy accent, which suggested to me that they're a immigrants. I would say that was a fair amount of the population in Navoo Hollow. I don't know why it's that way except that's probably where they could afford to live when they came here. They came probably to work in the mines."

-Mike Hancock

"I remember going up Navoo Hollow, all them people, John Canigiani called that Russian Hollow…. People took care of their properties. The hillsides, they used to cut the hillsides with the scythes. They had grapevines and pear trees…We used to go up there and they'd make wine. I watched them make wine. The Hollow was clean, the creek was clean then….. They were Russian and Slovak, but he (John) called it Russian Hollow. There was a lot of Yetsconishs there. They had 12 kids. I think they were all Russian and then on up from the border of Yetsconish's they were Russians. The Helas were Russians. There was a bunch of Helas in there. They were Russian and got along. But there was like Mr. Turek there. He was something."

-Jim McKevitt

"Most of them (from Navoo Hollow) attended St. Edward's Catholic Church and that was your social life, the church and the activities of the church. And then the church built that picnic grove up Johnson's Hollow. That's where everybody gathered on Sundays with the church picnics, because they had the dance floor and the pavilions, the bingo hall and the food hall and where the men could buy their alcohol and all the games such as penny pitch.

St. Eusebius was downtown next to McCrory's (Funeral Home). St. Edwards was for the people from Eastern Europe because those people spoke Slovak and Polish and Croatian. St. Esuebius had their own church because they weren't from Eastern Europe. They were more Irish and southern Italians. But then in the 60s they were combined into St. Edward's which then became Holy Spirit."

-John Vargo

"I'd say that most of them (in Navoo Hollow) were from the Slovak countries. Czech, Slovak, Yugoslavia, Hungary, Poland, Russian, in those countries, you know. They came over in early 1900s. And it was just, they had to get out of where they lived because they weren't living there. I mean, just nothing but war over there. Every year, there's another war coming. I want to tell you about them, all of them. I just mean them all, I mean, Polish. Yugoslavian and Czechoslovakians, and there was some other ones. They mentioned Russia. They became the best American citizens you could ever want….Many of them would refuse to talk their native language when their kids were around. They wanted to make sure their kids understood English and became an American and not fall back into what they were before."

-Bill Williamson

"Navoo Hollow, a lot of foreign, European immigrants lived in Navoo Hollow back when I was a kid. A lot of those immigrants were Russians or other European extractions. I remember I used to think boy, they have a break because they have Christmas after we do. They get to get their Christmas trees cheaper because they get marked down and then the Russian boys and girls could get cheaper Christmas trees. But there was a very different atmosphere. In fact there was almost a standoffishness in the youth at least. We used to play a lot of ball up in an area called Ridgway. It was about two thirds of the way down town hill on the side. Never would any of the boys with the exception of one or two come up out of Navoo Hollow to play. They were like sequestered back in there. I was half afraid to go up Navoo Hollow. It was rough."

-Jack Young

The political scene in Fayette City in the 1940s was active and anything but boring. This was never more apparent than in the race for Burgess at the opening of the decade.

In 1940 U.F. Higinbotham, Fayette City's beloved dentist and the son of the Fayette County Commissioner Arthur Higinbotham, was midway through his term as Burgess when he swore in the newly elected officers of the reorganized Borough Council. Joseph Moravek was voted President. Michael McDonough was voted secretary and treasurer. Other Board members included John Canigiani, Joseph Bell, and James Thirkield. John Whitelaw was renamed chief of police. In the Fall of the following year, the office of Burgess was on the ballot. Higinbotham had opted to run for Justice of the Peace instead of for another term as Burgess. John Canigiani won the Democratic primary for Burgess and was projected to win the election in November since there were no candidates in the Republican primaries. The citizens of Fayette City, however, had something else planned. In a so-called "sticker campaign" Higinbotham was elected Burgess with 295 ballots versus Canigiani's 203. Higinbotham was also elected Justice of the Peace, the office that he actually sought. In response to his double election Higinbotham said "Two offices definitely are too many. Don't ask me what I'm going to do about it. All I can say is: 'This to so sudden.'". After a moment of reflection, he went on to say "Oh, gee, what will my wife say when she finds out there are two offices to keep me away from home." In January of 1942, Dr. U.F. Higinbotham was sworn in a Fayette City's Justice of the Peace and Burgess. By the Spring of that year, Higinbotham resigned as the Justice of the Peace to focus on his job as Burgess. The Governor of Pennsylvania, Arthur H. James, appointed Edward D. Steinman, Jr., the son of the owner of the Fayette City Journal, to serve as Justice of the Peace until January of 1944. Higinbotham never did get to serve out his second term as Burgess. In September of 1943, he died suddenly at the age of 38 after complications from an appendectomy. The Fayette City Borough Council elected James M. Hough, a former Council President, to serve as Burgess in place of the Higinbotham. George Ferris was elevated to Council President and Edwin Hindmarsh fill the vacant Council Position. Alvie "Rip" Usher was reappointed chief of police

By the middle of the decade, Hough was still Burgess and the Borough Council consisted of Jim Eley, George Ferris, William Gardner, Claude Davis, Edwin Hindmarsh, M.P. McDonough, H.B. Barker and Carl Frantz. Earl Opfar served as chief of police for a short period of time but left for other opportunities allowing Usher to serve as chief once again. But another election was on the horizon. James Hough ran unopposed for Burgess. Alfred Makepeace who had won the primary for school board director passed away and was replaced on the ballot by George Roy. The election in November of 1945 was a clean sweep for the Democrats with the exception of Republican Wilbur Evans's victory as Inspector of Elections.

The new Borough Council was sworn in in January of 1946. Edwin Hindmarsh was voted President, and McDonough Secretary and Treasurer. Rip Usher was once again appointed chief of police. Before the end of the year a major dispute erupted regarding the salary of the Borough's health officer (a new position recently mandated by the State government). The Burgess was dead against giving a health officer $20 a month

Burgess		
James M. Hough	280-196	476
Council		
George Ferris	251-206	457
Lawrence Mugrage		218
James Eley		268
Leroy Gardner		241
Frank Dewar		240
Raymond Barker		233
Edwin Hindmarsh		245
Tax Collector		
Charles L. Humphries		316
James V. Welch		192
School Director		
George Roy		292
George G. Hancock	238-150	388
Albert Walton		240
Justice of the Peace		
Wilbur B. Evans	235-185	420
Judge of Election		
Charles Kuhns	279-200	479
Inspector of Election		
Sue Opfar		300
Wilbur B. Evans		174
Auditor		
Miller Boag		2

Fayette City Journal
November 9, 1945

since he received no payment as Burgess for doing his job. Hindmarsh suggested that they take enough off the cop's salary to pay for the health officer. Usher immediately offered to turn in his badge if they did. William Gardner, another Council member, agreed with the Burgess stating that $20 a month is too much for health officer since there wasn't enough work to be done. Hindmarsh sharply replied, "Is a cop worth $185 a month?" to which Gardner replied "Absolutely." Tensions on the Council were clearly on the rise and destined to only get worse.

By the middle of 1947, tensions had reached a boiling point. In February of the preceding year, the Borough Council passed an ordinance outlawing parking on Connellsville Street. Traffic on the steep hill made parking on either side of the street untenable. The ordinance was not popular with everyone and was seldom enforced by the chief of police. At a Council meeting in April of 1947 two council members, Leroy Gardner and William Gardner, demanded to know why the no parking ordinance on Connellsville Street was not being enforced. An excerpt of the discussion is provided at the left. At the Council's next meeting a week later, Burgess Hough and chief of police Usher tendered their resignations. Hough had two years and eight months left in his term. The following week, James Thirkield was unanimously appointed on a resolution by William Gardner to fill the unexpired term of James Hough. Thirkield, a resident of Fayette City for 44 years, was immediately sworn in as the new Burgess. Earl Opfar was once again hired as chief of police to replace Rip Usher. Before the year was out, however, Opfar resigned for a better job and Rip Usher was appoint chief of police for the fifth time. Monongahela's Daily Republican newspaper referred to the "oft-changing police situation in Fayette City" when it announced the change. Fayette City's reputation for law enforcement had been firmly locked up.

The elections of November 1947 brought three new members to the Borough Council. In January of 1948 John Canigiani, Lawrence Mugrage and Frank Rihtarcik were sworn in joining George Ferris, the President, and M.P. McDonough, the Borough Secretary, on the Council. Rip Usher was appointed chief of police. During 1948 the Council voted for one of the largest tax increases Fayette City had ever seen: a $5 head tax and a 2 mill increase on property. The Council also added a ten-cent tax per ton on coal mined or dumped at tipples in the Borough as a means of discouraging any further coal mining.

> Next the oft discussed parking situation on Connellsville Street flared up with two of the councilmen demanding that ordinances in the borough be enforced.
>
> Following is some of the discussion that was had on the subject.
>
> William Gardner: "The Burgess should fine violators of parking laws." He continued, "The Burgess is making a fool out of council."
>
> Leroy Gardner: "I think the Burgess should fine someone when the cop gives them a ticket."
>
> William Gardner: "The Burgess has left Wilbur Evans go three times."
>
> Hindmarsh: "I understand that is because the street isn't properly marked."
>
> William Gardner: "Why does he fine one man then and let another go. I can't see no sense in coming here and holding a meeting if it doesn't mean anything."
>
> Leroy Gardner: We don't need a cop in this town, he doesn't do anything.
>
> William Gardner: "I make a motion that the President of Council contact the Burgess and tell him to enforce the law."
>
> This motion was seconded by Leroy Gardner with no one voicing any opposition.

Fayette City Journal
April 25, 1947

Before the end of the decade, Rip Usher once again resigned as chief of police. Charles Weiss, Charles Hazlett, and Joe Cvetan applied for the coveted position. Although Weiss had the backing of many of the townspeople, Joe Cvetan was unanimously appointed the position by the Council in front of a packed room of visitors who attended to see the outcome. As a departing shot to the Borough Council, Usher refused to return the uniform the Council had furnished him a few months ago. This act of definance led the Council to pass a resolution forbidding the future purchase of uniforms by the local Council with public funds. The 1940s were indeed a colorful and spirited decade of political activity.

"There was a big house there right below (where I lived). And I looked at it. I don't know why, but I started to throw stones from above onto the roof. Well, I thought this was a lot of fun back then and continued with my attack. At a point I turned around for more rocks or more stones to throw. There he was, the town policeman or one of his assistants in full uniform with gun and all. I don't remember if it was Rip Usher or some other one before Rip was policeman. Off to jail we went. I don't remember if he put me in handcuffs or not. I think he might have. I sat there to jail for almost an hour or two thinking of all the horrible things they are going to do to me. After an hour or two of confinement, the policemen returned and asked what I learned from this experience. He told me he will let me off if I promise never to throw rocks or stones on people's houses again and if I would go with him and apologize to the house owner and asked him for his forgiveness. I quickly agreed. And I've never been in jail again."

-Bill Williamson

"It was a quiet little town and not much went on. There was no crime. We had one policeman. I think his name was Rip. They called him Rip, and his last name was Usher. He was very tall and wore a hat and patrolled the streets. He didn't have a car. I remember his gun being in a holster on his hip. And he would patrol the streets and again, there wasn't much going on in Fayette City, but he was a fixture there. In the wintertime he'd wear a leather jacket which was fur trimmed with his policeman's hat. It looked like a cowboy hat. Everyone knew Rip. We were afraid of him. We knew we had to behave, or we'd get put in jail."

-Shirley Ferree Stilgenbauer

FAYETTE CITY BOROUGH COUNCIL
Budget Resolution

Be it Resolved by the Council of Fayette City Borough:

That, having complied with the legal requirements, the annual budget as set forth in Schedules A and B, on file in the office of the Borough Secretary, is hereby adopted:

That for the expenses of the Borough for the fiscal year of 1945 the following items are hereby appropriated from the revenues available for the fiscal year for the following specific purposes, thereby constituting the necessary appropriation measure to put the budget into effect:

GENERAL FUND
Estimated Receipts

Cash balance for appropriation	$5,591.74	
Taxes from Current levy	5,024.70	
Taxes of prior years	1,900.00	
From miscellaneous sources	1,366.00	
Total estimated Receipts and Cash		$13,882.44

Appropriations

General Government: Administration	415.00	
Tax Collection	400.00	
Borough building and Offices	400.00	1,225.00
Protection to Persons and Property: Police	2,075.00	
Fire	725.00	2,800.00
Health and Sanitation: Board of Health	25.00	
Sewers and Sewage Disposal	200.00	225.00
Highway: Streets and Bridges	5,125.00	
Street Lighting	1,450.00	6,575.00
Miscellaneous	250.00	250.00
Unpaid bills of Prior years (to be paid in 1945)	250.00	250.00
Total Appropriations from General Fund		$11,325.00

SINKING FUND
Estimated Receipts

Total Cash and Securities	$2,996.26	
From Taxes	2,885.62	
Total estimated receipts, Cash and Securities		5,884.88

Appropriations

Interest and State Tax	494.00	
Bonds to be retired	1,000.00	
Total Appropriations from the Sinking Fund		$1,494.00

That any resolution conflicting with this resolution be and the same is hereby repealed insofar as the same affects this resolution.

Certification

I hereby certify that the foregoing is a true and correct copy of the resolution passed by the Borough Council this 27th day of February, A. D., 1945   M. P. McDonough, Borough Secretary

3-23-c

The Small Things

Civic groups, schools, churches, and the political scene fostered an environment that enabled an exceptional community spirit to flourish in Fayette City in the 1940s. Community spirit, however, was most evident in the smaller things, the everyday person-to-person interactions that strengthened the bonds between neighbors. Two very disparate examples of these interactions are offered here.

Nearly all the men in Fayette City had nicknames given to them by their peers. It was a rite of passage, in a way, to have a nickname bestowed upon you, although not all nicknames were flattering or welcomed. You were now part of the community with your own unique moniker known only within the borders of Fayette City. A nickname often became so strongly associated with someone that, except for one's closest friends and family, people would forget the persons given name. A list of men's nicknames from the 1940s is provided in Appendix V.

The second example of theses everyday interactions was illustrated by the fact that everyone seemed to look out for one another. Fayette City was such a small community that everyone knew everyone by name (or nickname), where they lived, what they did for a living, where they went to church, what they did right, and where they may have fallen short. It was hard for anyone to have secrets, especially when some townsfolk could be best characterized as nebshits according to narrator Jack Young. But you knew that your neighbor was going to be there for you, to celebrate a wedding or birth, to mourn the loss of a loved one, to help with food or clothing, to run an errand, or to just lend and ear. These simple acts of kindness are the surest fruits of true community spirit.

> **Nebshit**
> Definition: Pittsburghese slang. One who is extremely nebby; one who is always involved in the business of others and is often a gossip.

"It seemed like every man and child, a boy, no girls, no mothers, had nicknames. No daughters had nicknames. Everybody else had nicknames. My nickname was strawberries. I had earned that because at one time I loved strawberries. I was at a relative's for some sort of dinner and my uncle was saying a blessing and it was getting rather long. I allegedly said to my mother when he finished his prayers, can I get his strawberries? Strawberries became my name...The barber was Fuzzy Opfar. The other barber was Doodles. The ballplayers everyone had a nickname. I think it's really interesting that nicknames were never given to girls. Shorty Brown, Lugs Russell, Ziggy Zajack, Pagetti Haywood, Brother Opfar. Almost their given name by the time they got to be an adult."

-Jack Young

"Oh my gosh, I am so glad I was raised here. I'm so glad that my children were raised here, and my grandchildren because it was still a nice place to raise your kids. When I was growing up, and even after I was married, I used to know everybody in down town, Sisleytown, up Navoo Hollow, up Johnson's Hallow, and up on the hill. I knew almost every house where a person lived. When I was a kid and we were out playing, if we did something wrong the neighbor could yell at us. Your parent wouldn't get mad like they do nowadays. If you yell at that kid, it was not my kid's fault. You know, my kid wouldn't do that. Blah, blah, blah. No, one of the neighbors would call and say hey, Ella Marie's bababababa. My mother naturally she believed the neighbor. I would get smacked before or even get a whipping, whatever you want to call it. But nobody got mad. You can holler to the neighbor, "Hey, did you see Ella Marie? Would you tell her to come home, it's time to eat?" It was like yelling back and forth. And back then you could leave your door open and just have the screen door and even leave the screen, cause we only had those hooks, leave it unlocked....This town was a great town to be raised in."

-Ella Marie Auther Davis

"Fayette City was a town, like I said, where everyone looked out for each other. You were safe in Fayette City. But your parents always warned you about strangers. This happened in Cherkins pharmacy drugstore. We called them drugstores then. While I was in there, looking at the candy, I was little but I remember, there was this man behind me. He said that he wanted to buy me the candy. Mr. Cherkins, he saw what was going on and he went and called my mother on the telephone. We lived above the Journal office. To the Cherkins Pharmacy, that was right by Joe Bells, within minutes, my mother was there, grabbing me. He saw you know what was going on and he called my mother…. Everyone looked out for everybody's kids. They also told your parents on you too, they did. They liked doing that."

-Georgia Jean Arrow

"Going up town hill there was Elaine Perry, Turk Perry's mother, I think. She would sit at her window all the time looking at people going up and down town hill. She was crowned the nebshit of town hill. That term is recognized in western Pennsylvania, maybe not many other places."

-Jack Young

"There was not much going on in Fayette City. My sister and I, my cousins Betty, Audrey and Judy Dewar and Georgia and Johnny Nicholson were basically the only kids in the downtown part of Fayette City. We'd run the streets and we kind of ran the town, if you will. Everybody knew us. Everybody wanted to feed us and give us cookies and crackers. The girls would run up and down the streets in our mother's high heeled shoes. So we all lived in this, again, very, very small town. It was a two-minute walk to one another. I remember those days. They were fond memories."

-Shirley Ferree Stilgenbauer

"It was a great place. It was a great place to live. It was a family town, you know. Everybody knew everybody else. It was just a family town. Most of the men in town worked at the steel mill in Allenport. Nobody had much of anything, but then we didn't need much, you know."

-Nancy Ferree Johnson

"Everybody knew everybody else and helped everybody else out. Just, just get along good. Just get along. That's all. That's all I knew. That's all I can say about all that. It was a good place to grow up. We grew up in one of the best of places and the best of times. A lot of people will never know what we enjoyed. There was nights when you would go down to Fayette City, you couldn't walk on the sidewalk there'd be that many people there. You didn't realize it then, but boy, you sure miss it now."

-Raymond Moody

"Everybody knew everybody's business. They looked out for the other kids. If someone saw you doing something wrong, your parents found out about it not long after you did it. You couldn't hide no secrets. It was it was a happy town. Like they had their beer gardens. They used to be like seven or eight beer gardens. Seven or eight churches."

-Larry Moskala

"The other thing, you know, you almost as a kid, you almost really couldn't get into trouble because if you did something you weren't supposed to be doing at one end of town until you go home at the other town your parents knew about it…. Everybody kind of knew everybody's business. I mean, there weren't too many secrets about things. But I don't remember that being a big problem."

-Georgia Nicholson Slezak

"Up on town hill, you walked down the sidewalk and you talked to everybody that's out on a porch….You knew everybody. They knew you. You knew their family, good and bad. I remember one time I was running down, we were going to the movies or something. I tripped on the road. It was broke, or something. Scraped my knee. Two ladies came off the porch to see if I was alright or needed a band aid and stuff. And I thought, people don't do that anymore. They're strangers, or they're afraid they might get sued for something. But it was a wonderful town to grow up in. It really was. You knew everybody, good and bad."

-Kathleen Walton Stimmell

"It seemed like every family in Fayette City looked after all the children when they played near or on their property. Everyone knew everyone. Us kids were treated as their own when in their presence. Just a wonderful, friendly place and time to go up."

-Bill Williamson

"On a Saturday, I would get up and tell my mother I was going to ball field. I had to be back when my dad got home from work. She had like a front porch grapevine system. I remember many times up on town hill, up on Connellsville Street, somebody on the front porch would say, "Strawberries! Your mother just called and said if I see you to tell you get home right now." You always had somebody looking out for you."

-Jack Young

"I think it was a pretty tight community. By that I mean everybody appeared to sort of look after everybody else kind of thing. Now that's, that's my point of view. I know that if I got in trouble downtown, my mother knew before I got home. So somebody would call her and tell her….It just seemed like everybody knew your business."

-Grace Hough Martin

REFERENCES

DiCiccio, C. *Coal and Coke in Pennsylvania*. Commonwealth of Pennsylvania, Harrisburg, 1996.

Fayette County Genealogical Society of Pennsylvania | Facebook
https://www.facebook.com/FayetteGenSociety

History of the Fayette City Christian Church provided by Audrey Tiernan Repka.

History of the Fayette City First Methodist Church 1842-1952 provided by Lauri Miller Thompson.

The American Legion a U.S. Veterans Association
https://www.legion.org/

The United Presbyterian Church, Fayette City, PA, 100th Anniversary Program provided by Eleanor Welsh Owens.

Urban Dictionary: Nebshit
https://www.urbandictionary.com/define.php?term=Nebshit

Wikipedia contributors. "Community spirit." *Wikipedia, The Free Encyclopedia*. Wikipedia, The Free Encyclopedia, 29 Jul. 2021. Web. 7 Feb. 2022.

Wikipedia contributors. "Lions Clubs International." *Wikipedia, The Free Encyclopedia.* Wikipedia, The Free Encyclopedia, 18 Jan. 2022. Web. 7 Feb. 2022.

CHAPTER 8 Fun and Games

Although the economic conditions of the 1940s were a vast improvement over those of the prior decade, everyday life was still difficult. Work in the steel mills and local coal mines was hard and most people often struggled just to get by. The challenges of everyday life made it all the more important for the residents of Fayette City to find those opportunities to have fun and enjoy themselves, even if in the smallest of ways. For example, Fayette City never turned down an opportunity for a parade, whether a baby parade, a fireman's parade, or a more somber Memorial Day parade. Swimming in the Monongahela River, with all of its dangers, was a favorite pastime, as was competitive horseshoe pitching. Baseball, of course, was not only the national pastime, but also the local pastime. These activities and more will be described here beginning with how the children found their enjoyment.

For the Kids

Fayette City lacked many formal facilities for kids to play despite the baseball field at the far end of town and some clay tennis courts near the water works. The cemetery on town hill was a favorite spot for kids to play to the dismay of the town's leadership. An empty lot near St. Edwards Church known as Ridgway's was a prime spot for a pickup ballgame. The local school didn't have a gymnasium, but it did have a small playground where kids would often gather on days off or in the summer to plan out their day. A favorite playground activity was sliding down the school's fire escape. The fire escape wasn't like the common external ladder and stair type. It consisted of a large round metal tube that exited from a small door in one of the second story school rooms, made a 90-degree turn, and then sloped two stories along the side of the building to the ground. The secret that every kid knew was that if you polished the tube with ordinary wax paper, that you would shoot out of the fire escape like a speeding bullet. In the summertime, it wasn't uncommon for rolls of wax paper to mysteriously disappear from the kitchens of homes across town and end up discarded on the school grounds.

Release the Belgium, sort of a team form of hide-and-go-seek, was a popular game in the various neighborhoods around town. The origin of the game is uncertain although it appears to be unique to Western Pennsylvania. Some history buffs have speculated that veterans who fought in the "Flanders Fields" of Belgium during World War I inspired the game upon their return home, an interesting, if unverifiable, hypothesis.

Burgess Issues Warning To Hill Youths

Burgess James Hough has issued a warning to all those who are making the local cemetery a playground and refuse dump that they will be prosecuted to the full extent of the law if they do not stay off cemetery property.

Hill district parents should see to it that children do not play on the cemetery property because they are running over graves, damaging markers, and destroying the property in many other ways. Parents whose children trespass on this property are liable to prosecution as well as the children.

*Fayette City Journal
March 30, 1945*

Another favorite game, particularly in the down town neighborhood, was kick-the-stick. This game was not just unique to Western Pennsylvania but appears to be unique to Fayette City. The game originated at the wharf at the intersection of Market and Front (or Water) Streets and resembled a poor-man's version of baseball. Bases were marked off with home base located at the base of the sidewalk steps where Market and Front Streets meet. First base was the cement pillar supporting the train trestle above. Second base was the steps at the opposite corner of Market and third base was an arbitrary spot in the middle of Market Street. A stick fished out of the River served as the "baseball" and was strategically placed against the steps at home plate. The batter would, as the name of the game suggests, kick the stick and run the bases as in a game of baseball. In a time when few people could afford a baseball and bat, a stick and a little imagination just had to be sufficient.

A particularly favorite time of year for the youth and young adults was Halloween. Halloween in Fayette City was more than just one day (or night). Kids usually started to trick or treat a couple of weeks in advance so that by October 31st they had worn out their welcome in the neighborhood. The older kids, on the other hand, focused more on the "trick" part of trick or treat. In the weeks leading up to Halloween, tic-tacking, or the throwing of corn against people's homes, was a favorite activity. Attempts to discourage the activity by appealing to the need to conserve food were unsuccessful. Tipping over garbage cans and soaping car windows were part of the fun too. Since most of Fayette City's school teachers including the principal lived within shouting distance of the school, they were often a prime target of the pranksters. In an attempt to quell the pranksters, each year the Burgess of Fayette City would post a warning on the front page of the Fayette City Journal notifying the pranksters that if they were caught damaging or destroying property they would be prosecuted to the fullest extent of the law. The annual warnings appeared to have little effect as the fun continued unabated.

Beware!

Beware Youngsters! Burgess James Hough issued a warning this week, after complaints have come to him in regards to Hallowe'en capers that are being performed in the borough.

Youngsters are upsetting and taking garbage cans and removing porch furniture, breaking bottles and in many numerous ways are destroying private property. and the Burgess warns that anyone caught will be taken by the police to the Burgess and fined.

The Burgess does not want to interfere with innocent fun, but when that fun becomes malicious mischief, it is time for action.

Parents are urged to keep their children out of mischief during the remaining days of the month until Hallowe'en.

Fayette City Journal
October 19, 1945

Beware Pranksters!

This is the time of the year when Hallowe'en pranksters are keeping local citizens busy watching their property, so the local Burgess James M. Hough has issued a stern warning that anyone caught destroying property will be dealt with according to the law.

In the case of a minor, the parents will be held liable and prosecution will follow.

Fayette City Journal
October 18, 1946

DON'T THROW CORN!

High food prices will not be lowered nor will hunger be lessened if food is wasted. The "Corn Night" of years ago is definitely a thing of the past and arrant waste is seen in reviving the custom. Parents of the children who think this is a harmless Halloween season prank should explain to them its serious nature and forbid the practice at once.

Fayette City Journal
October 10, 1947

WARNING!

Fayette City's burgess, James Thirkield, warned Hallowe'en pranksters this week that he will not tolerate vandalism that tends to destroy or damage property.

He asks that parents warn their youngsters against damaging property of others and also asks that parents cooperate in every way possible to keep youngsters from being destructive.

Fayette City Journal
October 7, 1947

"The only one (teacher) we've kind of harassed was John Wheeler. He lived up on the same street as the Nelson sisters. Halloween, it was just really rough on him. He is the one that got pranked all the time because he was the principal first of all. He knew who was doing it. He just went along with it. Somebody would take a **** in paper bag and then light it on fire and put it on his porch. And there was a ton of corn on his porch from tic-tacking. It wasn't anything real mean. But I think a bag full of **** was kind of a rough thing to do."

-Barry Hindmarsh

"At Halloween, we started October 1 as kids….We'd go around and people had to guess who we were. I'm sure if we got started on October 1, by Halloween people were fed up with us kids coming around, knocking on the door, you know, hoping to get a treat or something. That was always a big time. And then some of the bigger kids got into what we called it tic-tacking. They would throw corn at the windows. I think the worst thing that happened would be soaping somebody's windows or something. There was no terrible destruction or anything that I remember."

-Georgia Nicholson Slezak

"When we went trick or treating the teachers always gave out the best stuff. We didn't do one day, we did weeks, a week anyway."

-June Cramer Yevincy

"At Halloween you had trick or treat. Most of the boys did tricks. I remember one Halloween, I must have been in sixth or seventh grade. We were tricking. We were pulling some dirty stuff up on town hill. We upset people's garbage cans on their front doorsteps and threw tomatoes at their doors. Just generally raised hell. And we were going up towards Mount Auburn Cemetery from downtown and we went past Williamson's house, which was pretty close to where the Russell's lived. And then we went up and we came back the same route. We were going to split up. We made a pact that if anybody got caught, they'd never tell who was with them. I was a ringleader, and that was my edict. When we came back, Bill Williamson's older brother, Butch Williamson, grabbed me and everybody else scattered. He wanted to know who was with me. I wouldn't tell him. So "I'm taking you the constable." So downtown across from the Fayette City Methodist church was where that constable was…They were questioning me about why I was doing that and who was with you. I said, I'm not telling. Then they said, "Well, if you're not going to tell us we're sending you to reform school." So then I squealed on everybody. That was the end of my braggadocio leadership."

-Jack Young

Kennywood

The community picnic at Kennywood Amusement Park near Pittsburgh was always the biggest event of the summer, even during the War years. Each year the Volunteer Fire Departments from Fayette City, Washington Township, Belle Vernon and North Belle Vernon sponsored the event and worked with Park management to arrange special entertainment for the attendees. The Fire Departments also arranged for transportation to the Park since many, if not most, people had no vehicle of their own. In 1945, street cars from Allenport were arranged for Fayette City citizens. The street cars departed Allenport at 8:30AM and returned from the Park at 9:00PM. Riders were dropped off at the base of the hill below the Park and faced a steep climb to the Park's entrance. In later years, trains departed from the train depot in Fayette City and took riders to finals stops like Braddock, Rankin and Homestead. Trolleys or street cars would then take the riders to the Park. Round trip tickets cost about $1.50 for adults and 90 cents for children.

On "Kennywood Day", local merchants would close up shop since practically no one would be in town to shop. Families often carried their meals to the Park in ice chests and baskets and staked out a prime spot in one of the Park's many pavilions. It wasn't unusual to leave the food unguarded while everyone enjoyed the rides and activities, although occasionally someone's grandmother would camp out in the pavilion to watch over her handywork.

Local merchants sold strips of Kennywood tickets which kids coveted. Each ride required a certain number of tickets, so the more tickets you had, the more rides you could ride. Kids under sixteen who entered the Park before 2:00PM were given free tickets from the firemen.

In 1946, Kennywood boasted 38 major amusement devices, a completely overhauled pool, an extended miniature railroad, an open-air Dance Pavilion, and a new Bubble Bounce attraction for its 49th season. Over 3000 people attended the community picnic in 1946 making it the most attended community picnic ever. The end of the War and the return home of so many soldiers no doubt made it a particularly memorable affair.

Next Thursday is the Day! All the kiddies are going along with Maw and Paw and the usual picnic basket.

Committees report that everything is in readiness for the annual outing of the Fayette City, Washington Township and Belle Vernon Fire Companies at Kennywood Park.

Special street cars will be available to transport picnickers to the Park next Thursday, it was announced.

Committee chairmen have completed arrangements with the Street Car Company for special cars which will leave Allenport and Speers at 8:30 a. m. July 26.

On the return trip, the street cars will leave Kennywood at 9:00 p. m.

The fare will be $1.55 round trip from Allenport and $1.40 round trip from Speers. Only round trip tickets will be sold and even those will be limited, so hurry and get your tickets before they are gone.

Special cut-rate amusement strips are on sale at various stores here and in the Township. Local merchants will remain open all day Tuesday and close all day Thursday, picnic day.

Fayette City Journal
July 20, 1945

176

"It was fun going to Kennywood. We used to go on a train. There was a station up here and a lot of people packed their own baskets. Most people packed their own baskets. So you rode the train to Braddock. We rode to the train to there. Then from there we got on a streetcar and it took us in to Kennywood. That was a lot of fun."

-Ella Marie Auther Davis

"On Kennywood day, we would get on the train early in the morning. We could buy these strips of tickets. I think they were a quarter, they were at that time. They were affordable, but it was a luxury. We'd get on the train and spend the day in the park. My grandmother, Martha Walton, everyone called her mom Walton, she would cook for days. The men would carry these big coolers. They were big and heavy, like a five gallon or more jug of lemonade. There were no refreshment stands there. We would deposit our food and our grandmother at the food pavilion. We'd go and ride. My grandmother would sit there and she would watch the food so no one would take it. Then we would come back and we would have lunch, usually a meat loaf, deviled eggs, beets, a great big pot of potato salad, homemade bread, angel food cake. Those are the things I remember most of all. I believe it (the train) went directly to the Park. After we got off the train there was a big hill we had to climb."

-Shirely Ferree Stilgenbauer

"We used to go to Kennywood. If I recall, we used to crossover the River on the ferry and get on a train. I think that's how we did it, and went to Kennywood on the train. When we got off the train, there was like a trail went from the train track up over the hill, and you'd go up into the back part of Kennywood Park, like there was a gate in the back….That was always a big, big event for us. We went every year. We'd go down to Kennywood on a train like that. And then we'd have a lot of tickets, which was all your dad or mom could afford. When the people were leaving at nighttime, we would scrounge around to get someone who had a car so we could ride home later. So we'd scrounge around and collect them tickets. Then we stayed there until the last minute. That was a good day. Kennywood was big day…Everyone went."

-Jack Gargan

PICNIC DRAWS BIG CROWD

Although the war still causes an inconvenience to local people, many took advantage of the special street cars which awaited them at Allenport and Speers which went directly to Kennywood Park for the local community picnic.

However, a large share of the local residents drove to the picnic in their private cars, sharing with their neighbors, the empty seats.

Although a little rain fell here at home, the day was clear and perfect at the park.

Many forms of entertainment and thrills awaited the picnickers, such as the free act on the Lagoon Lake. Dancing was enjoyed by the younger set while kiddies rode the pippin, roller coaster, ferris wheel, etc.

Seven street cars carried the picnickers of the three districts to and from the park. All in all everyone enjoyed themselves and planned to attend again next year.

Fayette City Journal
August 3, 1945

PICNIC IS HERALDED SUCCESS

Heralded as the most successful community outing every held in this district was the annual picnic to Kennywood Park held last week.

Over three thousand people from the Fayete City, Washington Twp., Belle Vernon area attended the affair which was sponsored by the fire departments of the area. Train tickets were sold to 1161 people and an estimated 2,000 journeyed to the park in automobiles.

Following the free show at the Park Lagoon, prizes were awarded to the following people: Nick Mae, Joe S. Gonne and Jack Holder of Belle Vernon; Rudy Kobaska, Pill Nouiselli, Mrs. Robert Hamer of Washington Township; Garnet Price, Donald Vizza, Jakie Miller of North Belle Vernon; Lillian Coogan, Joe Alberta and Mike Hancock of Fayette City.

Perfect weather marked the outing with no accidents being reported.

Fayette City Journal
August 2, 1946

"Everybody would gather at the train station with their picnic baskets. The men in the town would move the baskets onto the train. We'd all get on a train, ride all the way to Kennywood. I don't know if you remember or not, but the train had like a landing a deck. I remember a wooden area was like a platform. The men would unload all the picnic baskets. Everybody would pick up their basket. And there was a steep hill at the platform into the park and we had to climb that hill, walk up that hill to get into the park. We would ride the rides all day long. At the end of the day, we'd get back on the train with our picnic baskets again and ride the train home."

-Nancy Ferree Johnson

"My brothers and I, we sold tickets for Kennywood for the fire department. They sold tickets to get into Kennywood. We got, I think it was a penny per strip of what we sold. We sold them for I think it was four strips for $1….We would sell tickets before Kennywood started and we would get a penny a strip. That was when they first started and then they jumped it up to you know whatever a fixed figure and they went. But when it first started, we went to Kennywood and they would sell tickets. Oh, we had a good time down there. They had a pavilion set up for the Fayette City firemen. That's where we would go to eat."

-Willard Jones

"You got on the train. You smelled the coal dust. And you went to Kennywood. You got off. You packed a lunch. They had picnic tables in the back. You put your lunch on the picnic table. You went and rode and then you come back and ate your lunch and it was still there. Nobody touched it. You couldn't do that today, I doubt it. And we came home on the train. The older people come in the, when I say older people I mean the 20 year olds, the ones that were dating, they come in and went to the ballroom to dance at night."

-Joanne Cunningham Manetta

Families waiting for the train to Kennywood circa late 1930s.
Photo courtesy of Nancy Ferree Johnson.

"We would pack up picnic baskets. At the time my grandmother was still living. Of course, when you got off the train, you had to take the streetcar to get over to Kennywood. And you took all the food with you....I remember my grandmother, mom, we called her mom because my great grandmother was still living. She was grandma. So my grandmother was mom. And mom would sit down. It was underneath and behind the old mill, I think. The old mill was here. The Jack Rabbit was here. And I think there was a road that went down. There were picnic tables. Well, my grandmother, God love her, would sit there all day with this food while we're running around."

-Judith Dewar Shearer

"Oh, they (Kennywood picnics) were big affairs. They were. The picnic lunches, baskets that were on the table that we used to run around and see if we could snatch something off of the tables, you know, because they just left it there and went to ride. We didn't make any messes, or anything, we'd just take a cookie or something like that. So, the community day at Kennywood was the big thing here. They had the train come in, you know, the train went down there. That's how we got there. Nobody would drive down there."

-June Winters Baldwin Jaquette

Swimming

Swimming was a popular summertime activity during the 1940s. Unfortunately, reaching the closet public swimming pool, Redds Beach, from Fayette City required catching a bus to Charleroi, and then changing buses to Cokeburg. So most of the kids and adults in Fayette City settled for swimming in the Monongahela River. The Mon, as many called it, wasn't known for its pristine waters. This was especially true of the River near Fayette City due to upstream runoff from the abandoned nearby coal mines, and waste waters from Allenport Mill and the chemical factory at Newell. But what other options were there?

The locals had two favorite spots for taking a dip: the Rocks and the Sandbar. The Rocks was located almost directly across from the Mill at south end of town. The Rocks lacked a beach but had deep water at shore's edge that made jumping from rope swings or the remains of an old mine tipple an activity for the adventurous. The Sandbar was located at the north end of town where Downer's Run from Johnson Hollow passed through a tunnel that ran under the railroad tracks and then emptied into the River. Sadly, swimming at the Sandbar was a segregated activity. The south side was reserved for residents of Fayette City and surrounding neighborhoods while the north side was open to anyone including any Negros, or coloreds, from nearby Arnold City or Belle Vernon. (The terms "Negro" and

"The daring guys would swim out, whenever the push barge boats, pushing the barges up to Pittsburgh. That was before diesels. They had paddle wheels on the back of the boats. The real gutsy guys would swim out and get as close as they could to the waves coming off those paddle wheels. I recall the names of each of those boats were painted across the side of it. The one that had the biggest wave was the Sailor...It would really raise hell going up and down the river. That was the thing to swim across the river and also swim in the waves of the Sailor, and you earned your spurs in Fayette City."

-Jack Young

"A lot of times we would swim up like going out of Sisleytown. There was like a rope swing and stuff down there. And we would swim out, that was an attraction, that rope swing out into the River. And then we'd try, whoever could swim the River was like a hero once you could swim that. That was a good swim across the River. But you learn to swim there because the current, you know, it was a different swim. You had to kind of be a pretty good swimmer. I did it a few times. Some other guys that were a little bit braver than me, they'd get on them paddle boats. They'd dive out over the over the paddle wheel, dive out over that. I never did it. I'm not getting out on that boat. That's when you're bored, you do stuff like that....But we did swim out to them. There was a big boat. Seems to me it was called the Sailor. It put out the biggest waves in the back. We'd see that coming. We'd try to swim out so we could catch them waves out further. Yeah, it's crazy. It was dangerous doing that. Yeah, but we did it. Well, that's a long time ago. If my mother knew that, she'd probably, I wouldn't be here now. That's for sure. I learned how to swim in the River and I would always try to look, not look like I was swimming when I went home. I'd let my clothes dry, hair dry, wear a hat and all that. So then we went to a picnic out at Spillway Lake, and that was pretty popular at the time. Everyone did it. So we were out there and there's a boardwalk out there and a bunch of kids there, which I knew. So my mother's watching me and whatnot. I just jumped off the side of the thing. I turned around she says you thought all this time you was fooling me but you was going swimming every day. But then she was happy that I could swim because my mother was a good swimmer. So she was happy that I learned how to swim. But she did like me learning in the River."

-Jack Gargan

"I remember swimming to the paddle boats and getting behind the boats and riding the wave...They'd make big waves, the paddle boat...One time, you never forget things like that. I got to close. It almost sucked me into the paddle. I went into the waves too quick."

-Joe Vargo

"colored" are used here in keeping with period references to African Americans in the Fayette City Journal. The terms were used by all parties and carried no negative connotations.)

The Rocks seemed to attract the young men more so than the kids. Perhaps it was the beach across the River in Allenport where the young ladies used to congregate in the summer. In any event, the young men often tried to prove their mettle by swimming across the River. The bravest would wait for one of the large paddle boats like the Sailor, Homestead, or Edgar Thompson to pass by before taking the dive in hopes of riding the waves churning from the back of the boat.

It's a wonder that more people didn't drown in these endeavors. To be sure the River did claim its share of lives. This was never more evident than during a two-week span during the summer of 1945 when three people drowned. The first to drown was a 17-year-old colored young man from Arnold City. The following week James E. Miller drowned when he was pushed from the ferry by a loose car on his way to work in the Mill. Days later another 17-year old drowned while swimming from the Colonial Docks a mile and a half upstream from Fayette City. The lack of available boats to take part in the rescue missions led the Fayette City Lions Club to purchase for the Fayette City Fire Department boats and trailers as soon as they could be obtained.

> Tragedy struck in Fayette City on Wednesday of this week when the Monongahela river claimed its first local victim of the present summer season.
>
> Clarence Jones, 17, colored, resident of Arnold City was drowned as he sought relief from the present heat wave, by swimming at the North End of Fayette City known as the sand bar.
>
> Apparently not a very good swimmer, Jones ventured too far from safety and was not able to make his way to shore. Another swimmer, Mathew Sabolek of Arnold City, attempted to rescue him, but was unsuccessful as the victim was hysterical and pulled Sabolek under where he was forced to let Jones go.
>
> Fayette City firemen were immediately notified and along with other residents a search for the body was begun. The tragedy occurred at 3:30 and at 6:05 the body was located by the use of grappling hooks. Howard Wilburham was the one who located the body and in the skiff with him were Albert Roberts and Don Hall.

Fayette City Journal
June 15, 1945

"Some days we would go to the Sandbar on the north side of town, where Johnsons Hollow creek emptied into the Monongahela River. This place got a bad reputation when a young Arnold City man or boy, or youth, stepped off the north side of the sandbar that was very deep and had under currents. Sad day for me to see them bring in his dead body hours later."
-Bill Williamson

Swimming in the Monongahela River became a thing of the past around 1953 when Stefanick's Crystal Pool opened and quickly became the preferred swimming spot for kids and families from all over the area.

Between 1964 and 1967 the dam at Lock 4 near Charleroi was replaced in order to raise the water level by six feet and eliminate Lock No. 5 near Brownsville. The higher water level submerged the Sandbar and took with it the memories of generations.

"We, as children, were not allowed, we really shouldn't have gone near the River, but we did. We would wade our feet, and we would pick up stones, and throw them in the River and make them jump. And then, again, we didn't dare go swimming, although some of the older boys went swimming. I remember one year, I forget what his name was, went swimming and disappeared. I remember them dragging the River. It was sad. We didn't really swim. We just would wade our feet. It was much later that they put the pool in in Fayette City....But we would sneak down there. It was like everybody knew what we were doing. We weren't getting away with anything. We thought we were. Everyone knew one another in Fayette City. And everybody knew what everybody else was doing. But people looked out for one another."

-Shirley Ferree Stilgenbauer

"The River, as a boy, or as a girl, but mostly the boys, you made your mark if you could swim across the River. My mother didn't permit me to swim in the River. Fayette City had two swimming locations. One was down near the waterworks. That was called the Sandbar. And then as you went up toward Sisleytown, there was another location called the Rocks. It was appropriately named. People would dive in, off the Rocks into the river and at the Sandbar you could wade out. One of the reasons, my mother just, she didn't want me to swim in the River and I never did go into the River. A good friend of mine, Tommy Evans, called Mussy Evans, had an older brother Kenny. Kenny Evans, he drowned at the Sandbar when I was a youth. Now my mother would allow me to swim in the creeks or "cricks", whatever you want to call it, particularly ones coming out of Johnson Hollow. The good thing is I didn't go into River. The bad thing is I went into those sulfur creeks. You'd come out looking all orange and everything. It was probably more dangerous to go into those creeks, but that's where I ended up going."

-Jack Young

"(The Rocks) was just a bunch of great, big, huge rocks. And then it was sort of a beach like thing, you know, in front of it, like along the shoreline. We used to swim across the River to the beach right by Allenport mill when we were kids. I know that you probably have never seen it because they raised the River. I can't remember what year they raised the River but they took away that beach. People in Allenport used to go to that beach a lot and we used to swim across to that....When I was 11 years old, my mother, at that time, everybody wore bathing caps. The girls wore bathing caps, which didn't really keep your hair dry, but people thought they would. My mother bought me a red one so she could see from our house. I wasn't allowed out in the middle of the River. Okay. So I just didn't wear it. I was crossing that River for years before she knew. I think I was 11 when I went across the first time, but I was with other people. I never went over there by myself."

-Leila Breckenridge Seiner

"They went up to a place called the Rocks. It was, as you're going out of town, behind Sisleytown towards the River, there was a railroad track and you walked up there a quarter mile or so....And everybody that could swim real well would go there. I couldn't swim that well, so I wouldn't go in the River. The boys used to swim across the River and then they had swim back. For some reason I don't remember anybody drowning."

-Joanne Manetta Cunningham

"I'll tell you what happened. My sisters were supposed to watch me and for some reason, I don't know why, they weren't. But I was down in the water. I had been on the Sandbar where it came out. Well, I walked over, I went down and I could just push myself up. But I wasn't out. Well they're up on the top, my two sisters, up on the railroad and they're hollering down. I didn't know this but they're yelling. Melvin Schroyer grabbed me and picked me up…. I said Melvin save my life. Although there were other kids around, I just seemed to be the one who couldn't swim. I don't know why my sisters left me. And they're going "Don't tell mom. Don't tell mom." You know the old kid thing, don't tell mom I almost drowned. We loved to swim. We would go to Redd's Beach. This is still when I was in Fayette City. We would take a bus from Fayette City to Charleroi and in Charleroi you would have to switch to a bus that went to Cokeberg and that would take you out, at the time, it was Redd's Beach."

-Judith Dewar Shearer

"Before the swimming pool came there were two places kids used to swim in the River. One was called the Sandbar which was down there near where the waterworks was. And then the other was further up a little bit down across where Allenport Mill was called the Rocks. Back then, you know the mills were still dumping all kinds of oil and stuff in….And well, there were some drownings that happened, you know, to some kids.

I think the barge companies had dug out the channel for the boats. And then they dumped a lot of that sand. So they called it the Sandbar. But there was a creek that came out down there too. But you would actually sink down in the mud and everything if you weren't careful. I remember, I don't remember who the kids were, there was more than one drowning which was very frightening."

Georgia Nicholson Slezak

"The Rocks was where everybody swam. The guys swam much further there. It was…probably maybe a half mile up there, maybe not that far, a fourth of a mile walk up the tracks. We weren't allowed to go on the tracks because Mosier would get us. He was something with the railroad and they didn't want you to walk on the tracks. Sometimes we would walk up the road and went down over, but mostly we went up the tracks. It was just rocks and…then you went in the water. That was it….And then we also had the Sandbar down where the other creek comes in. There was a Sandbar there."

-June Cramer Yevincy

"Other things that I remember about Fayette City, we swam in the Rriver and shouldn't have. (We swam) down around the Sandbar area. If you weren't careful. there would be some drop offs in there. But we swam in there….I'll never forget the day that we were in there. It was a hot summer day, and I was in there and I got out too far. I was struggling to get myself back to the Sandbar. I'm trying to remember now who pulled me out of there. It was either, oh, that's who it was, McKevitt, Mac could have been…..We were down there in the summer. We spent time on the sides of the River, you know. I can remember we had hot dog roasts down there. And we had some gatherings. That's about really what all you had to do, you know."

-June Winters Baldwin Jaquette

"There was a place right down there where Johnson Hollow creek enters the River. They called it the Sandbar. Then down at the other end of town there was a place we called the Rocks. At the Rocks there was no beach at all. When you went in the River there you was over your head. We used to swim over to Allenport. There was a beach there at Allenport. That beach is gone now cause they raised the River. The Sandbar down there is gone too."

-Jim McKevitt

Horseshoes

Horseshoes, or barnyard golf as it was often called back then, was hugely popular in the years leading up to the War. Fayette City boasted a five-time state champion named George Curry. Curry was born in 1907 and won his first state championship in 1932 at the age of 25. After being crowned state champion, Curry hurled shoes for over five hours at an exhibition in Fayette City. He threw a total of 2,000 shoes and made 1201 ringers. At one point during the exhibition, he tossed 70 ringers out of 100. Curry would go in to win the state championship again in 1935, 1937, 1938 and 1940. Fayette City had other top competitors as well. Dale Carson of Fayette City finished third to Ted Allen and George Curry in Class A at the state competition in Philadelphia in 1939. Frank Craig, also of Fayette City, captured the Class B state championship that same year. Curry and Carson were also runners up in Class A in 1941 losing this time to Bill Kolb from Newark, NJ,

Fayette City's fascination with horseshoes hit a peak in 1940 when the town staged the annual Pennsylvania championship. Nine courts were erected near the ball field. Bleachers were also constructed to accommodate the crowd. Between 400 and 500 horseshoe pitching champions participated in the event.

In addition to playing singles, Curry would often partner with Don Evans in doubles competition. Evans's father, Willbur Evans, was the business manager of the horseshoe club at Fayette City and responsible for the building the lighted, clay horseshoe pits in a burned-out foundation on Connellsville Street, just yards from the Mount Auburn Cemetery on town hill. Don started throwing horseshoes under the tutelage of his father at the age of 14 and at one time pitched 51 consecutive ringers. When Don served in the Army during World War II he came in second among the GIs in a pitching contest in Manila. His second-place finish earned him a spot in the Pacific Olympics held in Tokyo on January 26, 1946.

The War effectively put an end to Fayette City's love of barnyard golf. Curry moved to Monessen after the War. But he and Don Evans would continue to perform at community events where they would demonstrate trick and fancy pitching. The pit where they honed their skills on town hill is long gone. But the memories of the spectators who saw them pitch continue to live on.

"My memory of horseshoes...you go up the street here where Pattersons lived. There was a foundation up there. Just the foundation. And see, I lived in Brownstown and I'd walked past. These guys would be down in there, a horseshoe pit set up in this foundation and they would pitch horseshoes. When I was a kid I was impress with it. I sat on that wall there watching them pitch horseshoes...I think George Curry, he was the guy. When he was throwing, I was just amazed. Ringer, ringer, ringer, and then there was other guys to. But I remember him for some reason. I think Don (Evans) threw horseshoes too."

-Jack Gargan

"I can remember if you go up the top of the hill before you get to the cemetery there was a foundation. It was knocked down and no top on it. And they had horseshoe courts down in there... It was a big deal then. A lot of these, everybody went and watched them through the top of the road there and watch them play. It was quite a few that played horseshoes right there."

-Willard Jones

"(Horseshoes) was just, that was just dying out when I was getting to the place that I would have liked to play. That horseshoe pit was across from Scully's store. Do you remember where Scully's store was? There was a big open pit there that they played in there. I think Evans owned, must have owned that."

-Raymond Moody

"Horseshoes was a big attraction before TV. We had a great horseshoe pit up there by the Evans's property. The Evans ran it. It was great because they had lights. They had tournaments there. As soon as the war came it shut down. The two Evans brothers, they were really great horseshoe players, really, really good. One was better than the other, but I don't know which one.

There was a building there that sold flowers for Decoration Day. We used to call it the Decoration Day. Now it's Memorial Day. It was across from where the Evans lived. The Evans owned that store. They sold geraniums and flowers you could put in. Right beside that was the foundation of a building that evidently burned down. They made a horseshoe court out of that down inside that building with clay pits. It was really good. I mean, I'd go up there and watch those guys put ringer on after ringer. It just blew your mind."

-Bill Williamson

"There were several places around town where they had a pitch set up. They had them down at the ball field too. I was never involved with it. I don't know that anybody in my family was. But they had horseshoe tournaments, I know. I remember that."

-Mike Hancock

185

Baseball

Although Fayette City's success on the baseball diamond dates back to the beginning of the twentieth century, no greater heights were achieved than during the 1940s. In the early part of the decade Fayette City's attention was focused on Jim Russell, a hometown boy who had made it to the Major Leagues and played outfield for none other than the Pittsburgh Pirates. Russell's every move, whether a visit to his parents' home on town hill or a vacation to New York City, was documented in the Local Topics section of the Fayette City Journal. Any big changes in Russell's career, like when he was signed by the Pirates, was traded to the Braves, or spent time in the hospital, were splashed across the front page of the Journal. When Russell did visit Fayette City, it was not unusual for him to bring along a teammate or two from the Pirates to enjoy his mother's home cooking. A particularly favorite teammate of Russell's was the slugger and fellow outfielder Ralph Kiner. When Kiner and Russell visited Fayette City the town would be a buzz with kids trying to get an autograph or just a glimpse of their heroes. Fayette City was indeed proud of its hometown hero, so much so that during the 1944 season they arranged a "Jimmy Russell Night" during a game at Forbes Field against the St. Louis Cardinals. More than 100 fans from Fayette City led by James E. Hamer and Lee Ridgway attended the game. Before the game started, the group presented Jimmy with a gift of appreciation for what he had done on the field and off the field for the community.

Carl Russell, Jim Russell, and Ralph Kiner in the dugout at the Fayette City ball field. Photo courtesy of Steve Russell.

Jim Russell wasn't the only one in his family with the talent for baseball. His two younger brothers, Jack and Carl, were also skilled on the diamond. Jack and Carl served in the military during World War II unlike their big brother who was exempt from the military due to a childhood illness. During the War, the local baseball scene was practically nonexistent since the top baseball talent and leaders, like the Russell brothers, were waging war in Europe and Asia and not on the ball field. But when the War ended, baseball in Fayette City once again rose to prominence. After being discharged from the military, Carl and Jack Russell tried their hand at minor league baseball. In fact, Carl signed a contract with the Selma, AL, Pirate farm team in the Southeastern League presenting the possibility of a brother act in the Pirate outfield. Unfortunately, neither Carl nor Jack made it to the Big Leagues and both brothers eventually returned to Fayette City to play for the local teams.

Fayette City fielded a team in 1945 managed by Marion DeRienzo and featuring pitcher Leonard Gaskill. The team's moderate success portended better days ahead.

Local Ball Club Wins Sixth Tilt

Manager Marion DeRienzo's fast stepping baseball club won its sixth straight game at the expense of East Pike Run, last Friday evening.

Leonard Gaskill hurled brilliant ball, striking out eleven batters. Big Stompher injured his ankle in the fourth inning on a foul tip. He was relieved by Charles McKevitt, who turned in a grand job.

The high spot of the baseball tilt was James Fitzpatrick's great catch of a fly ball in center field. Loose fielding lead to East Pike Run's downfall. In the sixth inning, the game was called off because of darkness.

Those playing for Fayette City were Gaskill, P; Bednar, 1B; DeRienzo 2B; Stompher C; Coogan LF; Traynor SS; Fitzpatrick CF; Baldwin 3B; McKevitt LF-C; and Yetsconish RF.

Fayette City Journal
July 7, 1945

In 1946 a team called the Fayette City Independents was organized with Jesse Smith as manager and Marion DeRienzo as captain. Expectations were high for the team with more talent than had ever been seen in Fayette City. The Independents played their opening tilt on May 24, 1946 with Lester Liviskie on the mound and Carl Russell in the lineup. At times throughout the summer both Russell brothers would play for the Independents taking turns at pitching and playing the infield. They didn't win the league in 1946 but showed that Fayette City could field as good a ball team as any other city. A banquet was held at the end of the season to celebrate the team's success. Speakers for the event included Bernard Sara, Wilbur Long, George Stublarac, Gilbert Young, and Joe Alberta who had taken over as manager of the team. Expectations were high for 1947 when the local post of the American Legion was expected to sponsor the team.

The year 1947 would prove to be pivotal year in the lore of Fayette City baseball. The American Legion Post 484 sponsored a baseball entry in the Mon Valley League. Other teams in the League included Webster, Donora, Collinsburg, Belle Vernon, New Eagle, Monongahela and Fairhope. By mid-summer, the new Legion team was in a tightly bunched group between the clear front runner New Eagle and last place Collinsburg. The Russell brothers, although only playing part time, kept the team competitive with their pitching, hitting and fielding. Walt Plevniak led the team with RBIs.

After playing together for two years, the core members of the 1946 and 1947 teams were ready for a breakout season in 1948. With the Russell brothers playing full time, the Fayette City Legion team finished atop the Mon Valley League. The best of five championship series came down to Fayette City and the Allenport Millmen who finished in fourth place in the regular season. The two teams split the first four games forcing a fifth and deciding game. The final game certainly lived up to expectations. The game was played in Stockdale in front of the largest crowd ever to watch a game of the Mon Valley League. Allenport won the game in the eleventh inning

Fayette City Tops Donora Nine

Lanky Carl Russell enjoyed one of his better pitching days for the Fayette City Legion in the Mon Valley League last Friday when he set down Donora CIO 9-6 at Donora, allowing nine scattered hits and fanning 11. Darkness halted the game in the eighth inning.

The younger brother of Jim Russell, Pittsburgh outfielder, also helped along the Legionnaires' cause with four hits to pace a 14-hit attack followed closely by Leland (Pegetti) Haywood who had three. Walt Plevniak slammed a triple. Pat Murphy led Donora with a double and single.

In the only other game reported league-leading New Eagle turned back Fairhope 6-3.

The summary:

Fayette City	013 410 00—9	14
Donora CIO	000 102 12—6	9

C. Russell and Kroskie; Barbac S. Bolek and J. Bolek.

MON VALLEY LEAGUE STANDING OF THE TEAMS
July 26

	Won	Lost	Pct.
New Eagle	26	4	.867
Monongahela	17	12	.586
Donora	16	16	.500
Fairhope	14	15	.483
Belle Vernon	14	16	.467
Webster	13	16	.448
Fayette City	14	18	.438
Collinsburg	9	21	.300

Fayette City Journal
August 1, 1947

on a two-out single by John Koval to score Bob Fisher giving Allenport a 6-5 victory. The game, however, was not without dispute. Fayette City vehemently protested an umpire's ruling on a bunt early in the game. Nevertheless, the Fayette City Legionnaires had shown that they were a team with which to be reckoned.

Local Nine Loses To Allenport

Unless a protest is upheld and a replay of the fifth and final game is ordered, the 1948 Mon Valley League baseball championship today belonged to Allenport CIO.

The Millmen, fourth-place finishers during the regular season competition, turned Cinderella men Sunday to outlast pennant-winning Fayette City American Legion 6-5 in 11 innings at Stockdale to wrap up the crown before one of the biggest crowds of the MV season.

The Legionnaires, it was learned, planned to file a protest with Loop Commissioner Floyd France of Monongahela, claiming a mis-interpretation of the rules by Umpires Frank Kovach and Tracy when an Allenport batter bunted and was called safe after he had stopped and retraced his steps.

Fayette City Journal
September 24, 1948

With their success in 1948, the Legionnaires had high expectations going into the 1949 season. The Legionaries were sitting atop the Mon Valley League standings by mid-season, but the disputed call in last year's championship game still stuck in their craw. A charity event was planned in July for League umpire Adam (Tracy) Klawcho of Belle Vernon who had been hurt in a mining accident a few months back. Klawcho just happened to be the same umpire who made the call against the Legionnaires in last year's final game. Fayette City refused to participate in the charity event to the dismay of many in the Mon Valley.

The Legionnaires would go on the win the regular season pennant in 1949 and, once again, face Allenport in the championship series. The two teams split the first four games, once again, forcing a fifth and final game on Fayette City's home field. The last game was a low scoring affair with Big League prospect Hal Livingstone on the mound for Allenport and Carl Russell on the mound for Fayette City. Allenport took a 3-0 lead going into the bottom of the ninth. But Fayette City could only muster 2 runs giving Allenport their second consecutive Mon Valley League championship.

The Legionnaires weren't the only team fielded by Fayette City in 1949. The Fayette City Merchants, sponsored by local merchants as the name suggests, played in the Mon-Yough League. Several players from the Legionnaires played on the Merchants as well. Under the leadership of manager Dickie Barker, the Merchants won the Mon-Yough League championship.

The year 1950, the end of the decade, would prove to be exceptional by any standard. Fayette City once again fielded two teams: the Fayette City Legionnaires in the Mon Valley League and the Fayette City Merchants in the Tri-County League. The Mon Valley League consisted of the Legionnaires, Allenport, Charleroi, Monongahela, New Eagle, Finleyville, and Webster. The Tri-County League consisted of the Merchants, Allenport, Monessen, California, Newell, Fellsburg, Whitset, Long Branch, Smithton, and Brownstown. The Legion team was managed by Joe Alberta while the Merchants were managed by Dickie Barker. Jack Russell, Damon Turek, Oliver Niemela and Ted Schneider played for both teams. For the third consecutive year the Legionnaires finished atop the Mon Valley League with Carl and Jack Russell and Walt Plevniak once again leading the way. Allenport, Fayette City's arch nemesis for the previous two years, finished in second place. This time, however, Allenport failed to make the final championship series after being defeated by the team from Charleroi in an earlier round. With Allenport out of the way, the Fayette City Legionnaires defeated Charleroi three games to one to win their first Mon Valley League Championship. The Fayette City Merchants also won their league giving Fayette City two champions and the title of "biggest little baseball town in Western Pennsylvania". Both teams were feted at a banquet held in the social room of Fayette City's Methodist Church. Local politicians and sports dignitaries from around the Mon Valley attended to sing the praises of Fayette City's young men.

In 1951 the Legion Team moved up to the faster Fayette County Big Ten League while the Merchants took the Legionnaires' spot in the Mon Valley League. Teams from Fayette City would go on to have more success on the diamond, but nothing would ever compare to the glorious summer of 1950.

"I ate, drank and slept baseball. Fayette City had a very good sandlot program. Before I was big enough to play, I would go down to the field where the older people were playing. I volunteered to be a bat boy or a water boy carrying water from the field up to McFall's well out in right centerfield. Or I'd be a ball boy chasing balls that were fouled off, sometimes over into coal cars along the back of the playing field, which was located about a half a mile outside of Fayette City toward Belle Vernon. And so from that early youth being there all the time, I just loved baseball. In Fayette City, Jim Russell was a major league ballplayer, the Russell family. In fact they lived very close to me up on town hill. The Father, Doc Russell, had three boys and a daughter. The three boys all played and of course, the oldest one Jim played for the Pittsburgh Pirates and the Boston Braves and the Los Angeles Dodgers. And I would always go to watch the other two brothers play in Fayette City. Fayette City became sort of a home of champions. When I eventually got old enough to play, there was American Legion. I didn't play on that team. I played on the Fayette City Merchants. We had two teams in Fayette City. In one year we both won championships."

-Jack Young

"Oh baseball. We had two teams, the Merchants and the Legion. A lot of guys from across River played on our team, on the Fayette City teams. We'd go to the ballgame, at six o'clock it started. That's where all the guys were. So that's where all the girls went. Right? You don't think we went down there to watch the baseball game in that heat, do you?"

-June Cramer Yevincy

"You had two baseball teams in Fayette City. We used to chase the baseballs. Do you remember all the boxcars that used to be down by the ball field? It was a depot like for the boxcars. And we use to, somebody would hit a homerun and they go to the boxcars. And you had to chase them balls down, I remember, for a quarter. That would get you a big order of french fries and a bottle of Pepsi up at Humphries. That was living."

-Joe Vargo

"I remember our big our big entertainment was baseball games. Well, the Fayette City Merchants and then there was the Fayette City Legion. I don't know how they got two two teams....But then of course, they had some other players...I know there was a couple of fellas played that were from Charleroi. But we went to all those baseball games. The Russell boys, the Russell boys all played football or baseball. Of course, Jimmy, you know, he got his chance with the Pirates and went on from there. But Carl and Jack they had the beer distributors place. And that was down on the Second Street. Jimmy Russell would bring somebody home with him....I remember we saw Ralph Kiner....Ralph Kiner, you know, he was the big home run hitter at that time. He would bring a player home once in a while up on the hill."

-Judith Dewar Shearer

"Best thing ever happened to Fayette City. I mean, it, was great for me because it was right at the time I was learning to drive. My dad loved baseball and every place that Big 10 baseball team went to play, we went, because that was my thrill taking him. I liked baseball too. It was a great baseball town. It was back in the day. In fact they had two teams then. They had the Merchants and then the team that played in the Big 10, if I remember correctly. There was two teams. Can you imagine that in Fayette City? Two men's teams?"

-Jack Gargan

"Live sandlot baseball returned to Fayette City with the American Legion the primary startup team after the War. They won many league championships and were usually second if they didn't win. Many war heroes were on those teams. Some had survived the war. Some had severe war wounds. I remember one guy whose shoulder and face were so scarred up. He played baseball, was a very good baseball player. I was a scorekeeper back then, and substitute player many of those years until I entered college. Joe Alberta was the manager and did a great job. Then Dicki Barker, a great sandlot player, with Bundles Package organized the Fayette City Merchants with two of my friends, best friends, Jack Young at shortstop and Bill Janeri at second. I think Donald Dinger Young may have played with the Merchants also. Dinger signed as a pitcher with the St. Louis Cardinals and managed a number of Fayette City teams later. He was my best friend ever. We played ball all the time in the back of his yard with the Scrogg's fishpond a home run. We would go to the ball field many times in the mornings, and watch the Russell brothers Carl and Jack catch and throw....Back then the ballpark was laid out the complete opposite than it is now. The old field had home plate where centerfield is now."

-Bill Williamson

"The other big thing was baseball in Fayette City. it was a big thing on Tuesday nights. We had the Fayette City Legion and the Fayette City Merchants. They had a lot of good ballplayers, the Russell boys, Jimmy and Carl, played on that. There was a fella from, I believe he was from Allenport, Ray Ermlich. I can't remember if he was the Merchants or the Legion. I think he married Dana Baldwin who had been a neighbor. They had two separate teams in Fayette City. Oh yeah. I don't know who financially supported them. But they were drawing really big crowds."

-Georgia Nicholson Slezak

Jim Russell

Jim Russell was born on October 1, 1918 in Fayette City, PA, the son of James Walch "Doc" Russell and Lillian Johnson Russell. As a child, Russell contracted rheumatic fever and developed an infection in his heart, which would keep him out of military service and would ultimately shorten his baseball career. Russell dropped out of high school and went to work in the local coal mines to help supplement his family's income.

Jim stood 6'1" and weighed 181 pounds. He developed his baseball skills with the help of his father Doc, a skilled baseball player in his own right, and by playing on local sandlot teams.

 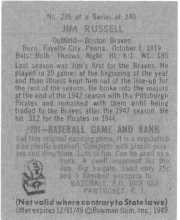

1949 Bowman Baseball Card front (left) and back (right).

Jim was a natural right-handed hitter but learned early to hit left-handed so that he could make contact with his brother Carl's nasty curve ball. Jim's switch-hitting skills and speed on the bases and in the field eventually caught the attention of baseball scouts. Russell was signed to his first professional baseball contract in 1937. After several years in the minor leagues including stints in Butler, Beaver Falls, Youngstown, Springfield (IL), St. Joseph (MI), and Memphis (TN), Russell was selected by the Pittsburgh Pirates in the minor league draft. He spent the 1942 season with Toronto of the International League where he batted .295. He was called up to the Pirates at the end of the season where he appeared in five games. Russell would spend the next five years as a fixture in the Pirates outfield. His best season came in 1944 when he played in 152 games, hit .312, and garnered 181 hits, including 34 doubles and 14 triples and some votes for National League Most Valuable Player.

1950 Bowman Baseball Card front (left) and back (right).

In the 1947 offseason, Russell was traded to the Boston Braves in a five-player trade. In exchange for Russell, pitcher Al Lyons, and catcher Bill Salkeld the Pirates received infielder Danny Murtaugh (the future manager of the Pirates) and outfielder Johnny Hopp. Russell, as the starting center fielder for the Braves, had a career highlight on June 6, 1948 in a game against the Chicago Cubs when he homered and doubled from both sides of the plate. The Braves made it to the World Series in 1948. Unfortunately, Russell missed the last month of the season and the World Series when he was stricken with bacterial endocarditis brought on by the rheumatic fever he had in his youth.

Jim spent a second season with the Braves in 1949 but was unable to reach the same level of play due to his heart problem. On Christmas Eve 1949 he was traded to the Brooklyn Dodgers along with Ed Sauer and cash for Luis Olmo and was assigned to the Dodgers top farm team in Montreal. Immediately after the trade Russell contemplated quitting baseball rather than play again in the minors, particularly in cold weather Montreal. After a change in heart, Russell spent the next two seasons splitting time with the Dodgers and the Montreal minor league team. He finished out his career playing the 1952 and 1953 seasons with the minor league Portland Beavers of the Pacific Coast League.

Russell played a total of 1,035 games in the Major Leagues with a career batting average of .267 and 959 hits including 175 doubles, 51 triples and 67 home runs.

While Russell had a solid career on the field, he was known to be involved with some colorful incidents off the field. During the war years, Russell was rumored to be one of the ringleaders in the threatened strike of the Pittsburgh Pirates. When Russell was eventually traded by the Pirates some observers speculated that he was aligned with the pro-union faction of the team. Another intriguing incident occurred in August of 1949 during Russell's stint with the Braves. After performing poorly on road trip in Chicago, Russell reportedly ended up on the receiving end of teammate Earl Torgeson's right hand. Torgeson suffered a sprained thumb while Russell was left with two black eyes. With rumors of discontent in the clubhouse, Russell was traded by the Braves at the end of the season.

After retiring from baseball, Russell spent several years as a scout for the Dodgers and the Washington Senators. He and his two brothers Carl and Jack operated the Russell Brothers Beer Distributorship in Fayette City before selling it to a competitor in the 1960s. Russell was also a long-time coach for the local American Legion Baseball team working with dozens, if not hndreds, of young men hoping to make it to the big leagues. Russell died of a heart attack in 1987 at the age of 69 leaving a legacy for all the aspiring young baseball players in Pennsylvania's Monongahela Valley.

1952 Topps Baseball Card front (top)
and back (bottom).

REFERENCES

Heberling, J.A., Kudlik, J.J., Carlisle, R.C., Heberling, S.D. *Contextual Essays on the Monongahela River Navigation System.* U.S. Army Corps of Engineers, Pittsburgh District, Pittsburgh, 2012.

Jim Russell – Society for American Baseball Research (sabr.org)
https://sabr.org/bioproj/person/jim-russell/

Milller, James E. *Daisyville.* Unpublished work provided by Lauri Miller Thompson.

Paglia, Ron (2012, November 15) Baseball was natural draw in Fayette City. *Tribune Review.*

Paglia, Ron (2013, January 17) Russell remains a major interest to baseball buffs. *Tribune-Review.*

Wikipedia contributors. "Jim Russell (baseball)." *Wikipedia, The Free Encyclopedia.* Wikipedia, The Free Encyclopedia, 18 Aug. 2021. Web. 24.

194

CHAPTER 9 Not Mayberry

Everyone who lived in Fayette City during the 1940s was grateful for its rich community spirit and the exemplary generosity and strong work ethic of their neighbors. But like any other town, Fayette City had its shortcomings and challenges. After all, Mayberry exists only on television. Most of Fayette City's shortcomings were plainly and painfully visible to all. One very insidious shortcoming, however, was mostly invisible to the casual observer.

The Visible

The Borough of Fayette City faced many of the same issues that most nearby towns, no doubt, faced during the 1940s. Garbage collection, property maintenance, outhouses, ash disposal, and stray dogs were just a few of the high-profile examples that plagued the municipality and routinely made the front page of the local weekly newspaper.

Citing concerns about stagnant water causing malaria and hay fever, the local Board of Health in 1946 notified the Borough Council to have weeds on Borough property cut and to inform town residents that weeds on their property must be cut as well. The Board further emphasized its case by noting that failure to do so would be punishable by law in accordance with a local ordinance.

A year later, in 1947, a State Health Enforcement Officer warned Fayette City property owners that outdoor toilets were creating a public nuisance and must be removed. Although the Borough had a long-standing ordinance prohibiting outdoor toilets, the Borough Council largely neglected to enforce it. The State Officer insisted that the situation be remedied.

Complaint Made On Ash Dumping

Complaints are being made that local residents are throwing ashes out on the streets or in alleys.

Several people have made the statement that they are burning their garbage to save the expense of garbage removal, then these same people are scattering ashes throughout the borough streets in order to save ash removal charges.

A borough ordinance prohibits the dumping of ashes within the borough limits and a warning is given to those who are practicing this plan of disposing of ashes that they are liable to a fine which will more than exceed the cost of having your ashes hauled away this winter.

Fayette City Journal
November 15, 1946

NOTICES

NOTICE

DUMPING ASHES or rubbish in the Borough of Fayette City is prohibited by an ordinance. Anyone violating this ordinance will be prosecuted to the full extent of the law.

Burgess,
James M. Hough
1-25; 2-1,8-c

Fayette City Journal
January 25, 1946

Garbage collection was an ongoing problem for the better part of the decade and in 1946 the Borough Council finally decided to tackle the issue. A plan was devised to survey local residents about their needs for garbage collection. Many residents were already having their garbage hauled away for between $18 and $24 per year. In the Council's new plan the fee for the first year would be $12 year and then adjusted thereafter to cover the cost of purchasing a new truck and hiring help. Contracts setting a rate of $1 per month were subsequently presented to the public.

Closely related to the problem of garbage collection was the issue of disposing of ashes. Since most homes were heated with coal, residents had to find a place to dispose of their ashes. In order to save on garbage collection, many residents would burn their garbage, further compounding the ash problem. Despite an ordinance against dumping ashes in the Borough, many people would surreptitiously and under cover of darkness scatter their ashes throughout the town. A favorite dumping ground seemed to be the empty lot at the south end of town, so much so that it was known as "Ash Park". When this lot was modified to enable one-way traffic in and out of town in 1947, residents were forced to find a new home for their ashes.

The biggest issue facing the Borough in the 1940s appeared to be an abundance of loose or stray dogs. The canines were known to run amok in neighborhoods upsetting garbage cans, destroying flower beds, and occasionally attacking people, particularly children. Cases of rabies in the mid-1940s led to dogs being quarantined and stray, loose dogs being shot on sight. Complaints from residents compelled the Burgess to post multiple annual notices in the Fayette City Journal warning residents about the issue. Unfortunately, these annual warnings seemed to do little to stem the problem.

At least one other activity presented a challenge to the peace and quiet on the city streets. As mentioned previously, Fayette City was known as the town with seven churches and seven bars. The churches weren't the problem, but the bars sometimes were. With a total population of only 1500, seven bars were more than enough to quench the thirst of even the most prolific drinker. The bars would often be visited by the mill workers on their way home from a hard day at work. The busiest time of the week, however, was Saturday, specifically Saturday night. Fayette City had an old and deserved reputation for "rowdiness" that often comes with imbibing a little too much and Saturday nights did nothing to change it. For some residents, Saturday night in the summer became sort of a spectator sport. Most of the bars were in the down town area and within a few yards of each other. Residents could simply sit on their porch or look out their window and keep score of who was drinking and where they were drinking. Inevitably, some

Warn Dog Owners As Drive Opens

Many complaints have been received by borough officials that dogs are being permitted to run at large in the borough and they are destroying gardens, property, etc.

This week the Burgess issued and order stating that dogs must be kept tied at all times. He will enforce an ordinance that states that dogs running at large will be picked up, and held for 48 hours, after which, they will be disposed of if not claimed.

The burgess also stated again this week that anyone desiring to open a street or alley for the purpose of sewage, gas or water must first obtain a permit from his office.

Fayette City Journal
September 5, 1947

Burgess Sets Quarantine On Animals

Burgess James M. Hough last week issued a quarantine on dogs and cats when a local dog was found to be a rabies victim.

When a local dog was acting queerly the owner took it for an examination. The examination showed rabies and the animal was immediately disposed of.

The burgess warns that any dog who is found running the streets will be shot.

Fayette City Journal
July 5, 1946

NOTICE TO DOG OWNERS

Numerous complaints are coming to me about dogs running at large, particularly at night, upsetting garbage cans and, destroying flowers, etc. The Pennsylvania Dog Law states that all dogs must be kept tied between sunset and sunrise.

The County Dog Law enforcement officer has been apprised of this condition and, unless stopped at once, proper action will be taken against those owners whose dogs are found running at large between the above mentioned hours.

J. M. THIRKIELD
Burgess

Fayette City Journal
September 24, 1948

people, mostly if not entirely men, would have a little too much to drink and end up in the seldomly used jail cells in the Borough building for the evening. Conservative elements in town, including the editor of the Fayette City Journal, often sought to return to the days of prohibition. But for the most part, citizens took the situation in stride with the understanding that these men worked hard, were otherwise good neighbors, and deserved a brief respite from their daily labors.

> "Some of the (jail) cells are still in there, I think. You get down there after Saturday night and torture everybody that was in jail. You can look right in the jail. Doots McGowan, he was number one. He was the number one guy in jail on Saturday night. He was always drunk. It was wild in town. Well, you figured all the bars that was here was open. The only bar that wasn't open on Saturday night was old Markish's on the corner....Riverview Grill, right on the corner, across from Moravek's store on the corner."
>
> -Jim Eley
>
> "There were two bars on Main Street. Let's see. One, two, actually three, four if you count the Legion. But there's also a house on Main Street, right across from Samberg's department store, a house with a sun porch on it...My grandparents lived there for a while. That sun porch jetted out just far enough that we could sit in there and see all the way down Main Street. Members of my family, I was only a little kid of course, but two members of my family who were older used to sit out there and keep track of the drunks who came out of the local bars because you can see all the way down all the bars and see who came in and went out. I had relatives who kept score. I won't reveal who they kept score about it, but they sat in that house."
>
> -Mike Hancock

The Invisible

(Author's note: This section was particularly difficult to write. Racism, when you get right down to it, is an ugly word. But there is no denying that racism was a part of the culture of Fayette City in the 1940s. The comments and stories from the narrators were mostly unsolicited and illustrate the changing ethos of the time as seen through the eyes of a child, as the narrators were then.)

Many of the original settlers of Fayette City were of English descent who migrated north from Virginia using the abundant waterways leading to the Monongahela River. The settlers brought with them not only a familial connection to other Virginians, but also an understanding of how slavery was viewed in the South. Consequently, during the Civil War many residents of Fayette City were staunch supporters of the Confederacy and proponents of slavery. Not all residents held this belief though and divisions within the local churches led to at least one physical altercation between members.

Some residents of Fayette City showed their support for the Confederacy by manufacturing shot and shipping it to the troops in the South. The building where the shot was reportedly manufactured was a wooden, three-story, multi-family dwelling on Fourth Street near the intersection with Union Street. The building known of the "Shot Tower" by locals was torn down decades ago and only fragments of a foundation remain.

At the end of the Civil War in 1865 the steamboat "Fayette" brought news from Pittsburgh of General Lee's surrender. At the boat's landing in Fayette City it was greeted by a shower of stones that broke the boat's windows and a passenger's arm. For its support of the Confederacy Fayette City was dubbed "Little Richmond", a nickname that it would bear for decades.

Sadly, Fayette City's support for the Confederacy eventually evolved into the formation of a chapter of the Ku Klux Klan. Local towns<u>men</u> were not the only members of the Klan. A Fayette City chapter of the Women of the Ku Klux Klan was formed in 1927 under the name of Helping Hand Klan No. 207. Fayette City became a so-called "Sundown Town" complete with metal plaques posted at the north and south entrances to town warning Negros that although they might be allowed in town during the day, they must leave by sundown. The plaques were removed at some point during

The Shot Tower on Fourth Street in Fayette City.
Photo courtesy of Vanessa Moskala Pugh.

"The KKK was around here... There was no blacks in Fayette City. During the Civil War they called this Little Richmond.... They weren't allowed in Fayette City. They didn't come to Fayette City. But McCrory did bury the blacks because when they died back, and I'm not positive, but when they died back in the Depression, McCrory I think he really helped the black families out up there in Arnold City... There weren't any blacks in Fayette City. Blacks knew not to come into this town. Now when I was in the army, a man, he was black, I told him where I was from. He was from Cleveland. And he knew exactly where Fayette City was. And how did he know? He must have had relatives in Arnold City. I think he had cousins up in Arnold City. His cousins probably told him, they can't go down to Fayette City."

-Jim McKevitt

"When I went to Marion (school), I hate to say, this sounds awful. But there were black kids out there...in my class. And I had never been in a class with you know with any black kids. They were nice kids, the Thrasher kids. I think they both have died. Richard Thrasher and his sister Shirley....She became a, I think she got a doctorate in something. But I did see where she died a few years ago. That was something for me."

-Judith Dewar Shearer

"I guess (Fayette City) did have their sort of prejudices and things. But as kids growing up, I didn't know this until later. But later I learned that black people were not allowed to live in Fayette City at that time and they had to be out of town by sundown. So consequently, I never had any black students in my class until high school. But when we had them, I mean they were just, they were our classmates. We didn't ever give skin color a thought. And the other interesting thing for me later in life during the Vietnam era, we were stationed in Shreveport, Louisiana. And I did freelance anesthesia in three different hospitals. At that time, they wouldn't take black people to the recovery room. Well, I stood my ground with them. I said, No, not on my watch."

-Georgia Nicholson Slezak

the 1940s, but their existence was firmly ensconced in the memories of some of the narrators for this book. (More than 10,000 Sundown Towns were known to exist in the United States between 1890 and 1960. Most of them were in the mid-western and western parts of the nation. More than three dozen Sundown Towns were known to exist in Pennsylvania over this period.)

Support for the KKK in Fayette City seemed to be concentrated in a few prominent citizens. But by the 1940s, the Klan's influence was clearly on the decline, as it was in other parts of the country.

Obviously, no Negro families lived within the Borough of Fayette City. The Black families closest to Fayette City lived in the coal patch town of Arnold City about a half mile up Johnson Hollow. In the 1940s, some Fayette City businesses would serve Negro visitors from Arnold City, while others would not. Some churches would welcome Negro visitors, while others would not. Just the appearance of a Negro person in town, though, was enough to send school children scurrying to their classroom window to catch a glimpse of the rare, dark-skinned person. In fact, Fayette City was so insulated from outside influences that many children were never really exposed to Negros until they graduated from high school and joined the workforce in the steel mills and coal mines. The closure of the local high school in 1946 started to bring about some significant changes. The upperclassmen, grades nine through twelve, were sent to neighboring Marion High School or Charleroi High School where they had Black classmates for the very first time. The fears that had been instilled in them by some of their teachers and, no doubt, by some parents were quickly dispelled.

> **PRESBYTERIAN CHURCH TO HAVE NEGRO PREACHER THIS SUNDAY MORNING**
>
> ---
>
> The First Presbyterian Church of Fayette City will present Robert L. Maffett, a negro student at Western Theological Seminary, on Sunday morning February 24.
> Mr. Maffett is a second year student at the Seminary and comes here highly recommended. His appearance is timely as this week is National Brotherhood week. Services will be held at 11 a. m. Everyone is welcome to attend.

Fayette City Journal
February 22, 1946

A favorite form of entertainment in the local school and in the community was the minstrel show. It seemed to be a tradition for the third-grade class to perform a minstrel show for the school. Shows with titles like "Melody Minstrel Show" and "Tom Thumb Minstrel Show" were performed in "true minstrel style". Children in black face sang, danced, and told jokes for parents, friends, and fellow classmates. The grade school students even performed a minstrel show for the Lions Club in the fellowship hall of the local Methodist Church. For the children, the performances were nothing more than good fun and entertainment. They were simply unaware of any connection with the racial stereotypes on which the shows were based. The minstrel shows weren't only limited just to child actors. Adults also performed minstrel shows for the community in the opera hall of the Odd Fellows Building. Minstrel shows continued their popularity in Fayette City well into the 1950s before eventually disappearing for good.

> **Minstrel Show**
> Definition: A type of stage entertainment featuring songs, dances, and formulaic comic routines based on stereotyped depictions of black Americans and typically performed by white actors with blackened faces. It developed in the US in the early and mid-19th century and was widely performed until the mid-20th century but is now regarded as highly offensive.

One unifying activity for all races seemed to be sports, specifically baseball. In 1946, the newly formed Fayette City Independents baseball team hosted the Clairton Elites, a Negro team from nearby Clairton. Ironically, the baseball field was just a few yards from where the Sundown sign once stood at the north end of town. A year after Fayette City's game with the Clairton Elites, Jackie Robinson broke the color barrier in Major League Baseball. Change was indeed coming to the United States and to Fayette City, but perhaps just not fast enough for many.

STUDENTS ENTERTAIN LIONS

A joint meeting of the Roscoe and Fayette City Lions Clubs was held in the local Methodist church Tuesday evening with over fifty in attendance.

One of the finest programs ever presented was had in the form of a minstrel show by the Fayette City grade school pupils. The minstrel was very well received by both clubs and the youngsters congratulated for their fine work.

President Paul Jesick was in charge of the meeting and William Mascara was song leader.

Following the regular meeting the directors met and named delegates to the state convention and announced the June 3 meeting as father son and daughter night.

Nomination of officers for the new year was made and election will take place the first meeting in June.

Fayette City Journal
May 9, 1947

"I remember going to the minstrel shows in the community center on Main Street. Oh, I remember those….They all sat in like a half circle facing the audience. They had black faces on, you know, their faces were all black, and they had the white lips. And then what they would do, somebody would say something, and somebody would answer back and they'd go and hit their hands on their pants and you know, start laughing. Then everyone in the audience laughed. The sixth graders up at Fayette City school they put on a minstrel show in the community center this one time. A friend of mine, that's John Vargo, he had a racoon cap. He wore it to school and there was a point in the show where someone fired a rifle to shoot a raccoon and the person behind the scene threw the raccoon cap up in the air and it fell on the stage.

There was the KKK in Fayette City that I was told by more than one person. Names were prominent citizens….They were the higher up. Someone told me that my Uncle Bill was one. I asked this person, I says well, was my dad one? And they said you know, I'm not sure about your dad.   There were fireman's parades. They were a big thing in town with all the fire trucks coming through. And oh, that's whenever, one of the parades, it was a big parade, because there was a lot of people in town. And I went to Hamer's dairy bar to get a soft ice cream cone. I was about seven or eight years old at the time. There was a long line. And there was a tall black man who was in front of me. He was just standing in line to get an ice cream cone. That's all. And to this day, I still remember I'll never forget it. I remember what Mr. Hamer said to him. He says we don't serve your kind. I remember the black man leaving the line and going out of the store. He didn't say a word.

Our dad told us when he was little, the KKK members came into his parents' home, uninvited. His mother told all the kids to hide. The leaders said it's okay, Mrs. Arrow, we only came in to get warm. We aren't after your husband."

-Georgia Jean Arrow

"I remember that there was no colored people allowed in Fayette City. They were scared to come to Fayette City. Now I can't remember whose place it was, they burned a cross on their property. But I only remember my mother and them talking….I want to say they were going to let colored people come in. Somebody was gonna let colored people come in and they burned a cross on their property. I just remember my mother and them talking about it. I don't know whose property it was. Just burning a cross sticks in my mind."

-Ella Marie Auther Davis

Minstrel show in the Fayette City school auditorium, circa early 1950s. Photo courtesy of Judith Dewar Shearer.

Minstrel performers. From Fay-View 1946 Annual.

Fayette City School Notes

The students in the third grade of the local school presented a show entitled "Melody Minstrel Show." The parents and friends of the students were entertaind on Thursday evening while the students enjoyed the performance on Friday afternoon.

Lana Gayle Zubovic was the Mistress of Ceremonies while Tony Hawker played the part of Bone Flipflop, Herbie Vargo as Mose Scallawag, Mary Jo Janeri as Rosebud Patticake, Sonnie Sue Alberta as Petunia Skillet, Marlene Makepeace as Blossom Flower Bed and Tommy Package as Remus Panhandle. Soloist for the affair were Judy Lorinchak and Ronnie Delbarre. The chorus included James Hough, Paul Fedora, Thelma Moats, Teddy Bill Kinney, Buddy Ferris, Marlene Schroyer, Dicky Scott, Barbara Roth, Francine Gill, James Fowler, Jerry Gardner, Martha Allen, Francis Gaskill and David Calcek.

The children performed in true minstrel style with many jokes, songs and dance, and greatly enjoyed giving the performance.

*Fayette City Journal
April 9, 1948*

"I was in one of the minstrels where they had, all the people on the stage had black faces. I must have been awful little. I was probably still in elementary school...I think we sang the Mama Doll song. But anyhow, that really blew my mind that actually in my lifetime, I went to a minstrel, and performed in the minstrel."

-Linda Russell Nelson

"The colored people were only permitted in town to go to the liquor store and the post office. Maybe once every couple of years there would be a colored funeral. But they weren't permitted to live in Fayette City...Mr. Wheeler was our sixth-grade teacher and principal. One day he said next year, you're going to be at Marion Junior High. You're going to be in with colored kids. You remember you're from Fayette City. The last colored man that tried to live here is at the bottom of that River encased in cement. Isn't that an awful thing to tell 11-year-olds?"

-John Vargo

"Well, they (Negros) just weren't around. We didn't have anybody in town. The older men would say, see anybody come in they were going to kill them. I mean they were bigots, terrible, absolutely terrible. Why did they hate black people? I have no idea. Not all of them, just as few of them, you know. But that's all it takes, a few bad apples. You know, I never understood it....One of my good friends in Charleroi was a colored boy. His name was Robertson. His sister, who was younger than me, she was in my class. We were good friends. If I was black too, I'd have probably tried to date her. She eventually was a dancer in New York, you know, the high stepping dancers...The rockets!! She and my cousin, Mary Carolyn, were rockets....One night, we're not going to work, we're going to go to a ballgame. I must have been a senior then in high school because I didn't really have any interest in driving a car. I could pedal my bike wherever I wanted to go. Anyway, I had a driver's license. So I never thought about it, driving home with me, because I had to get some clothes or something, because we were going to a basketball game or some Charleroi game somewhere and it was away. And he was riding with me. I offered him to ride with me and brought him home. The next day, my mother says, "Do you know he was black?" I said what? I said, I never thought about it. I said, what makes any difference? Well, you know, we don't have any around here... I never ever, ever......I didn't care if he was green, you know. No difference to me what he was.

There's another college experience I had that disturbed me a lot. We had on the dorm I was living in, I have, had one boy in my room and two black boys in another room on the third floor. And so we would go on something or came from a sporting event or something. So let's go down to this Italian place and have a beer. So we went down there and told them to come on in. Then our attendant refused to serve them...Terrible. I said, Why don't you served them? I don't serve black people. And me, like a friggin fool, you know, they turned around went out and got back in the car. I stayed there and had a beer. I should have just got up and said let's go to your neighborhood and get a beer."

-Bill Williamson

Fayette City School Notes

The students of the local school, parents and friends were entertained last Friday afternoon with a "Tom Thumb Minstrel Show" which was presented by the third grade at the local school auditorium. Many songs, dances and jokes made up the program for the afternoon.

Carolyn Boag, as Mrs. Brown, acted as interlocutress for the entire show.

The Black Faces for the affair included, Ella Marie Auther, Tommy Dent, Joe Vargo, Mike Hancock, George Vargo and Glenn Shepler.

Dancers for the occasion were, Patty Rice and Joyce Eley, students of Mr. Jacques Van Ipe of Pittsburgh.

The chorus included, Mary Carolyne Williams, Helen Jean Wilbraham, Connie Lee Stickle, Alan Cunningham, Connie Miller, Elizabeth Scott, Rhetta Branthoover, Francis M. Smith, Fred Martin, Martha Tiernan, Mickey Yelanich, Billy Dwyer, John Nicholson and Dick Breckenridge.

Fayette City Journal
April 25, 1947

Big Ball Game Here Sunday

Fayette City Independents, local ball team will play host to the Clairton Elites, a negro team from Clairton this Sunday August 25 at 2:30 p. m.

The game which will take place at Marine Field promises to be one of the best that has been played here this Summer. The Elites have a record of 35 wins against 10 losses while the Fayette City nine has won 17 and lost 9 tilts.

Local people are urged to attend the game and support the local ball team which has won 4 out of their last 5 games.

Joe Alberta, local manager who has replaced Jesse Smith who resigned, reports that Planey is scheduled to start on the mound.

Fayette City Journal
August 23, 1946

"I understood, not that people drilled it into me, that Fayette City had a sunshine and sunset rule that black people could be in Fayette City during the daylight hours, but when the sunset, they had to be out of town. As far as I knew, nobody lived in Fayette City who was black. I went to Charleroi High School. In Fayette City, there's no black children. When I went to Charleroi High School, I think I had about four in my graduating class with 200 and some. I think there were four or five black people. But Fayette City was really, I think, when I was in the Navy, I was sort of ashamed of what Fayette City had been all about."

-Jack Young

"I can remember, I used to hear them old guys saying, "Well, the sun is down, the ****** better be gone. They used to tell them "Let this let the sun rise on your head, but don't let it set on you head". I mean for years the colored people were afraid of this town. They really were. I mean whenever I went to high school some of the colored kids said "Oh no, we ain't going to that town. That's a white town."

There was one (a sign) at each end (of town) I guess. Let the sunrise on your head, but don't let it set on your head. They were bronze plaques. I don't who ever took them, but they cut them down and took them....It had Fayette City on it and it was up on the post. One on each end of town. The one was right there where you turn into the water company. That's where Fayette City ends. It started right there. And then the other one was right up here at the top of Sisleytown hill...I should have took pictures."

-Jim Eley

REFERENCES

Fay-Vew 1946, Fayette City High School Annual provided by Becky Miller.

Wikipedia contributors. "Minstrel show." *Wikipedia, The Free Encyclopedia.* Wikipedia, The Free Encyclopedia, 20 Feb. 2022. Web. 26 Feb. 2022.

Moskala, E.J. *From Freeport to Fayette City: A History of a Small Town in Southwestern Pennsylvania from Its Founding in 1800 to Its Zenith in the 1920s.* Amazon Publishing, 2019.

Loewen, James W. *Sundown Towns: A Hidden Dimension of American Racism.* The New Press, 2005.

CHAPTER 10 The Sesquicentennial Celebration

The exact year that Freeport, Fayette City's original name, was founded is somewhat open for debate. Some sources state that it was founded in 1799 while other sources suggest it was a late as 1806. The discrepancy may just be due to different interpretations of the word "founded". What is certain, however, is that Fayette City celebrated its centennial in 1900. Just five years after the grand celebration welcoming the railroad to town, Fayette City held another impressive celebration for its 100th birthday complete with fireworks, a parade, a bicycle road race, and a variety of speeches from distinguished guests. Both celebrations would pale in comparison to what Fayette City had planned for its Sesquicentennial Celebration in 1950.

The Sesquicentennial Queen and her court.
Photo courtesy of Linda Russell Nelson.

The Sesquicentennial Executive Board was led by Burgess James M. Thirkield. Other members of the Board included Leroy Gardner, Mrs. Joseph Williams, Howard McCrory, Mrs. Wayne Hawker, Mrs. Aland Dent, Mrs. John Wilson, George Hancock, Miss Betty Evans, John Wheeler, Frank Dewar, and Jack Stockton. An 18-page Program for the event was printed by The Journal Company, owners of the Fayette City Journal, and sold for fifteen cents. The Program contained details of the weeklong celebration including lists of everyone who contributed to or performed in the events. A few pages of the program are reproduced here. The Program also contained a slew of advertisements from nearly every business in Fayette City and from some businesses in neighboring towns. Everyone was encouraged to take part in the celebration in some form or fashion and almost everyone did.

The festivities started on Sunday, July 30th and ran through Saturday, August 5th. On July 8th, a few weeks before the formal activities started, the Fireman's Drum and Bugle Corps hosted the Beers-Barnes trained animal circus at the Community Athletic Field. Fifty percent of the ticket sales for the event went to the Corps' new uniform fund. A few days prior to the start of the Sesquicentennial, the coveted position of Queen of the Sesquicentennial was announced. Contestants for the Popularity Contest sold strips of three tickets for the Historical Review at $2.00 per strip. For each strip sold, the contestant received 1,000 votes. Seventeen girls entered the contest. Miss Mary Ellen Barker won the title of Queen tallying a total of 180,000 votes. Lyda Kirkpatrick with 150,000 votes and Kathleen Walton with 130,000 votes finished second and third, respectively. Mary Ellen received $50 in cash and a wardrobe valued at $50. As runners up Lyda and Kathleen received $25 and $10, respectively, and titles of maids of honor in the Queen's court. Other members of the court included Norma Jean Holmes, Leah Marriott, Miriam Pegg, Audrey Dewar, Dolores Miller, Mona Lee McDonald, Sophia Fedora, and Mary Moats. The Queen

> Miss Mary Ellen Barker won the coveted title of the Fayette City Sesquicentennial Queen, as a result of having sold the most tickets for the Historical Review during the Miss Popularity Contest which closed Monday.
>
> Mary Ellen had a total of 180,000 votes to her credit, topping her closest competitor by a margin of 30,000 votes, and will receive a reward of $50 in cash and personal wardrobe valued at $50 and will preside as queen at the Sesquicentennial festivities.

Fayette City Journal
July 28, 1950

and all of the members of her court were featured on a float in Thursday's parade. Although the contest was deemed a huge success, it did not pass without controversy. Rumor had it that the winner had help selling tickets from a couple of her very well-known and influential relatives.

The formal activities of the Sesquicentennial started on Sunday, July 30th with Masses at the two Catholic Churches, St. Edwards and St. Eusebius, and a special hour of worship at all of the Protestant churches. A song fest was held in the evening at the Review Field constructed near the Water Works at the north end of town. The song fest was conducted under the general supervision of the Fayette City Ministerial Association which included representatives from all the Fayette City Churches. Father Charles W. Ribick, pastor of St. Edwards Church directed the community choir as they sang "God Bless America", "Fairest Lord Jesus", and the national hymn. Thomas Dobson, choir supervisor of the Christian Church, then led some group singing. Colonel David W. Isaac provided the address. The community choir closed out the event by singing "Dear Land of Home" and "Going Home".

Monday was Educational Day. Activities included the opening of a historical museum at the Fayette City School, a tour of the Allenport Mill, judging of the hobby show at the School, and an elaborate Historical Review of Fayette City at the Review Field. A "Midway" was set up on Market Street between Fourth and Second, as had been done traditionally for the annual Fireman's carnival. A special feature of the Midway this year was the kangaroo court, a makeshift jail constructed beside the Riverview Grill. Men were thrown in jail if they shaved without a permit. Women were jailed if they wore makeup without a permit. And just for fun, almost anyone could be thrown in jail at the whim of the jail keeper until they met the jail keeper's demands. Abraham Lincoln, or at least his spitting image in the form of local resident "Huck" Gardner, made a guest appearance on the Midway and at other events during the week.

Historical Review at the Review Field.
Photo courtesy of Linda Russell Nelson.

Monday's big event was the Historical Review at the Review Field. The event cost more than $2,000 to produce and had more than 100 persons in the cast. Prior to the Historical Review, James H. Duff, Governor of Pennsylvania provided the address. In a speech that could be given today in some circles, Duff said "We are today the leaders of the free people of the world" and that "willingness to accept responsibility is a characteristic of our heritage." He went on to say that "a second quality is that of being dependable once that responsibility has been accepted. Only so long as you are and continue to be responsible and dependable, can we continue to have celebrations such as this. You are facing as critical a time as your ancestors ever faced. We have responsibilities as great as those whose legacies we inherited." Following the speech, the Governor crowned Mary Ellen Barker the Queen of the Sesquicentennial. The Queen was accompanied by her ten attendants. Five-year old Ross Brightwell carried the crown on a satin pillow with the aid of Gale Arrow.

Tuesday's Homecoming Day was celebrated with a tour of the historical museum at the School, a concert by the Charleroi High School Band, a baseball game hosted by the Fayette City Merchants, another performance of the Historical Review at the Review Field, and a water event . The water event was held on the River at the Fayette City-Allenport ferry. The Fayette City and

Governor Duff and Mary Ellen Barker. Photo
courtesy of Linda Russell Nelson.

209

The Queen and her two junior attendants, Linda Russell (left) and Carolyn Barker (right).
Photo courtesy of Linda Russell Nelson.

Fairhope Volunteer Fire Companies fought from two rafts. The Company holding on to their raft the longest was declared the winner.

Wednesday was set aside for the youth of Fayette City. The festivities began with a soap derby just after noon for boys ages 9 to 14. Some competitive sporting events for the kids were held at the Review Field followed by a baseball game between the Fayette City Legionairres and New Eagle at the Community Baseball Field. The day was capped off with a final performance of the Historical Review at the Review Field.

As the weekend approached, Thursday celebrated both Labor and Industry. Speeches by R.E. Sance, the Works Manager for the Pittsburgh Steel Company, and Eugene Maurice, District Manager of the Congress of Industrial Organizations, were made at the Review Field. The Fayette City Merchants played another game at the Community Baseball Field. After the game, the Fayette City Trojans Drum and Bugle Corps hosted a competition with other local groups at the Review Field. The highlight of the day, however was the afternoon Float Parade. The Parade started at the entrance to Johnson Hollow and made its way through the streets of Fayette City. The Parade included an assortment of floats, vehicles, and horse-drawn carts as crowds five-deep on the sidewalks watched.

Friday was dedicated to the local merchants who sponsored an all-day "Old Fashioned Bargain Day". A pet parade was held at the foot of the school steps where silver dollars and blue ribbons were awarded the winners. The Fayette City Merchants played their second game of the week at the Community Baseball Field. The day ended with a Celebration Ball featuring Tommy Tucker and His Orchestra at the Fairhope Skating Rink.

Pet Parade judging at the school steps.
Photo courtesy of Linda Russell Nelson.

After a six days of festivities, the Grand Finale had finally arrived. Saturday's activities began with what now had become an annual event – the Lions Club Baby Parade. In keeping with the spirit of the Sesquicentennial Celebration, no entry fees were required this year. However, cash prizes were still given to the winners of the various groups, as had been done in the past. The Fireman's Parade was held in the evening and featured volunteer fire departments from around the region. The week-long activities were capped off with a spectacular display of fireworks at the ball field. The decade that started with the threat of a world war ended with a community that was never more united, never more proud, and never more optimistic about its future.

Sesquicentennial Baby Parade entrants.
Photo courtesy of Linda Russell Nelson.

"It was a really, really, really big deal. It (the Sesquicentennial Celebration) was, in one respect, the last gasp in a rapidly changing society, the end of the small industrial town, the last gasp of it. I didn't look at it that way at the time, obviously. But looking back on it, that's what it seemed like it was to me. It was terrific. The planning went on for months. They had as many activities and things to do as, as you can think of. It lasted a whole week, and every day was packed with activities, different parades and things. From the selfish point of view, most of it took place right out our front door because the location for most of the activities was Second Street between the school and the River. So right in front of our house....It seemed like everybody in town was involved. They had square dances, and they had regular dances, and talent shows. They had baby parades. They had a drum and bugle corps parade and a firetruck parade. I can remember they had nickel hot dogs. There was stuff going on down there all the time. I mean, there were games going on, baseball games, but also other kinds of games involving little kids that I didn't pay a whole lot of attention to. But there was something going on down there almost all the time. They had food down there. I remember that. Of course, I was of the age that you remembered food.

I was a bit of an amateur artist. My job was to organize an art show where people would submit their drawings or paintings or whatever they were for her display and then a contest with judges who would judge.

One of the funny things about it (the Sesquicentennial) was they had a rule that the men all had to have beards or else they'd have to pay a fine of 50 cents or something like that if they showed up without a beard. That's one of the things my dad had to do was to police the guys and their beards. They had a jail cell set up right in the middle of Second Street where the guys who didn't have a beard, didn't want to pay the fine, had to go in and spend an hour. Now, there are pictures of that around. I haven't seen any. But I'm sure there are pictures of that. It was just a breathtaking activity for a little town like that, a little town where everybody who was involved with that was an amateur, that sort of thing. They still managed to pull it off."

-Mike Hancock

"The main thing that I always remember about that was Huck Gardner. He was Abraham Lincoln. I always said from that day to this day, he looked more like Abraham Lincoln than Abraham Lincoln did. That's how good he looked, you know. It was just, and I always said that one thing sticks in my head all the time about that man there. He played the part. He had a good time. He was Abraham Lincoln, believe me. He was, if he had walked in here, you'd think he was Abraham Lincoln.

Oh, there was so much stuff there....It was a continuous carnival where it would go on for about a week or so....Every night it was a carnival. So every night there was something different going on somewhere like competitions maybe. I think at the ball fields they had stuff going on there. They had dances, bands playing and people drinking. Everyone was in a good mood. The way the world should be today is the way that was. We will put it that way. You probably had a few skirmishes, but not much. It was just a great thing to be part of. I went there every day, that's for sure."

-Jack Gargan

"Yeah, a lot of people in town. A lot of floats. There were floats, and this covered wagon. I don't know who's that was that. My grandfather Tiernan was arrested in the Sesquicentennial and put in the jail. I think he was in his late 80s. He was put into jail because he didn't have a tag on or something. They had a little made up jail. And they put him in and my dad had to go bail him out."

-Audrey Tiernan Repka

"It was a big time in this town. It went from Sunday to Saturday night. Something going on every night of the week. I mean, the governor was here and I think the name was Governor Fine at that time. It was celebrating 150 years as a town. There were a lot of people here in this town that year. I mean, that week was just full of things going on. All the churches, they had a church service at the ballpark. All the churches went together and had one service, even the Catholic Church. It was a big time....They had a big stage built down in the freight yard there...The fireman's parade was on Saturday. They had the county farmers convention that week. It was a big affair. I think it lasted two and a half three hours almost. It was big then. They had the ball field full of firetrucks after the parade and a big event. I've never seen the town celebrate anything like that after that. They had a lot of planning....I wasn't very old at that time. We ran that pageant that they had. Then of course every organization in town had some type of booth where they sold food or something. It was during the week of the Sesquicentennial. I remember husking corn for...the Church I think. The Presbyterian Church sold corn on the cob. We would husk the corn and clean it for them. It was a big week. I can remember it real well."

-Jim Eley

"I don't even know what Huck's right name was. But when the Sesquicentennial was here, he wore a black coat down like where they used to wear them years ago, and a big black top hat. Honest to god, he looked just like Abraham Lincoln. I have a picture with him and me on Market Street, up where McKevitt's is now. They had a lot of memorable things in the schoolhouse where people could go through and look at it. We had these hats on that they sold. They looked like Robin Hood. It was so much fun, that Sesquicentennial. Paul Moravek, they had the Clover Farm store right on the corner, it was called Clover Farm, and then they had the jail there where they would lock up people just for the fun of it...It was just so much fun, that Sesquicentennial!"

-Ella Marie Auther Davis

"I was part of the attraction, running a ring and cane game at that thing. I didn't get to see much of it, you know, everything, because I was working for the Legion baseball team. I was running this game you played. You had canes, you had canes, wooden canes, that you stood up in the wooden fixture. And you threw round hoops. If your hoop went over a cane, you got to keep that cane. So I think it costs five cents for one throw and 10 cents for three throws. But we made a lot of money on it back then. That was a lot of money. I ran this for the American Legion, and I believe they won the league championship that year. I know they did now because I saw another report. The town was exploding during the celebration. Our men we're back and party time was here...The parade was huge, circuses, and fair rides and shows covered the area by the water plant and I believe the ball field. Drum and bugle teams marched and played. The cheers of happiness and celebration filled the air up and down the valley."

-Bill Williamson

"I was in the, what do you call, the Queen's court. We had to, we were to sell tickets for the things that were going on. The ones that sold the most tickets got to be in the court. But I don't think I sold the most. I was right in the, well I don't know what you call it, bridesmaids, queensmaids. But it was a really good time. It was a nice thing. They had things going on and it was like a carnival and everything."

-Kathleen Walton Stimmell

Sesquicentennial Program

CHURCH DAY
SUNDAY, JULY 30, 1950

MASS AT ST. EDWARD'S CHURCH .... 8:30 A. M., 10:30 A. M.
MASS AT ST. EUSEBIUS CHURCH .... 9:15 A. M.
SPECIAL HOUR OF WORSHIP AT ALL PROTESTANT CHURCHES .... 11 A. M. to 12:00 Noon
SONG FEST AT REVIEW FIELD .... 8:00 P. M.

EDUCATIONAL DAY
MONDAY, JULY 31, 1950

OPENING OF HISTORICAL MUSEUM AT FAYETTE CITY SCHOOL .... 11:00 A. M.
OPENING OF KANGAROO COURT AND MIDWAY .... 12:00 NOON
TOUR THROUGH ALLENPORT PLANT OF PITTSBURGH STEEL COMPANY .... 2:00 P. M.
JUDGING OF HOBBY SHOW AT FAYETTE CITY SCHOOL .... 4:00 P. M.
ADDRESS BY GOVERNOR JAMES H. DUFF .... 8:00 P. M.
    (AT REVIEW FIELD)
HISTORICAL REVIEW AT REVIEW FIELD .... 8:30 P. M.
FUN ON THE MIDWAY .... 12:00 NOON—12:00 MIDNIGHT

HOMECOMING DAY
TUESDAY, AUGUST 1, 1950

TOUR OF HISTORICAL MUSEUM AT THE SCHOOL .... 11:00 A. M.
LUNCHEONS AT THE VARIOUS CHURCHES .... 12:30 P. M.
BAND CONCERT BY CHARLEROI HIGH SCHOOL BAND .... 2:00 P. M.
WATER EVENT .... 4:00 P. M.
HISTORICAL MUSEUM WILL BE OPENED AT THE SCHOOL .... 6:00 P. M. to 8:00 P. M.
MERCHANTS BALL GAME AT FAYETTE CITY BALL PARK .... 6:15 P. M.
HISTORICAL REVIEW AT REVIEW FIELD .... 8:30 P. M.
FUN ON THE MIDWAY .... 12:00 NOON—12:00 MIDNIGHT

YOUTH DAY
WEDNESDAY, AUGUST 2, 1950

SOAP BOX DERBY .... 12:30 P. M.
COMPETITIVE SPORTS AT REVIEW FIELD .... 2:00 P. M.
HISTORICAL MUSEUM WILL BE OPENED AT THE SCHOOL .... 6:00 P. M. to 8:00 P. M.
BASEBALL GAME AT FAYETTE CITY BALL PARK .... 6:15 P. M.
    (Legion vs. New Eagle)
HISTORICAL REVIEW AT REVIEW FIELD .... 8:30 P. M.
STREET DANCING (Near School) .... 9:00 P. M. — 12:00 MIDNIGHT
FUN ON THE MIDWAY .... 12:00 NOON—12:00 MIDNIGHT

LABOR AND INDUSTRY DAY
THURSDAY, AUGUST 3, 1950

FLOAT PARADE .... 2:00 P. M.
SPEAKING AT REVIEW FIELD .... 4:00 P. M.
    P. E. SANCE, WORKS MANAGER OF PITTSBURGH STEEL COMPANY
    EUGENE MAURICE, DISTRICT MANAGER OF CIO
DRUM AND BUGLE CORPS COMPETITION AT REVIEW FIELD .... 7:30 P. M.
FUN ON THE MIDWAY .... 12:00 NOON—12:00 MIDNIGHT

MERCHANTS DAY
FRIDAY, AUGUST 4, 1950

GALA OPENING OF OLD FASHIONED BARGAIN DAY—ALL DAY EVENT
PET PARADE .... 2:00 P. M.
MERCHANTS BALL GAME AT FAYETTE CITY BALL PARK .... 6:15 P. M.
CELEBRATION BALL WITH TOMMY TUCKER AND HIS ORCHESTRA .... 9:00 P. M.
    (AT FAIRHOPE SKATING RINK)
FUN ON THE MIDWAY .... 12:00 NOON—12:00 MIDNIGHT

GRAND FINALE
SATURDAY, AUGUST 5, 1950

BABY PARADE .... 2:30 P. M.
FIREMEN'S PARADE .... 7:30 P. M.
FIREWORKS .... 10:30 P. M.
FUN ON THE MIDWAY .... 12:00 NOON—12:00 MIDNIGHT

The Borough of Fayette City, Pennsylvania,

Commemorating its 150th Anniversary

— PRESENTS —

Fayette City Historical Review

SCENE I—INDIAN SCENE

In this scene the narrator tells of the first citizens of Fayette City, the Indians of this region. The curtain parts, showing an Indian village. The Indian braves do a dance of Thanksgiving for a good harvest.

SCENE II—THE WHITE MEN COME

Narrator tells of the first white settlers of the region. The curtain parts, showing a minuet on the porch of Col. Cook's home in honor of the visiting George Washington.

Narrator tells of the Whiskey Rebellion. The curtain parts showing a mob scene protesting the tax levied on the chief product of the region by Alexander Hamilton, the Secretary of Treasury, and the new United States Government.

Narrator describes the planning of Freeport, or Fayette City, in 1800. Colonel Cook and Joseph Downer are shown measuring lots with their clothes line.

SCENE III—CHURCHES AND SCHOOLS

Narrator relates the history of our local churches and schools. An early school and church scene is enacted on the stage.

SCENE IV—INDUSTRIAL SCENE

Narrator tells of the industries found in Fayette City during its 150 years. Representatives of each industry act out the work of the industry as it is mentioned by the narrator.

SCENE V—FIRE AND DISASTER

Narrator tells of the fires which destroyed much of Fayette City about 1900. The dance of the flames pays tribute to the men whose lives were lost in these disasters. The narrator mentions mine explosions of this period. Death scene.

SCENE VI—TRANSPORTATION

Narrator tells of the importance of the Monongahela River in transportation. Various types of boats cross the stage in the background. The rough treatment of the Steamer Fayette, by the Southern sympathizers of Fayette City at the close of the Civil War period is related. The Waltz, typical dance of the Civil War period, is staged.

Narrator tells of the coming of the Railroad in 1896. Gay Nineties Scene is enacted with the girls doing the Cancan Dance.

SCENE VII—NATIONALITY SCENE

Narrator tells of the coming of many nationalities to Fayette City at the turn of the century. The nationalities are honored in dance.

SCENE VIII—FINALE

Narrator relates the history of the town during the present century. Scene is presented honoring heroes of two World Wars. Pageant closes with the crowning of the Popularity Queen of Fayette City.

-: CAST :-

NARRATOR .... Rev. H. D. Hough
ORGANIST .... Mrs. Carl Frantz
PIANIST .... Miss Kathleen Scullion

Scene I
INDIAN PERIOD
SQUAWS

Mrs. John Russell
Mrs. Robert Park
Miss Catherine Russell
Mrs. William Opfar
Mrs. Edward Moskala
Mrs. H. C. Cunningham
Mrs. Wilfred Young

INDIANS

Joseph Alberta
Philip Motsay
Allen Park
Bernard Lee Sarra
Robert Jones
Jack Young
Kenneth Karcesky
Willard Jones
Joseph Sarra
Robert Cunningham
Donald Young
Dennis Livi
Raymond Moody
Duane Miller
Charles Grados
Mike Hancock
Kenneth Lindey
Merle Miller
Robert Smith

INDIAN CHILDREN

Wilma Grados
Buddy Ferris
James Batwinis
Andrew Lorinchak
Linda Wilson

Scene II
THE WHITE MEN COME

Mr. Jasper Hare
Mr. Miller Boag
Mr. James Yates
Mr. Thomas Evans
Mr. Herman Trader
Mr. Wooda Brightwell

MINUET

Directress Mrs. John Barnes
Pianist   Mrs. Sara Mong
Assistant Pianist
      Miss Sue Rittenhouse

Mrs. Virginia Allen
Mr. Ralph Allen
Mrs. Blanche Lynn
Mr. Otis Rittenhouse
Miss Mary Leighty
Mr. John Barnes
Mrs. Nellie Arison
Mr. Clayton Arison
Mrs. Jane Forsyth
Mr. Howard Forsyth
Mrs. Evie Silbaugh
Mr. Kenneth Silbaugh

Scene III
CHURCHES and SCHOOLS

CHURCH CHOIR

Gerald Devers
Mr. Fred Weightman
Mr. Joseph Moravek
Mrs. Wellington Baldwin
Mrs. Park Russell
Miss Mary Winn
Miss Margaret Winn
Mr. John Murt
Mr. Domenick Canigiani
Miss Georgia Nicholson
Miss Janet Mathewson
Mrs. John Bowers
Mrs. George Troth
Miss Florence Sobek
Miss Ann Sobek
Miss Janie Roy
Mr. James Marriott
Mr. John Traversari
Mrs. Fred Brightwell
Mrs. Samuel Miller
Miss Helen Scullion
Mr. Joseph Dorcon
Mrs. George Hancock
Mrs. Bertha Roberts
Mrs. Aldo Stagi
Mrs. William Elliott

SCHOOL SCENE

Wanda Winters
Jane Hargar
Thurman Smith
Donald Schroyer
Andrew Lorinchak
Kay Beris
Kay Auther
Charlotte Lindey
Helen Grados
Charlene Turik
Margaret Calcek
Audrey Devers
Gail Cramer
Judy Dewar
Dixie McCrory
Audrey Tiernan
Harold Russell
Norman Russell

Scene IV
INDUSTRY

Mrs. Clarence Young
Mr. Lester Liviskie
Mr. Albert Roberts
Keith Stark
John Edward Arrow
Mr. Edwin Hindmarsh
Mr. Herman Trader
Robert Stimmell
Robert Young
Robert Blacka
Claude Nutt
Frank Devers
Mr. Edward Applegate
Oliver Niemala

Scene V
FIRE AND DISASTER
FIRE-DANCE

Kathleen Walton
Audrey Dewar
Betty Dewar
Lillian Smith
Mona Lee McDonald
Mary Ellen Barker
Virginia Scullion
Joan Cunningham
Elizabeth Mae Hamer
Ethel Grummer
Mary Yusko
Elsie Carney
Virginia Moats
Mary Moats
June Cramer
Sara Allen
Grace Watson

DEATH SCENE

Mr. Jasper Hare
Mr. Miller Boag
Mr. James Yates
Mrs. William Opfar
Mrs. Wilfred Young
Mrs. Edward Moskala
Mrs. Charles Morgan

Scene VI
TRANSPORTATION

WALTZ SCENE
CIVIL WAR PERIOD

Mrs. Raymond Miller and
Mr. Peter Gardner

Mrs. Vernon Smith and
Mr. Gerald Devers

Mrs. Russell Jones and
Mr. Kenneth Humphries

Mr. and Mrs. Leroy Gardner
Mr. and Mrs. Bernard Sarra
Mr. and Mrs. Frank Dewar
Mr. and Mrs. Jack Stockton
Mr. and Mrs. Randall Evans
Mr. and Mrs. Joseph
  Williams
Dr. and Mrs. Victor Jesick

CANCAN DANCE
GAY NINETIES

Dana Baldwin
Helen Yusko
Mary Layton
Leah Marriott
Julia Dohanich
Dorothy Zelenski
Mariam Pegg
Mary Ann Puskas

Cast - Continued

Scene VII

NATIONALITY SCENE
ENGLISH
COUNTRY DANCE

Kathleen Walton
Audrey Dewar
Betty Dewar
Lillian Smith
Mona Lee McDonald
Mary Ellen Barker
Virginia Scullion
Joan Cunningham
Elizabeth Mae Hamer
Ethel Grummer
Mary Yusko
Elsie Carney
Virginia Moats
Mary Moats
June Cramer
Sara Allen
Grace Watson

POLKA

Mrs. Raymond Miller and Mr. Peter Gardner
Mrs. Vernon Smith and Mr. Gerald Devers
Mrs. Russell Jones and Mr. Kenneth Humphries
Mr. and Mrs. Leroy Gardner
Mr. and Mrs. Bernard Sarra
Mr. and Mrs. Frank Dewar
Mr. and Mrs. Jack Stockton
Mr. and Mrs Randall Evans
Mr. and Mrs. Joseph Williams
Dr. and Mrs. Victor Jesick

IRISH

Dana Baldwin
Helen Yusko
Mary Layton
Leah Marriott
Dorothy Zelenski
Julia Dohanich
Mariam Pegg
Mary Ann Puskas

Scene VIII

FINALE

Mr. Donald Mossburg
Mr. William Gardner
Mr. George Yusko
Mr. Edward Sobek
Mrs. Edward McGee
Mrs. Robert Park
Mr. Robert Pivarnik
Mr. George Gardner
Mr. Thomas Osborne
Mr. Randall Evans
Mr. William Ciavarra
Ronald Martin
Audrey Devers
Georgia Nicholson
Mrs. Wellington Baldwin
Mr. Fred Weightman
Mr. Joseph Moravek
Mrs. Park Russell

Miss Mary Winn
Miss Margaret Winn
Mr. John Murt
Mr. Domenick Canigiani
Miss Janet Mathewson
Mrs. John Bowers
Mrs. George Troth
Miss Florence Sobek
Miss Ann Sobek
Miss Janie Roy
Mr. James Marriott
Mr. John Traversari
Mrs. Fred Brightwell
Mrs. Samuel Miller
Miss Helen Scullion
Mr. Joseph Dorcon
Mrs. George Hancock
Mrs. Bertha Roberts
Mrs. Aldo Stagi

Celebration Ball Patrons

MR. and MRS. JAMES M. THIRKIELD
DR. and MRS. E. B. SLOTERBECK
DR. and MRS. A. S. SICKMAN
DR. and MRS. ALAND C. DENT
MRS. LOUIS MILLER
MISS FLORENCE GATER
DR. and MRS. J. R. CONNELLY
MR. and MRS. WILLIAM EVANS, SR.
DR. and MRS. W. E. TREZISE
MR. and MRS. J. H. RENSTROM
MR. and MRS. GEORGE HANCOCK
MR. and MRS. WALTER RIDGWAY
MR. and MRS. LOUIS SAMBERG
MR. and MRS. JOSEPH CIAVARRA
MR. and MRS. HOWARD OPFAR
MR. and MRS. GEORGE MILLER
MR. and MRS. CHARLES KUHNS
DR. and MRS. J. J. BUCH
MISS MARY KAY MARINAK
MR. and MRS. PAUL MORAVEK
MR. and MRS. FRANK RIHTARCIK
MR. and MRS. JAMES DAVIDSON
MR. and MRS. JAMES E. HAMER

MR. and MRS. HOWARD McCRORY
MR. and MRS. GEORGE M. McCRORY
MR. and MRS. STEPHEN FIGEL
MR. and MRS. LEROY GARDNER
MR. and MRS. GEORGE ROY
MR. and MRS. MATT MARKISH
MR. and MRS. JOSEPH WILLIAMS
MR. and MRS. JOHN RAZZANDO
MR. and MRS. JOHN CANIGIANI
MR. and MRS. PATRICK HYNES
MR. and MRS. THOMAS CONWAY
MR. and MRS. JACK STOCKTON
MR. and MRS. ALSON ROY
MR. and MRS. JOSEPH ALBERTA
MR. and MRS. GEORGE DOHAN
MR. and MRS. ROBERT PREMOSHIS
MR. and MRS. HAROLD HUMPHRIES
MR. FRED WEIGHTMAN
MR. and MRS. DONALD STEPHENS
MR. and MRS. THOMAS DENT
MRS. EDWARD D. STEINMAN, SR.
DR. and MRS. FRANCIS SMITH
MRS. ROBERT WILLIAMS

Fayette City Sesquicentennial Executive Board

GENERAL CHAIRMAN .... MR. JAMES M. THIRKIELD
CO-CHAIRMAN .... MR. LEROY GARDNER
VICE CHAIRMEN .... MRS. JOSEPH WILLIAMS
MR. HOWARD McCRORY
SECRETARY .... MRS. WAYNE HAWKER
ASSISTANT SECRETARY .... MRS. ALAND C. DENT
TREASURER .... MRS. JOHN WILSON
FINANCE DIVISION CHAIRMEN .... MR. GEORGE HANCOCK
MRS. ALAND C. DENT
PUBLICITY DIVISION CHAIRMEN .... MRS. JOSEPH WILLIAMS
MISS BETTY EVANS
SPECTACLE DIVISION CHAIRMEN .... MR. JOHN A. WHEELER
MR. FRANK A. DEWAR
SPECIAL EVENTS DIVISION CHAIRMAN .... MR. JACK STOCKTON

Fayette City Sesquicentennial Committees

Finance Division

FINANCE DIVISION CHAIRMAN .... MR. GEORGE HANCOCK
FINANCE DIVISION CO-CHAIRMAN .... MRS. ALAND C. DENT

UNDERWRITING

Mr. George Hancock   Chairman
Mrs. Edward Batwinis
Mrs. Edwin Hindmarsh
Mrs. J. H. Renstrom
Mrs. Ben Holliday
Mrs. Stephen Figel
Mrs. Don Mossburg
Mrs. George Rainey
Mrs. Howard McCrory
Mrs. Joseph Ciavarra
Mrs. George Dohan
Mrs. Louis Miller
Mrs. Howard Opfar
Mrs. Norman Humphries
Mrs. Harry Shanks

CONCESSIONS

Mr. James M. Thirkield
Mr. Howard Opfar
Mr. George Roy

NOVELTIES

Mrs. Edwin Hindmarsh Chairman
Mrs. Ben Holliday
Mrs. Clarence Young
Mrs. Robert Brinegar
Mrs. Thomas Conway
Mrs. Gilbert Young
Mrs. John Phillips
Miss Leah Marriott
Miss Elizabeth Mae Hamer
Miss Virginia Scullion
Mrs. Samuel Miller
Miss Janice Weightman
Miss Jean Gardner
Mrs. Alson Roy
Miss Geraldine Jones

QUEEN CONTEST

Mrs. Read Brightwell   Chairman
Mrs. Ben Holliday
Mrs. Melrose Stewart
Mrs. Stanton Farquhar
Miss Frances Vesely
Mrs. Jacob Zubovic
Miss Jean Gardner
Mrs. Edward Applegate, Jr.

OFFICIAL PROGRAM

Mr. George Hancock   Chairman
Mrs. Aland C. Dent
Mr. Howard McCrory
Mr. Jack Stockton
Mr. Joseph Moravek
Mr. J. H. Renstrom
Mrs. Joseph Williams
Mr. James M. Thirkield
Miss Betty Evans
Mrs. Wayne Hawker
Mrs. Jack Stockton
Mr. Joseph Williams

KANGAROO COURT

Mr. Fred Holder   Chairman
Mr. Paul Moravek   Co-Chairman
Mr. Paul Jesick
Mrs. Edwin Hindmarsh
Mrs. Stephen Figel
Mr. J. H. Renstrom
Mr. Jack Beattie

Publicity Division and Committees

PUBLICITY DIVISION

Mrs. Joseph Williams Chairman
Miss Betty Evans   Co-Chairman

PRESS

Miss Geraldine Jones   Chairman
Mrs. Mildred Janeri
Mrs. Edwin Hindmarsh
Mrs. Joseph Alberta
Miss Jo Ann Blatnik
Mrs. Nick Turik
Mrs. Leroy Gardner

PROMOTIONAL

Mr. Frank McCurdy   Chairman
Mr. Willis Johnson
Mrs. Thomas Conway
Mrs. Patrick Hynes

DECORATIONS

Mrs. Edwin Hindmarsh
Mrs. Leroy Gardner
Miss Geraldine Jones
Mrs. Mildred Janeri
Mr. Nick Turik
Mr. Joseph Williams
Mr. Bernard Sarra
Mr. Leroy Gardner
Mr. George Breckenridge

DISTRIBUTIVE

Mr. Joseph Williams   Chairman
Mr. Bernard Sarra
Mr. Nick Turik
Mr. George Breckenridge

RADIO

Mrs. George Roy   Chairman
Mrs. George Troth
Mr. James Hamer
Mr. Raymond Barker

Special Events Division and Committees

SPECIAL EVENTS
Mr. Jack Stockton   Chairman

RELIGIOUS PARTICIPATION
Rev. H. D. Hough   Chairman
Rev. Charles W. Ribick
Rev. W. D. Savage
Rev. Briant O. S. B.
Rev. John Bowers
Rev. Arthur Warner
Rev. C. R. Ellenberger
Rev. George L. Bayha

EDUCATIONAL DAY
Mrs. George Troth   Chairman
Miss Margaret Restrom
            Co-Chairman
Mrs. George Rainey
Mrs. Howard McCrory
Mrs. Ellis Sisley
Mrs. George Spalter
Mrs. Robert Williams
Mrs. James Larimer
Miss DeEtte Maude
Mr. George Rainey
Mr. Thomas Marriott, Sr.
Mr. Thomas Marriott, Jr.
Mr. Walter Ridgway, Jr.
Mr. Harvey Barker

HOMECOMING DAY
Mrs. James M. Thirkield
            Chairman
Mrs. Richard Auther
            Co-Chairman
Mrs. Vernon Smith
Mrs. Mildred Janeri
Mrs. Louis Miller
Mrs. Bernard Sarra
Mrs. George Breckenridge
Miss Mary McDonough
Mrs. James Hamer

MERCHANTS' DAY
Mr. Jack Stockton
Mr. Joseph Moravek

PET PARADE
Mrs. George Rainey   Chairman
Mr. Charles Kuhns
Mr. Claude Nutt
Mr. William Nutt
Mrs. Philip Karcesky
Philip Karcesky, Jr.

BABY PARADE
Mr. Jasper Hare   Chairman
Mr. Louis Samberg
Mr. Paul Jesick
Mr. Andrew Bircsak
Mr. Howard McCrory

FIREMEN'S PARADE
Mr. Earl M. Opfar   Chairman
Mr. Edward Sobek
Mr. James Moody
Mr. Walter Zelenski

LABOR AND INDUSTRY DAY
Mr. James M. Thirkield Chairman
Mr. Howard McCrory
Mrs. Joseph Williams
Mr. Jerome Williams
Mr. Louis Samberg
Mr. William Beattie
Mr. Jack Stockton
Mr. William Ciavarra
Mr. Bevan Freshwater

**HISTORICAL
WINDOW DISPLAY**
Mr. Wayne Hawker

FIREWORKS
Mr. Leroy Gardner   Chairman
Mr. Frank Rihtarcik
Mr. Bernard Sarra
Mr. Wayne Hawker

CELEBRATION BALL
Mrs. Aland C. Dent   Chairman
Dr. Aland C. Dent Co-Chairman
Mrs. Donald Stephens
Mrs. George Dohan
Mrs. Park Russell
Miss Gertrude Markish
Mrs. Louis Samberg
Mr. William Ciavarra
Mrs. Thomas Conway
Mr. John Murt
Mrs. Richard Richardson
Mr. Jack Beattie
Mrs. Edward Vesely
Mrs. Joseph Alberta
Mrs. Stephen Figel
Mrs. Robert Premoshis

YOUTH DAY
Mr. Jesse Smith   Chairman
Mrs. George Hancock
Mrs. Wayne Hawker
Mr. Raymond Barker

STREET DANCING
Mr. George Roy   Chairman
Mrs. Earl Opfar
Mrs. James Moody
Mrs. William Opfar
Mr. William Opfar

Spectacle Division and Committees

SPECTACLE DIVISION
Mr. John A. Wheeler   Chairman
Mr. Frank A. Dewar Co-Chairman

TALENT
Mrs. Edward Batwinis Chairman
Mrs. Raymond Barker
            Co-Chairman
Miss Hildred Nelson
Miss Lucille Nelson
Mrs. Wellington Baldwin
Mrs. Clyde Wyatt
Mrs. Edward Vesely
Miss Sara Jean Scullion
Miss Kathleen Scullion
Mrs. John A. Wheeler

COSTUME AND MAKE-UP
Mrs. W. Glenn Burig Chairman
Marjorie Ferris

Mrs. Alfred Makepeace
Miss Mary McDonough
Mrs. Richard Richardson
Mrs. Russell Jones
Mrs. Oscar Paegert
Mrs. Elmer Russell
Mrs. John Wilson

SCENARIO
Miss Betty Evans
Mrs. Wayne Hawker

PROPERTIES
Mr. Robert Williams   Chairman
Mr. Wilbur Long   Co-Chairman
Mrs. James Welch
Miss Geraldine Jones
Mr. Edward Moskala
Mr. James Marriott
Mr. Willard Jones

CONSTRUCTION
Mr. Jacob Zubovic
Mr. James Moody
Mr. Joseph Butler
Mr. James Butler
Mr. Guy Sturgis
Mr. William Rutledge
Mr. George Bronson
Mr. John Wilson
Mr. Miller Boag

DESIGN AND SCENERY
Mr. John Murt   Chairman
Mr. Jack Beattie
Mr. E. H. Johnson
Mr. Floyd La Rue
Mr. William Usher
Mr. Kenneth Weight
William Janeri
Miss Pearl Kish

Due to Printer's deadline some names may be omitted. The Celebration Committee hereby offers its sincere thanks to those members of the cast and committees who did not receive program credits.

Scenes from the Midway. Photos courtesy of Judith Dewar Shearer (top) and Doris Moskala Breckenridge (bottom).

Scenes from the Midway. Photos courtesy of Linda Russell Nelson, Georgia Jean Arrow and Vanessa Moskala Pugh.

"I know that was a very big time. I think they were covering a whole period of history. I had a part, I was dressed up as a nurse for one thing, and then they had a baby beauty contest which I entered. We were judged up on the steps of the schoolhouse. They had that. I remember, Mr. Sarra, he was dressed up in a civil war uniform that they used as a union uniform. And I think his name is Leroy Gardner. I think he was dressed up as Abraham Lincoln. That was quite a big time, that Sesquicentennial. I forget how many days that went on and everything."

-Georgia Nicholson Slezak

"That was big doings….There was a parade. Everybody was in, every kid, every adult was in something. And, of course, they set up the thing just like they did for the Firemen's carnival….The men, if they shaved, they had to pay a fine. So my dad, he grew a mustache, the mutton bars and he grew a mustache. And then we all had to buy those hats. I had one….I think there's a picture of me in that hat….They had a thing with the schoolchildren. It was set like the old schools…The women and the men did a waltz dance, and they rented them hoop skirts and everything. And they did this waltz. I couldn't believe my father did that waltz. But he did. That was beautiful. That was beautiful. I talked to my sister Audrey a couple weeks ago. And I said something about the Sesquicentennial. And she said Oh, I remember. She said we did that dance. I said yes. You did the fire dance. I think it was Kauchatorian's music. She said Oh I remember…I remember they all had like lights, you know, different color things, like a flower would be a flame and they went around. It was beautiful. Just beautiful."

-Judith Dewar Shearer

"That was a big doings. It was nice. They had big parades. They had baseball every day, a big carnival and that. They had a lot of old cars in the parade. That was something to see….They had all kinds of games. There was the penny pitch, and they got to throw the balls in the middle of bottles and stuff like that. They had a lot of that going on….I can't remember that much of it….The fireman had a water battle with water barrels, squirting it back on a wire. Different companies would come in and use their water hoses to see who could get the barrel from one end to the other."

-Willard Jones

"Mary Ellen Barker Hazlett, she was the Queen. So she, of course, chose Carolyn (Barker) to be the attendant to carry the train. So Carolyn's mother called my mom and said, Well, since Linda and Carolyn do everything together, which we did, Linda gets to ride on the float, too. And then she gets to carry the train. So we went to Pittsburgh, and we got the dresses. So you can see those little dresses we had. And truthfully, I think I had that dress until a couple years ago. I don't know where in this house it might be. But my mom kept everything. We went and got matching dresses. I can remember the floats, riding the float. I can remember, wherever we were, we were out like on a field, like a baseball field or someplace, where we were carrying the train. It's a wonder I didn't fall off that float as silly as I was. But yeah, I got to ride on the float."

-Linda Russell Nelson

Scenes from the Float Parade. Photos courtesy of Linda Russell Nelson, Vanessa Moskala Pugh, Herb Vargo, and Judith Dewar Shearer.

Scenes from the Float Parade. Photos courtesy of Linda Russell Nelson, Vanessa Moskala Pugh, Herb Vargo, and Judith Dewar Shearer.

"Well, it was a nice, nice crowd. Who was the devil that grabbed Tinker and I and stuck us in the jail? We were in the jail there for a while, and they wouldn't let us out until we were kissing each other. Then they let us out. That was so much fun, that Sesquicentennial, it was. All of the costumes that people drew up...They brought out a lot of postcards and memorabilia from town, you know."

-June Winters Baldwin Jaquette

"Oh, I'll tell you what, that was a big deal for everyone in Fayette City. I mean, they prepared for weeks for that. I mean, it was the biggest parade. In fact, my sister, Gail, she was on the Queen's float, along with Carolyn Barker, Linda Russell and Ross Brightwell. The Queen was Carolyn Barker's mother's sister and I can't think of her name. People lined the streets five deep to watch the parade. Lots of kids of course were riding their decorated bicycles. That was a big thing in the parade. I remember where my mother and myself stood to the watch the parade. It was in front of the Presbyterian educational building. You know where that was, across from the old post office in Fayette City? People were four deep there. And this is where my mother had her purse pickpocketed. Someone took a $20 bill from her purse. And of course, they had the food booths, the wheel of chance, Bingo, and of course, penny pitch. All the kids loved playing penny pitch. Then all the old women playing bingo. And they'd be going "Shh, Shh. Can't hear, can't hear." They also wore hats."

-Georgia Jean Arrow

"Men had to have a shaving permit. If you were going to shave, you had to buy a permit. I don't know what it costs, but you had to have, the men had to have a permit. If you didn't have a permit, you ended up spending time in jail. Well, my dad didn't have a permit. So he spent time. They had this jail sitting right across on the parking lot just behind Riverview Grill, and it was all out in the open. It was all in great fun too. My dad had to spend time in jail. I think he had to spend an hour in jail because he didn't have a saving permit....It was it right in the middle of Market. The one guy, his name was Leroy Gardner, he grew a beard, and I would I swear to this day, he looked more like Abraham Lincoln than Abraham Lincoln did."

-Grace Hough Martin

"You had all them activities and that, and all them hotdogs stands, all the stands that they had. I remember Emma Alberta, she was a big, big worker for that, you know, and put that on. She was a hard worker, Emma Alberta was. She was married to Joe Williams. I remember Emma Williams. She was really exceptional, I thought."

-Joe Vargo

"All kinds of games were set up down the freight yard. They had a ball field down there. They put a lot of stuff on the ball field. They had the circus come in. They had a couple of different ball teams come. Fayette City had their own ball team at that time. Big parades going through town. Just running around have a good time."

-Larry Moskala

REFERENCES

Fayette City Sesquicentennial Program | PDF | Native Americans In The United States | Bar (scribd.com)
https://www.scribd.com/document/241754938/Fayette-City-Sesquicentennial-Program

Dr. Aland Dent

Howard McCrory

Emma Williams

George Hancock

James Namer

CHAPTER 11 The End of an Era

The 1940s was an extraordinary decade for Fayette City. Most of its young men and several of its young women served valiantly in World War II. Seven of Fayette City's brightest gave their lives for their country. Those who remained home during the War helped Fayette City distinguish itself from its neighbors for its generosity and organizational skills by routinely exceeding its goals in a variety of fund-raising drives.

Despite its small size, Fayette City had everything it needed (except for a bank) for a community to flourish. Doctors and dentists, funeral homes, a movie theatre, a post office, an excellent school, multiple churches, grocery stores, clothing stores, confectionaries, feed stores, hardware stores, barber shops, beauty shops, restaurants, gas stations, and of course seven bars were crammed into the tiny downtown area. The sidewalks could barely contain the lively crowds on a typical Saturday.

> "It seemed like everything was important. It all blended together and made a good living atmosphere. The problem is we were young and didn't know all that. It's not until later years when you don't have that and you miss it that you realize what you really had…. Everybody knew everybody else and helped everybody else out. Just get along good. Just get along. That's all I can say about all that. It was a good place to grow up. We grew up in one of the best of places and the best of times. A lot of people will never know what we enjoyed. There was nights when you would go down to Fayette City, you couldn't walk on the sidewalk there'd be that many people there. You didn't realize it then but, boy, you sure miss it now."
>
> -Raymond Moody

Most of the men worked in the steel mills or coal mines while their wives focused on their families. With the exceptions of the doctors and perhaps a couple of business owners, most everyone was on equal footing when it came to financial conditions. Everyone knew everyone and looked out for everyone. There were few secrets in the small community. As one narrator put it, "You knew your neighbors, good and bad, and everything about them." Kids could roam the neighborhoods from dawn to dusk returning home only if they were hungry. If a child managed to get in trouble during the day, his or her parents would know about before he or she got home.

Throughout the decade, the town's vibrant community spirit was on full display. Fayette City was blessed with many strong and committed leaders like those pictured on the adjoining page. Some other prominent leaders included, in alphabetical order, Joe Alberta, Joe Bell, John Canigiani, Mrs. Aland Dent, Jim Eley, George Ferris, Leroy Gardner, Dr. U.F. Higinbotham, Edwin Hindmarsh, Alfred Makepeace, Robert Premoshis, J.H. Renstrom, Jack Stockton, James Thirkield, Mrs. Bess Welch, and many others. Organizations such as the local chapters of the American Legion and the Free and Accepted Masons, the Volunteer Fire Department, and the newly formed Lions Club and Womans Club were committed to addressing the needs of the community. Each of Fayette City's seven churches had full

> "I just remember being free. When you think back on it now, you know, roaming all over the place. We would ride our bicycles up the Hollow. We would play all the time. I could go out during the day and my mother would say, well get home before dark. We'd play along the River and sometimes we'd sneak a ride on the ferry."
>
> -Judith Dewar Shearer

> "It was a good place to grow up. Everything was, I don't know, you knew who you were and who your family was and who your neighbors were, good and bad, and everything about them. There was hardly any secrets in a small town. But it was it was a great place."
>
> -Kathleen Walton Stimmell

and committed congregations. The Trojans Drum and Bugle Corps represented Fayette City with pride though out the region. Fayette City residents dominated state horseshoe competitions at the beginning of the decade and its baseball teams dominated the diamond at the end of the decade. Community spirit reached a crescendo at the end of the decade with the Sesquicentennial celebration of the town's founding.

But transformational changes were clearly on the horizon by the end of the decade. For example, Bell Theatre was the primary form of entertainment for the community during the 1940s. However, when first television set in the window of the Premoshis Hardware Store on Main Street captured the curiosity of everyone who walked by, the future of the theatre quickly came into focus.

Report Closing Of Local Station

According to a report carried in valley newspapers, the PUC has granted permission to the Pittsburgh and Lake Erie railroad to discontinue agent's service from the local station.

In contacting the local agent he stated that to date he has received no notice that this approval has reached company officials and therefore cannot state just when the station will be closed.

The president of the newly-formed Board of Trade stated that he contacted the legal counsel that was asking for a re-hearing on the protest that was lodged and to date no word has been received of a refusal to reopen the case.

Closing of the station which has been a topic of discussion among town folk for some time, will mean the passing of one more landmark of the good-old days when Fayette City was one of the leading towns in the valley.

Fayette City Journal
August 13, 1948

The closure of the local high school in 1946 and the jointure with neighboring Belle Vernon and Marion in 1951 had a profound effect on the insular nature of Fayette City. Up until 1946, students had essentially the same, small group of classmates from grades one through twelve. This often led to deep bonds between students that lasted a lifetime. With the closure of the high school and then the junior high school, students from Fayette City were now mixed in with a larger and more diverse population from beyond the town's borders.

The demise of the coal industry during the 1930s and 1940s shifted the emphasis to the steel mills for jobs. Most of the men in Fayette City worked at Pittsburgh Steel's Allenport and Monessen steel mills. It was just what everyone did. While the steel industry flourished during the 1950s and 1960s and even into the 1970s, it too had its own shelf life.

Perhaps the biggest change on the horizon involved transportation. During the early part of the 1940s, few people could afford an automobile. The train still shuttled people up and down the River valley. Before the end of the decade, however, the landmark train station in Fayette City would close and automobile ownership would become more commonplace. This increased mobility made it possible for everyone to easily find a job, or a place to live, or even someone to marry beyond the borders of Fayette City.

Interest in exploring life outside of Fayette City also had an unfortunate effect on the local newspaper, the Fayette City Journal. Local news became much less relevant as interest in the bigger cities took hold. The Pittsburgh newspapers and the larger local newspapers like the Valley Independent siphoned readers from the Journal forcing it to close before the end of the 1950s.

This potent mixture of factors would prove to have a profound and sustained impact on Fayette City. This impact, however, would be fully realized only with the passage of time. In retrospect, the 1940s truly were the end of an era.

"It (the Sesquicentennial Celebration) was, in one respect, the last gasp in a rapidly changing society, the end of the small industrial town, the last gasp of it. I didn't look at it that way at the time, obviously. But looking back on it, that's what it seemed like it was to me. It was terrific."

-Mike Hancock

APPENDICES

Appendix I: Women Narrators (Birth Year)

Baker, Pauline Ann Vargo (b1935)

Davis, Ella Marie Auther (b1938)

Jaquette, June Winters Baldwin (b1932)

Johnson, Nancy Ferree (b1933)

Manetta, Joanne Cunningham (b1935)

Martin, Grace Hough (b1941)

Moluski, Georgia Jean Arrow (b1944)

Moskala, Barbara Toth (b1945)

Nelson, Linda Russell (b 1946)

Owens, Eleanor Welsh (b1931)

Repka, Audrey Tiernan (b1937)

Shearer, Judith Dewar (b1938)

Slezak, Georgia Nicholson (b1935)

Steiner, Leila Breckenridge (b1943)

Stilgenbauer, Shirley Ferree (b1934)

Stimmell, Kathleen Walton (b1933)

Yevincy, June Cramer (b1934)

Appendix II: Men Narrators (Birth Year)

Applegate, Harry (b1945)

Eley, James (b1940)

Gargan, John (Jack) (b1935)

Hancock, George (Mike) (b1938)

Herspold, Brad (b1947)

Hindmarsh, Barry (b1941)

Jolley, Tom (b1954)

Jones, Willard (b1937)

McKevitt, James (b1932)

Moody, Raymond (b1936)

Moskala, Larry (b1943)

Vargo, Joe (b1937)

Vargo, John (b1944)

Williamson, Bill (b1934)

Young, Jack (b1934)

APPENDIX III: World War I Veterans from Fayette City (1914-1918)

Anderson John

Baldwin, John R.

Barker, Harvey B.

Beattie, John

Brightwell, Carl*

Brightwell, Wooda

Brosick, Joseph

Brown, Roy

Cadman, Luke

Chebein, Henry

Ciavarra, Joseph W.

Clark, George

Coogan, Leslie

Daugherty, James

Daugherty, Patrick W.*

Davidson, James W.

Davidson, John L.

Davidson, Thomas E.

Deaterly, Riley

Drennan, George

Dreyer, Chris W.

Dwyer, Llewellyn

Eland, Robert

Ferree, Guy W.

Fields, Edwin

Francis, William

Giffin, Walter

Gillingham, Harry

Greely, Thomas

Hamer, Edward

Hamer, Samuel

Hamilton, George

Harvey, Gray

Hency, Thomas

Hetherington, John W.

Hetherington, Joseph

Hetherington, Raymond

Humphries, Harold

Hynes, George

Hynes, John

Hynes, Patrick

Kalamaris, Mike

Karelli, John*

Kepple, Clyde*

Klinsky, John

Kuharic, Charles

Kuhns, Charles

Legg, John

Legg, Samuel

Livingston, Peter

Marriott, Thomas

Mathewson, Adam

Mathewson, David

Mathewson, James

McCready, Albert

McCready, Wm.

McCrory, Bird

McDermott, George

McKnight, Albert

McPherson, William

Morriston, Clarence

Opfar, Frank

Opfar, Howard, Sr.

Owens, Reese

Paegert, Albert

Palmer, Isaac

Parks, Alex

Pascoe, Andrew

Pascoe, James

Pascoe, Llewellyn

Pinks, Joseph

Rankin, Wm. C.

Renstrom, C. Henry

Rex, Edward

Rodgers, John A.

Rodish, Steven

Roy, George

Russell, Bruce

Rutledge, J. Wm., Sr.

Samberg, Louis

Shanks, Harry

Sillman, Emil

Smith, Albert

Smith, Clarence

Smith, O. Stanley

Steinman, Edw. Jr.

Stockton, Fred

Stollar, Dr. B. L.

Sturgis, Louis

Sturgis, Richard

Sheets, James

Thirkield, James F.

Todd, James E.

Trew, Fred

Usher, Louis

Vaughn, Walter

Wainer, John

Wilson, Harry

Williamson, Harry

Winn, Frank

Yates, Clarence

*Killed In Action

APPENDIX IV: World War II Veterans from Fayette City (1941-1945)

Abbott, Charles, Jr.

Abbott, Irwin

Alberta, Hector H.

Alberta, Jos. P

Aldridge, Willard

Applegate, Edw. L.

Applegate, Harry R.

Arrow, George

Arrow, John E.

Auther, Catherine

Auther, Dell S.

Auther, Kenneth*

Auther, Robert

Barker, Harold

Barker, William

Beattie, Jack

Beattie, Wm. L.

Beaumont, Ellis

Becketic, Adam

Bechicek, Peter

Bechick, Stephen D.

Bell, Edward

Bell, Donald

Bell, Jack W.

Bell, Melvin

Beris, Charles

Beris, Nickolas, Jr.

Blair, Dallas

Brightwell, H. Reed

Brightwell, Wooda F

Brilla, Paul

Calcek, Edward G

Campbell, Robert

Chunko, Michael

Chunko, Paul

Ciavarra, Wm. L.

Coates, Peter

Cooper, Paul

Cope, Quentin

Craft, Wm. H

Craft, Robert N.

Crea, John

Croushore, Don C.

Croushore, Jos. C.*

Cunko, Edward

Curry, Robert

Davison, Samuel

DeRienzo, Patsy P.*

Deck, Kenneth

Dewar, Wm. R.

Dohanich, John R.

Dorcon, Joseph

Dreyer, F.W.

Evans, Elizabeth S.

Evans, Sara

Evans, T. Randall

Evans, W. Don

Evans, Wm. S.

Farquhar, Stanton C.

Fedora, Geo. Jr.

Fedora, John

Fisher, James P.

Fitzpatrick, Clyde

Fitzpatrick, Reese J

Fitzpatrick, Wm. E.

Flemeng, Harold R.

Frantz, Earl A.

Gardner, James L.

Gardner, Peter P.

Gardner, Raymond J.

Gardner, Wm.

Gaskill John L.

Gill, Ralph

Grummer, Raymond*

Hawker, C. Ray

Hela, Andrew

Hela, Charles

Hela, John

Henry, Dwight

Henry, William

Hess, Glenn E.

Hicks, Howard W.

Hicks, James E.

Hicks, Samuel L., Jr.

Holliday, Benjamin, Jr.

Hough, Beatrix

Hough, Bennett J.

Huseman, Frank*

Huston, Clyde

Hynes, G. Wm.

Hynes, James J.

Ingland, Benjamin

Jamison, Roy, Jr.

Janeri, Joseph

Jesick, Thomas

Jesick, Victor B.

Johnson, E.H., Jr.

Johnson, Eugene

Keenan, Harold R.

Kenny, Theodore

Kovatch, Stephen

Kricsfaluski, John

Kruper, John A.

Kudlac, George

Kuharic, Carl W.

Layton, Wm. C.

Lazzari, Dr. John B.

Ledgerton, Eric S., Jr.

Ledgerton, Helen C.

Livi, Emil

Livi, James

Liviskie, James L.

Lloyd, Arthur R.

Lovich, Andrew P.

Lovich, Frank

Lukens, Holly J.

Makepeace, Ralph

Markish Frank J.

Marriott, Thos. R.

McCready, Robert

McCrory, John C.

McCrory, Raymond R.

McCurdy, Eugene F.

McCurdy, Glenn

McGee, Edward

McGee, Delores S.

McKenna, Frank, Jr.*

McKinley, Betty

McKinley, Harry P.

Melenyzer, Charles

Miller, Raymond L.

Moravek, John

Moravek, Paul

Moskala, Edward

Mosko, Edward

Mossburg, Donald

Mourikas, Harry

Mugrage Warren

Natola, Maynard W.

Nelson, John A.

Nelson, Harry

Novasel, Joseph

O'Brien, Charles

O'Connors, Joseph

Onufer, Joseph

Onufer, Stephen

Opfar, Earl

Opfar, Howard, Jr.

Osborne, Chas. R.

Osborne, Thomas

Package, Nicholas

Park, Howard

Park, John

Park, Robert

Park, William

Parry, Frank H.

Pasco, Geo. A.

Paskan, Mike

Petroka, Andrew

Petroka, George

Petroka, John, Jr.

Petroka, Mike

Petroka, Nick

Pivarnik, Elmer

Pivarnik, Robert

Renstrom, Sarah

Rhoades, Clarence

Ridgway, Richard

Ridgway, Walter

Rihtarcik, Carl L.

Rihtarcik, Frank

Russell, Carl

Russell, John A.

Rutledge, James

Rutledge, John R.

Scott, James

Scrip, Mike, Jr.

Scullion, Wm. S.

Sharrer, Chas. L.

Sheenan, Gloria

Shelper, Geo. E.

Shimko, Andrew

Shimko, Geo. T.

Skibo, Carl B.

Skibo, James E.

Slotterbeck J. Earl

Smock, Thurman E.

Snyder, J. Earl

Sobek, Carl P.

Sobek, Edward

Sobek, Jos. Frank

Sobek, Juluis S.

Sobek, Lawrence

Sobek, Stanley S.

Sobek, Thaddeus

Staley, Clarence H.

Stanley, Clarence H.

Stefanick, Paul

Steinman, Ed. D., III

Stephens, Bruce D.

Stephens, Varnon

Stewart, Wm. T.

Stublarak, Geo. D.

Suchta, Andrew

Supko, Stephen E.

Thirkield, Robert

Tissue, Clarence

Trew, Aberam L.

Troth, Geo. M.

Turek, Andrew

Turik, John

Turik, Nick

Usher, George

Usher, Fred

Vargo, John

Vargo, Samuel

Waugaman, Kenneth

Waugaman, Wm. S.

Weightman, Fred C.

Welsh, James

Whitelaw, John O.

Whitelaw, Jno. S.

Williams, James W.*

Williams, Jos. A.

Williams, Thomas R.

Williamson, George

Wilson, Charles W.

Wilson, Jackie

Wilson, James

Wilson, John A

Wilson, Robert T.

Winn, James P.

Winters, Jos. A.

Yakin Charles

Yakin, John

Yakin, Luke

Yelanich, Anthony G.

Yelanich, Stephen E.

Yetsconish, Chas.

Yetsconish, John

Yetsconish, Mike

Yetsconish Paul

Young, Harold

Young, James

Young, Wilfred

Killed In Action

Appendix V: Male Nicknames Compiled by Jack and Bob Young

Joe "Motor" Alberta, Jr. and Sr.

"Butch" Arthur

Don "Backy" Backstrom

Wellington "Tinker" Baldwin

Dickie "Nudgey" Barker

"Ram" Barker

"Fudge" Bednar

Chuck "Smiles" Berrace

Bob "Dalton" Blacka

Wooda "Senator" Brightwell

"Shorty" Brown

Bill "Wings" Calcek

John "Canny" Canigiani

"Chippy" Carlson

Norman "Tucker" Celaschi

Paul "Naul" Comedina

Les "Walter Mitty" Coogan

Jack "Wacky" Cramer

"Birdie" Cramer, Sr.

Curt "Curvin Curt" Davis

Jim Bob "Sandy" Davis

Tom "Bunky" Davis

"Mutsy" DeRienzo

Tet "Fedo" Emrick

Bill "Scodell Harris" Evans

Don "Counter" Evans

Tom "Mussy" Evans

Wilbur "Boobie" Evans

John "Pigeon" Fedora

Earl "Baa" Frantz

Gordon "Gog" Frantz

Bevin "Bevo" Freshwater

Earl "Freshie" Freshwater

Bill "Alfie" Gardner

Jim "Rags" Gardner

Ralph "Carridine" Gill

Leland "Pagetti" Haywood

"Ganz" Heinz

Steve "Judge" Hela

"Eagle" Henry

William "Sister" Hicks

Edwin "Hiney" Hindmarsh

George "Ducky" Hough

Harry "Buster" Hough

Ben "Cussy" Ingland

Bill "Jed" Janeri

Bob "Junior" Jones

Richard "Gomer" Jones

Phil "Kurk" Karcesky

Bill "Buggy" Layton

Ron "Ledge" Ledgerton

Kenny "Dippers" Lindey

Denny "Father Zircon" "Pogo" Livi

Hal "Lefty" Livingston

Joe "Poopy Joe" Livingston

Sheridan "Bodie" Livingston

Howard "Cocky" McCrory

Jack "Slick" McCrory

Frank "Ginky" McCurdy

"Doots" McGowan

Chuck "Buddy" McKevitt

Jim "Mac" McKevitt

Bill "Fagan" McKinley

Edward "Midgie" Moskala

"Butch" Mugrage

Don "Shep" Mossburg

Emerson "Red" Nichols

Don "Cutty" Niemela

Oliver "Fuddle" Niemela

Bill "Ollie" Nutt

Claude "Gike" Nutt

"Brother" Opfar

"Fuzzy" Opfar

Tom "Bundles" Package

Alexander "Sandy" Park

Howard "Hussy" Park

Alan "Fuseman" Parks

Bill "Sleepy" Parks

"Terp" Parry

Charles Oliver "Junior" "Booner" Pegg

"Yuddy" Pivarnek

"Spickets" Planey

"Pompy" Propes

"Dutch" Renstrom

Walter "Hoss" Ridgway

Jim "Dippers" Ridgway

Lou "Pud" Roy

Carl "Yane" Russell

Elmer "Abby" Russell

Jack "Lugs" Russell

Ross "Boxie" Russell

Bill "Motto" Scullion

Edward "Cap" Scullion

Tommy "Beans" Scullion

"Doodles" Sharrer

Ellis "Pop" Sisley

Earl "Bert" Skiles

Richard "Fred Wilt" Smith

"Jitters" Stefanik

Bill "Bicky" Stewart

Melrose "Memo" Stewart

Keith "Big Ben" Stark

George "Stubby" Stublarac

Joe "Swata" Svetan

Harry "Hard Rock" Theakston

Herman "Suntan" Trader

"Abe" Trew

"Rip" Usher

"Froggy" Vargo

Joe "The Bear" Vargo

"Hooks" Walton

Ray "Pumpkin" Watson

Dick "Weighty" Weightman

Jim "Beans" Welsh

Carl "Greaser" Westcoat

Johnny "Jo Jo" Wheeler

"Pee Wee" Williams

"Butch" Williamson

Bill "Bunny" Williamson

Charles "Pinky" Wilson

Walter "Curly" Wozniak

"Spanky" Yates

Bob "Bird" Young

Clarence "Youngie" Young

Don "Dinger" Young

Jack "Strawberries" Young

Wilfred "High Pockets" Young

"Ziggy" Zajack

Harold Wayne "Zeke" Zundel

Made in the USA
Coppell, TX
18 August 2022

81687379R00142